T0265634

CAREFULLY TAUGHT

American History through Broadway Musicals

CARY GINELL

APPLAUSE
THEATRE & CINEMA BOOKS
Essex, Connecticut

An imprint of Rowman & Littlefield
4501 Forbes Blvd., Suite 200
Lanham, MD 20706
www.rowman.com

Distributed by NATIONAL BOOK NETWORK

British Library Cataloguing in Publication Information available

Library of Congress Cataloging-in-Publication Data

Names: Ginell, Cary, author.
Title: Carefully taught : American history through Broadway musicals / Cary Ginell.
Description: Guilford, Connecticut : Applause Theater and Cinema, 2022. | Includes
  bibliographical references and index. | Summary: "Ginell's research of contemporary theater
  reviews and in-depth studies of productions' back stories play off his knowledge gained from
  his quarter century as a theater critic in Southern California. The combination is a complete
  overview of American history on the stage from the coveted balcony seat" —Provided by
  publisher.
Identifiers: LCCN 2022006504 | ISBN 9781493065400 (cloth) | ISBN 9781493065417 (epub)
Subjects: LCSH: Musicals—New York (State)—New York—History and criticism. | United
  States—History—Drama—History and criticism.
Classification: LCC ML1711.8.N3 G55 2022 | DDC 782.1/4097471—dc23
LC record available at https://lccn.loc.gov/2022006504

CONTENTS

FOREWORD

THE INTERPRETATION OF A NATION'S HISTORY THROUGH ITS THEATER may be as old as the art form itself. Certainly it was used by the Greeks in Athens and by Shakespeare in London.

The telling is not always historically accurate. Indeed, good dramaturgy usually demands that poetic license be taken. The audience must feel, though, that the theatrical telling of the story is faithful enough to provide a meaningful interpretation of the past. Historical drama is not, in general, designed to relate what *has* happened, but to use past events to make sense of present or even universal concerns. In America, musical theater in particular has been used as a kind of secular liturgical drama—a communal retelling of sacred stories using music to elevate the sense of transcendent truth that such myths demand.

In the early years of the twentieth century, many cities staged spectacular musical pageants in which the line between religious ritual and patriotic theater was greatly blurred. In 1914, the city of St. Louis, Missouri, produced *The Pageant and Masque of St. Louis*, a two-part presentation with a combined running time of five hours that told the story of the founding and development of the city through singing, dancing, and pantomime. The success of the production led to the founding of the St. Louis Municipal Opera (now called the Muny), which is now one of the nation's longest-running and most successful regional producers of musical theater. One of the playwrights of *The Pageant and Masque of St. Louis*, Percy MacKaye, went on to stage similar pageants in other American cities, helping to develop an audience for musical drama that would attend local productions of the Broadway musicals of the later twentieth century.

The stories musicals rehearse change with the culture, of course. In the so-called golden age of the Broadway musical, the myth was often the American Dream. The stories weren't always set in America, but the Broadway liturgy taught that optimism and hard work (qualities considered distinctively American by many in those American audiences) could charm a tyrant king in Thailand or convince the European aristocracy that a Cockney flower girl was a princess.

Yet, like *Antigone* or the darker moments in the Wakefield cycle of mystery plays, musical theater, even in the "golden age," wasn't afraid to explore the problematic moments of the nation's history. *Show Boat* and *Finian's Rainbow* dealt directly, if often clumsily, with the virulent racism in the country. *Of Thee I Sing* and *Let 'Em Eat Cake* skewered American politics and the politicians of the Great Depression. Even Rodgers and Hammerstein musicals, whose scores are often considered compendiums of national anthems, presented the problems of American society in subtext that recent revivals have uncovered and further explored.

Even as the "golden age" myths shifted in the 1960s, the myth of American exceptionalism continued to be celebrated on stage. If the loss of innocence was acknowledged in musicals like Sondheim's *Follies* or Kander and Ebb's *Chicago*, the wounded cynicism of these pieces still affirms the notion that things *should* be different. Part of the dramaturgical tragedy of these musicals is that American ideas and ideals do not necessarily hold true in America.

The musicals that, like Shakespeare's history plays, deal directly with public events that shaped the nation are often the most invested in American ideology, even in recent years. In 1969, the musical *1776* devoted one song, "Molasses to Rum," to the evils of the slave trade, but was still rooted in the idea that formation of the independent American republic is a self-evidently Good Thing. *Hamilton* unabashedly celebrates the legacy of the Founding Fathers, leaving its criticism of the nation's original sin of slavery mostly to choreography and a handful of throwaway lines.

A few deeply cynical history musicals have dared to question the founding myths of the nation. *Assassins* explores the problematic potential of an American Dream that places no limits on individual freedom and that positions those who haven't achieved their dreams as revolutionaries called to action. In the song added for the 1992 London production, the chorus tells us that with the assassination of President Kennedy "Something Just Broke," but the last lines suggest that perhaps what was broken was never entirely whole: "Something just spoke / Something that I wish I hadn't heard." In *Bloody, Bloody Andrew Jackson*, "The Saddest Song" articulates what Jackson (and the musical as a whole) suggests is a foundational idea of American governance: the manipulation of democracy via populism to benefit a few individuals at the top of the hierarchy. Despite small groups of enthusiastic fans, neither musical has enjoyed a long Broadway run.

This book includes titles like *Assassins* and *Bloody, Bloody Andrew Jackson* along with record-breaking, form-defining hits like *Oklahoma!*, *The Music Man*, *1776*, and *Hamilton*. Each show is a historical artifact that relates the history that unfolds with the plot, but also documents an example of historical interpretation in its own cultural moment. *Oklahoma!* tells a story about westward expansion and Oklahoma statehood, but it was written as a nostalgia piece in the dark days of 1943—the Curlys and Wills of the country were not wooing women on a farm but fighting World War II, and Americans needed to be reminded "what they were fighting for." *Bloody, Bloody Andrew Jackson* chronicles the life and career of the populist president, but the musical was itself a reaction to the violent patriotic populism fanned into flame by George W. Bush's administration after the terrorist attacks of September 11, 2001.

The teacher or student who uses this book will find this chronicle of historical musicals useful both as a pathway into the telling of history and as a bibliography of musical interpretation. Cary Ginell situates each title in the larger context of American history and explains what license has been taken with the facts as documented in the historical record. He follows this with a brief production history and analysis of the script and score. For those seeking a new title to fill out a theater season, prepare a syllabus, or even just to understand the way in which the musical has been used to tell the American story, this volume will undoubtedly serve as a useful reference. With the worldwide success of *Hamilton* still fresh in the minds of producers and writers, more musicals based on American history are undoubtedly forthcoming. This edition, I expect, may be only the first in a regularly updated resource.

Doug Reside
Curator, Billy Rose Theatre Division
The New York Public Library for the Performing Arts

Introduction

THE ART OF STORYTELLING HAS ALWAYS BEEN A CENTRAL FACTOR IN Broadway musicals, but despite the efforts of the genre's most creative playwrights, many of the most acclaimed musicals stemmed from real events from American history. This book includes summaries and analyses of forty of these musicals, ranging from legendary flops to epoch-changing triumphs, from off Broadway experiments that lasted only a few weeks to venerated classics that changed the industry forever.

I got the idea to write this book while I was performing in a pit orchestra for a community theater production of *Ragtime*. The show fascinated me through its integration of real and fictional characters, which resulted in my interest in the stories behind such disparate personalities as Harry Houdini, Emma Goldman, and Evelyn Nesbit, whose lives and personalities were interwoven into the story.

Since then, I became fascinated with other shows based on actual events or eras in American history and I decided to see if I could come up with shows that represented every era, dating back to the days of the American Revolution and spanning more than two hundred years of history. The shows encompassed such wide-reaching subjects as the drafting of the Declaration of Independence (*1776*), racism during World War II (*South Pacific*), notorious crimes (*Parade*), crippling strikes (*Newsies*), political campaigns (*Fiorello!*), and the construction of the Statue of Liberty (*Miss Liberty*). Historical eras permeated stories as well, using fictional characters to describe the era of territorial expansion (*Oklahoma!*), the entertainment world's transition from vaudeville to burlesque (*Gypsy*), the labor movement of the 1930s (*Pins and Needles*), and the counterculture of the 1960s (*Hair*). Some shows used history as a framework to deliberately incorporate anachronistic musical styles (*Hamilton*,

Bloody Bloody Andrew Jackson). Others satirized American politics (*Of Thee I Sing, Li'l Abner*) or focused on sensationalism in the media (*Chicago, Floyd Collins*).

My decision to focus on events and eras in American history resulted in the exclusion of many of Broadway's biggest hits, including *The King and I, Titanic, The Sound of Music,* and *Come from Away,* all of which incorporated actual historical figures (many of whom were American), but that took place outside of the United States. Those shows will be reserved for another book. Similarly, I decided not to include biographical musicals, a subject that has proliferated in the past two decades in shows like *Jersey Boys* and *Beautiful: The Carole King Musical,* although I have included biographically based shows like *Annie Get Your Gun, Gypsy,* and *The Will Rogers Follies* because they de-emphasized biographical detail in favor of depictions of specific eras in American history.

Each chapter presents basic details about the historical event behind each show, followed by a production history and an analysis of the score. Special attention is paid to historical personages and how they were portrayed, as well as the accuracy of the stories involved. The chapters are arranged in chronological order by subject, ranging from the American Revolution to the early 1980s, with no more than two decades separating each successive chapter.

Musical theater's main purpose is to entertain, but through these musicals and others, Broadway has served to combine the American musical with events portrayed on newspapers' front pages throughout its history in ways that are both entertaining and illuminating. I hope that this book will encourage teachers of history and musical theater to discuss these conflating elements, which will enrich the learning experience of students of both.

Cary Ginell
December 2021

1776

Historical context: The Second Continental Congress
Time period: May 8 to July 4, 1776
Broadway run: March 16, 1969–February 13, 1972 (1,217 p.)
Venue: Forty-Sixth Street Theatre
Book: Peter Stone
Score: Sherman Edwards
Cast album: Columbia Masterworks BOS-3310 (1969)
Major characters: John Adams (William Daniels), Benjamin Franklin (Howard Da Silva), Thomas Jefferson (Ken Howard), Martha Jefferson (Betty Buckley), Abigail Adams (Virginia Vestoff)

HISTORICAL BACKGROUND

The Battles of Lexington and Concord, which were fought on April 19, 1775, marked the beginning of the American Revolutionary War. Shortly afterward, on May 10, the Second Continental Congress first convened at the Pennsylvania State House (now Independence Hall) in Philadelphia. Representatives from the twelve colonies set about to decide what they should do should the British government not repeal or modify the Coercive Acts, punitive laws meant to punish Massachusetts for defying them through the Boston Tea Party. On June 14, Congress established the Continental Army, appointing George Washington as commanding general.

In 1776, the prevailing feeling among the colonies was to declare independence from Britain. Measures were taken to form delegations to authorize such a declaration to Congress. On June 7, Virginia's Richard Henry Lee (1732–1794) drafted a resolution that was presented to Congress to declare the colonies an independent nation. Over the next month, the Committee of Five worked to draft a declaration to deliver to Congress for a final vote, a formal explanation of why the colonies were separating from Britain. The musical *1776* deals with the period between Lee's resolution and the final vote on independence less than a month later. In all, fifty-six delegates, representing the thirteen original colonies, attended the sessions, with only thirty-nine delegates actually affixing their signatures to the document.

PRODUCTION NOTES

For a musical that purported to tell the true story of the drafting of the Declaration of Independence, *1776* played fast and loose with the details,

Ken Howard (Jefferson), Howard Da Silva (Franklin), and William Daniels (Adams).
PHOTOFEST

but in ways that contributed to the tension, drama, and wit displayed in the musical. The show's creator, Sherman Edwards, taught high school history before embarking on a career as a pianist and songwriter; he had more than a passing knowledge of the events of the American Revolution. Edwards knew that to present the Second Continental Congress as it actually existed would never work in a Broadway musical. In the original libretto to the show, Edwards included a "Historical Note by the Authors" that explained the play's documented elements as well as the dramatic changes undertaken. Those changes fell into five categories: "things altered, things surmised, things added, things deleted, and things rearranged."

The main aspect that Edwards altered was his distilling the size of the cast. The original Continental Congress consisted of fifty-six delegates, far too many for any audience member to keep track of or to be placed comfortably within the physical limits of a stage production. In *1776*, the cast was whittled down to twenty delegates to represent the thirteen colonies, many of whom only played minor roles. Only Delaware's three-man delegation was fully represented. The other colonies were represented by far fewer men than actually attended.

All of the delegates were based on real people, although some of their personal characteristics were generalized or combined with one another. John Adams (1735–1826) was hardly the "obnoxious and disliked" character he is portrayed as in the play. On the contrary, biographer David McCullough wrote that in 1776, Adams was actually one of the most respected members of Congress; there is no evidence of any delegate ever referring to Adams as being obnoxious. In the play, Adams, who would become the second president of the United States, was given some of the personality traits of his cousin, Samuel Adams, who worked behind the scenes as a kind of parliamentary whip in favor of revolution.

Edwards and book writer Peter Stone took many liberties with facts, but none that had a major impact on the story arc, which concludes with the dramatic signing of the document on July 4, 1776. In reality, the majority of the signings took place on August 2, but the dramatic effect of each delegate solemnly progressing toward the large table in front of John Hancock's bench on July 4 to sign the parchment, with the Liberty Bell tolling in celebration, became a powerful and emotionally satisfying conclusion to the musical. (In actuality, the Liberty Bell tolled on July 8, not July 4, after the Declaration returned from the printer.)

Historians have quibbled about the nature of the distortions, inventions, and fabrications of the musical, the most visibly obvious being the giant tally board that is the centerpiece of the set, employed to enable the audience to keep track of the "yeas" and "nays" as the voting progressed, thus ratcheting up dramatic tension. In fact, no such board existed, but its incorporation as a dramatic device was a stroke of genius on the part of Edwards, with each resounding "clack" of the board's sliders moving from one side or the other adding an exclamation point to each decision made.

In real life, Martha Jefferson (1748–1782) didn't come to Philadelphia to assuage her husband's sexual frustration; in reality, Thomas Jefferson (1743–1826) left the Congress to visit her because she had recently suffered a miscarriage. The Jeffersons were also not newlyweds, as was depicted in the play; they had been married for four years. Edwards, however, did not want to destroy the unity of the congressional setting and had Martha come to Independence Hall to visit her husband instead of having to change the play's setting.

Two major conflicts take place within the Congress during the play, one involving Pennsylvania's John Dickinson (1732–1808) and the other, South Carolina's Edward Rutledge (1749–1800). Much of how Dickinson was represented in *1776* is accurate. He was opposed to declaring independence, not because he felt fealty to King George III but because he objected to achieving independence through violence and thought the colonies should secure a foreign alliance before declaring itself a sovereign nation. In the final scene of the play, Dickinson dramatically abstains from voting, pledging to join George Washington's Continental Army, an event that actually happened.

Edward Rutledge is presented as the figurehead of the Southern, slave-owning states, who mocks Adams and the Northern delegates as hypocrites in the darkly dramatic song "Molasses to Rum" and then proceeds to hold the Declaration hostage until a passage opposing slavery is removed. In reality, Rutledge, who at twenty-six was the youngest delegate in the Congress, was not as dominant a figure as he is presented in the play, in which every Southern state defers to his position. In reality, slavery was supported not only by South Carolina and Georgia but also by unnamed "northern brethren," as Thomas Jefferson recalled in *The Jeffersonian Cyclopedia*. Contrary to historical fact, the South did not walk out and threaten to disrupt the entire process. Most delegates, both North and South, supported the deletion of the slavery clause, but the inclusion of this device helped audiences ask themselves: what if the clause had remained in the document? Had it not been excised, would we have even had a Civil War "four score and seven years" later?

To its credit, much of the dialog in *1776* is based on fact, most notably the letters John and Abigail Adams (1744–1818) wrote to one another and George Washington's dispatches from the field to the Congress, which are read aloud by Secretary Charles Thomson (1729–1824). John Adams was indeed fond of using the exclamation "Good God!" which has been preserved in a number of his letters and writings, while other lines of dialog were taken from actual notations from the journals of the Continental Congress.

The look of the play summoned up an idealized view of the privileged lives of well-to-do politicians of the day; however, historian David McCullough, author of the acclaimed book *1776*, said during a 2005 address given to the Union League Club of Chicago, "Everybody's in their shuffled shirts, powdered hair, and satin breeches, and they don't look quite real. They look like they were dressed up for a costume pageant." There was nothing in the musical to tell of the horrible conditions under which the revolutionary soldiers fought, something that might have enhanced the determination of Adams and his fellow delegates to make haste in completing the Declaration.

The musical would have been much less effective had it not been for the representation of the warm relationship between John and Abigail Adams, all of which was documented in the eloquent and tenderhearted letters they wrote to one another during this period.

What *1776* did more than anything else was to reveal the Founding Fathers as real human beings, underneath the powdered wigs and satin breeches, at a time when it was exceedingly demanding to simply live and survive, much less fight an entrenched, experienced invading army. The play reveals a side of General Washington that we don't usually see, thanks to the reading of his regular dispatches—far from the stony image we see on monuments, painted portraits, and the dollar bill. At the time, Washington was at his lowest ebb, frustrated by lack of success on the battlefield and the inexperience and suffering of his troops, many of whom deserted the Continental Army in droves. The reading of Washington's dispatches and the Adamses' letters, not the comical bon mots of Benjamin Franklin (1706–1790), the histrionics of Richard Henry Lee, or the posturing and complaining of the other delegates, gave *1776* its most effective, emotional moments.

The superior writing of *1776* was such that real drama was created in a plot where everyone already knew the outcome. By Act II, we wonder how on earth Adams will be able to convince the recalcitrant South and the stubborn Dickinson to join the cause. One state at a time, it happens, but the dramatic tension Peter Stone creates through his writing is palpable. At the end of the musical, we breathe a sigh of relief, overcome by a wave of emotional patriotism when the final signing takes place. Although there are many musicals, including the much-lauded *Hamilton*, that present history in a dramatic fashion, no one production uses creative license as majestically as *1776*.

SCORE

It could be argued that *1776* isn't really a musical but a play with periodic musical interludes. Only four songs appear in Act II, and, at one point, between "The Lees of Old Virginia" and "But, Mr. Adams," more than thirty minutes pass, the longest time of any musical, without a single note being played by the orchestra or sung by an actor. Sherman Edwards's songs are so well written and integrated into the story that one wishes that more of them were included, but unlike works by Rodgers and Hammerstein or Lerner and Loewe, the story inherent in *1776* is paramount and the drama might have been lessened had the deliberations been interrupted by additional songs.

The musical numbers range from lighthearted and romantic to frightening and profoundly sad, beginning with the strident ensemble piece "Sit Down, John," which serves as the third person "I am" song that defines the obstreperous character of John Adams. Adams's endearing relationship with his wife, Abigail, is revealed in the brief but tender "Yours, Yours, Yours," a musical love letter whose lyrics are adapted from the couple's actual correspondence as they pledge their undying devotion to one another.

In "The Egg," Adams, Franklin, and Jefferson debate over what bird should be the new country's national symbol. Adams favors the majestic eagle, Jefferson is in favor of the placid dove, and Franklin promotes the noble turkey. Although the play shows that they settle on the eagle during a break in the proceedings, in reality it wouldn't be until 1782 that the initial design for the Great Seal of the United States, which included the eagle, would be approved. The person responsible for the actual design was Charles Thomson, the dutiful secretary of the Second Continental Congress, who fashioned a drawing of a bald eagle clutching an olive branch in one claw and a bundle of arrows in another.

One historically accurate representation was the bargain struck by John and Abigail Adams in "Piddle, Twiddle, and Resolve," in which John asks Abigail to make saltpeter for gunpowder and she, in turn, asks him to send her pins needed for sewing. In another song, "He Plays the Violin," reference is made to Thomas Jefferson's musical abilities, which was factual. Jefferson played violin throughout his life and even took one with him during his travels so he would never be out of practice.

The dramatic musical highlight of the show is, with a doubt, "Molasses to Rum," sung with acidic fury by Edward Rutledge of South Carolina (Clifford David), a searing indictment of the hypocrisy of the Northern states and their support of the anti-slavery clause in the Declaration. The song reaches a fever pitch as Rutledge imitates the chant of a slave auctioneer, complete with cracks, a devastating and even horrifying song that freezes all of the members of Congress, until one, Dr. Josiah Bartlett of New Hampshire (Dal Richards) rises to his feet and cries out, in outrage, "For the love of God, Mr. Rutledge, please!" breaking the tension for the moment.

Dearest Enemy

Historical context: The American Revolution
Time period: September 16, 1776
Broadway run: September 18, 1925–May 22, 1926 (286 p.)
Venue: Knickerbocker Theatre
Book: Herbert Fields
Score: Richard Rodgers (music), Lorenz Hart (lyrics)
Cast album: Beginners Productions BRP1 (first full theatrical score) (1981)
Major characters: Mary Lindley Murray (Flavio Arcaro), Gen. George Washington (H. E. Eldridge), Gen. Sir William Howe (Harold Crane), Capt. Sir John Copeland (Charles Purcell), Betsy Burke (Helen Ford), Major Aaron Burr (James Cushman)

HISTORICAL BACKGROUND

The framework of the story is based on the events of September 1776 when British General William Howe (1729–1814), having defeated the Revolutionaries in the Battle of Brooklyn, landed in Kip's Bay, along the East River, forcing the Continental Army to withdraw to Harlem Heights (now Morningside Heights), thus ceding control of the lower portion of New York City to the British.

In March 1776, Howe was in Nova Scotia, regrouping after being besieged in Boston by the Continental Army and forced to withdraw. His new plan was to attack and take over New York City. Anticipating this move, George Washington (1732–1799) moved his army there to assist Major General Israel Putnam (1718–1790) to prepare for the attack. With Howe's troops closing in on both sides (from Staten Island and

Long Island), Washington was forced to retreat northward to Brooklyn Heights. Kip's Bay was a small cove located where Midtown Manhattan lies today, between Thirty-Second and Thirty-Eighth streets (it has since been filled in).

Robert Murray (1721–1786) was a local merchant who lived with his wife, Mary (1726–1782), on a steep glacial hill whose peak lay between where Lexington Avenue and Broadway are today. In the twentieth century the area became an upscale neighborhood now known as Murray Hill after its most prominent ancestral residents. According to legend, Mary Lindley Murray, the Quaker wife of Robert Murray, was able to forestall the deployment of Howe's troops by entertaining them, allowing Putnam and his army to get away.

Although Robert Murray was a Loyalist and did business with the British, his wife, Mary, was sympathetic to the Revolutionaries; many members of her family subsequently served in General Washington's army. On September 16, 1776, with Howe tracking General Putnam's retreating troops, Mary put into action a plan to save Putnam's army by entertaining Howe and his men at her home with refreshments and comely company, all the while knowing that Putnam's troops were less than a mile away. Once the troops entered their home, Mary and her daughters entertained while her maid kept watch from an upstairs window, instructed to deliver a signal when it was safe to allow their "guests" to leave.

The Murray Hill incident was recorded in the journal of a Continental Army surgeon named James Thacher (1754–1844). Some skeptics promoted the idea that Mrs. Murray was only trying to ingratiate herself with the British should they prove victorious, but the evidence shows that her actions were in genuine support of the revolution.

The story of a brave woman risking her life for a patriotic cause was particularly attractive to the suffragette movement when the musical was staged in 1925, only five years after women had been granted the right to vote. Although the story about Mary saving the Revolutionary forces from certain destruction has never been proved, it became something of a legend and was thus ripe for production as a musical comedy.

Production Notes

According to Richard Rodgers, credit for the idea to make a musical out of the Murray Hill incident went to his lyricist, Lorenz Hart. The pair had just started their collaboration with librettist Herbert Fields and were looking for a property to produce when Hart, an avid student of American history, was inspired by a plaque the trio saw while strolling along Lexington Avenue. (In 1994, the original plaque was replaced by another, courtesy of the Daughters of the American Revolution, which is located near the corner of Thirty-Seventh Street and Park Avenue.)

Fields expanded the story to include a fictional romance, Montague/Capulet-style, between the maid, who was given the name Betsy Burke and was now Mary Murray's feisty Irish niece, and the red-coated British captain Sir John Copeland. In the story, Betsy makes her first appearance wearing nothing but a barrel, after a dog makes off with her clothes while she is swimming. Copeland gallantly presents her with the barrel and they instantly fall in love. When Mary instructs her household of young ladies, who had been sewing uniforms for American soldiers, to "be nice" to their captors, who have commandeered the house as temporary headquarters, the Murray home becomes a potential brothel. Amid all of this, a second romance develops between Mary's flirtatious daughter, Jane, and British General Tryon's son, Harry.

Rodgers, Hart, and Fields submitted their idea to Fields's father, Lew, a Broadway producer who had been famous at the turn of the century as half (with Joe Weber) of the hugely popular comedy team of Weber and Fields. Despite this nepotistic connection, Fields père turned the idea down, telling the trio, "Whoever heard of a musical based on American history? The public won't buy it." Other producers followed suit, under the assumption that if it wasn't good enough for Fields's own father, it must be a bad idea. It took the success of Rodgers and Hart's revue, *The Garrick Gaieties*, which debuted in January 1925, to convince investors to financially support the show, and on September 18, it finally made its debut at the Knickerbocker Theatre.

In Helen Ford, Rodgers and Hart found the perfect actress to play the key role of Betsy Burke. At thirty-one, the vivacious Ford was one of the more popular musical comedy stars of the 1920s, getting her start on

Broadway at the age of eleven in *Grierson's Way*. By the time she appeared in *Dearest Enemy* she already had six other musicals under her belt. Flavia Arcaro, who played Mary Murray, was an actress known more for her appearances in silent films than on the stage.

Helen Ford's presence in the cast was sufficient to attract investors to the show, investors who might have been more reticent in putting money into a show whose score was being written by two unknowns. It would be the first of twenty-eight Rodgers and Hart musical collaborations.

During the show's week of tryouts at Ford's Theatre in Baltimore, its title was changed from *Dear Enemy* to *Dearest Enemy (An American Musical Comedy)*. Famed director John Murray Anderson, then at the beginning of his career as a writer, director, and producer, made sure the décor and costumes befitted the period, which pleased audiences and critics alike. Just before opening night, Rodgers, who was conducting the orchestra, got conked on the head by a can of peaches at a nearby delicatessen, knocking him cold. Fortunately, he was revived in time to conduct the overture.

At the time *Dearest Enemy* finally made its Broadway premiere, three other major shows were also making their debuts: Vincent Youman's *No, No, Nanette*, the Rudolf Friml operetta *The Vagabond King*, and *Sunny*, featuring a score penned by Jerome Kern, Oscar Hammerstein II, and Otto Harbach and starring Marilyn Miller, one of the decade's top stars.

SCORE

Rodgers and Hart's songs are just what you might expect from a musical comedy of the 1920s: lighthearted, tuneful, and witty. The influence of Gilbert and Sullivan is apparent in the opening number, "Heigh-Ho! Lackaday!" as the seamstresses sing merrily while they sew, happily waiting for their men to come home from the war. When the girls are told of their task—to flirt and entertain the British troops—they proclaim, "Hooray! We're going to be compromised" in the sprightly march "War Is War."

In his autobiography, Rodgers discussed his thoughts about the show and how its songs should not only be fresh and unhackneyed, but also should be able to fit into different situations, anticipating the full-fledged integration of song with story in *Oklahoma!* eighteen years later. "The repetition of a song, however, should never be used merely to plug the number in the hope of sending customers dashing to their nearest sheet-music or record store," Rodgers wrote. This conscious adherence to the concept for which he and Oscar Hammerstein would become famous made the score for *Dearest Enemy* more than just melodic accouterments to the story.

With memorable songs like "Some Enchanted Evening" and "People Will Say We're in Love" still in his future, Rodgers, at the tender age of twenty-three, was already consciously focusing on the show's love duets, with its central one, "Here in My Arms," sung by Charles Purcell and Helen Ford as Sir John and Betsy, introduced at the end of the first act. The lilting, hummable melody is exactly the kind of song you'd expect from Rodgers, one that follows you out of the theater and up the block. During the Act I finale, Sir John, now suspicious of Betsy's motives in seducing him, alters the song to a minor key. Another of the standout tunes was Betsy's melodious solo, "I'd Like to Hide It," in which she expresses her love for the soft-hearted Sir John, despite his being a sworn enemy of her countrymen.

Although original cast albums did not yet exist, a medley of tunes from *Dearest Enemy* was recorded on December 9, 1925, by the Victor Light Opera Company. It was released in Victor's "Gems" series, and included excerpts from the songs "Sweet Peter," "Bye and Bye," "Here's a Kiss," "Here in My Arms," and "Cheerio." The score was good enough that Rodgers and Hart were admitted membership in ASCAP, the American Society of Composers, Authors, and Publishers, which ensures that songwriters are compensated whenever their songs are performed for profit. In those days, ASCAP was an exclusive club; by being accepted into their ranks, Rodgers and Hart found themselves among the elite of American songwriters.

Dearest Enemy received pleasant but unremarkable reviews, with adjectives like "melodious," "gentle," and "gracious" applied to the show's score. Standing out among the notices was one written by Frank Vreeland in the *New York Telegram* that predicted that the team of Rodgers, Hart, and Fields would someday "form the counterpart of that one-great triumvirate of Bolton, Wodehouse, and Kern." But despite its favorable reception, *Dearest Enemy* failed to lead to other musicalized versions of American history. As in Rodgers's later work with Hammerstein, *South Pacific*, a pair of romances between mismatched couples on opposite sides of a conflict provided the show's main interest, instead of the conflict itself.

Ben Franklin in Paris

Historical context: Revolutionary War diplomacy
Time period: 1776–1777
Broadway run: October 27, 1964–May 1, 1965 (215 p.)
Venue: Lunt-Fontanne Theatre
Book: Sidney Michaels
Score: Mark Sandrich Jr. (music), Sidney Michaels (lyrics); includes
two songs by Jerry Herman ("To Be Alone with You" and "You're in
Paris")
Cast album: Capitol SVAS-2191 (1964)
Major characters: Benjamin Franklin (Robert Preston), Madame La
Comtesse Diane de Vobrillac (Ulla Sallert), Janine Nicolet (Susan
Watson), Louis XVI (Oliver Clark), Temple Franklin (Franklin
Kiser)

HISTORICAL BACKGROUND

As the new nation's first ambassador to France, Benjamin Franklin
(1706–1790) was entrusted with gaining support for the war effort
against England. Franklin was no stranger to overseas diplomacy. A representative of the Pennsylvania Assembly in 1751, he traveled to London
six years later to help settle a tax dispute involving descendants of William Penn, the owners of the Pennsylvania colony. After the Stamp Act
of 1765, Franklin testified against the measure in the British Parliament.
He returned to Philadelphia in 1775, in time to serve as a delegate to the
Second Continental Congress, participating in the Committee of Five,
along with John Adams, Thomas Jefferson, Roger Sherman, and Robert
Livingston, to draft the Declaration of Independence. On September

17, 1776, the day after the events described in *Dearest Enemy*, Franklin was appointed one of three commissioners to the court of France to negotiate a treaty of commerce with King Louis XVI and to enlist that nation's assistance in the Revolutionary War, which resulted in a military alliance, signed by France and the United States in February 1778.

On October 26, 1776, Franklin departed for France with his two grandsons, sixteen-year-old Temple (1760–1823) and seven-year-old Benjamin ("Benny" in the show) Bache (1769–1798). Temple was the illegitimate son of William Franklin, himself illegitimate, who named him for Middle Temple in England, where he was studying to become a lawyer. When the elder Franklin returned to the United States to become what would be New Jersey's last colonial governor, he left Temple, then only four years old, behind. Benjamin Franklin learned of the existence of

Robert Preston (Benjamin Franklin) and Ulla Sallert (Mme La Comtesse Diane de Vobrillac).
PHOTOFEST

his grandson while in London and took custody of him. He would raise the boy in his own household.

French aristocrats and intellectuals saw Franklin as the embodiment of New World Enlightenment. His personal charm, intelligence, sharp wit, diplomatic skills, and overall charisma made him a cause célèbre in France, his image emblazoned on artifacts like snuff boxes, medallions, and jewelry. Respected by politicians and scientists alike, Franklin was also adored by women, many of whom sought his companionship. Even at seventy-one, he was attractive to women and he to them, having a notoriously high libido.

Among Franklin's "dangerous liaisons" was Anne Louise Brillon de Jouy (1744–1824), a thirty-one-year-old French harpsichordist and composer who also played the piano, a new instrument then under development. Madame Brillon, who was married, flirted mercilessly with Franklin, calling him "mon cher papa." Other prominent women who befriended Franklin were Countess Sophie d'Houdetot (1730–1813), a French noblewoman, and the Princess de Lamballe (1749–1792), who became neighbors with Franklin when he moved to the Paris suburb of Passy, where he lived in a lavish home donated by a wealthy Frenchman, Jacques Donatien Le Ray de Chaumont.

PRODUCTION NOTES

Playwright Sidney Michaels chose to focus on Franklin's appeal to women as the focus of the musical, rather than the politics of his mission, painting Franklin as a lovable rogue who used his personal charm to gain France's cooperation and assistance in America's efforts against the British. In doing so, Michaels invented a composite of the females in Franklin's French life in the form of the forty-seven-year-old widow, Madame La Comtesse Diane de Vobrillac, Franklin's old flame, who was also a confidante to King Louis XVI. Franklin took advantage of their past relationship in hopes of getting access to the king, but Diane required proof of America's ability to win a battle against England first. Franklin hoped to rekindle their romance and, in the process, win the king's support. He talks her into going up in a hot air balloon with him, where she agrees to get another power to split the cost of financing the war effort. The pair ends up targeting Spain, and Franklin has to convince the Spanish ambassador to help fund American arms and supplies. The result was the Franco-American Alliance, which was signed in 1778 in support of America's efforts during the Revolutionary War.

To play the part of Franklin, producers George W. George and Frank Granat wanted to cast someone who could be seen as a ladies' man with the gift of gab, rather than the cuddly bon mots–quoting elder statesman depicted later in *1776*. Robert Preston, star of *The Music Man*, immediately came to mind. At forty-six, Preston was a quarter century younger than Franklin and made the decision to shave his head for the part, rather than wear a clumsy bald cap, which might slip during a performance. Shaving one's head was not a normal procedure for actors at the time.

In interviews, Preston noted Franklin's similarity to Professor Harold Hill in that both were great salesmen. "The only difference was that Ben was on the up-and-up; he was selling legitimate stuff, he was selling the country," Preston told *American Musical Theatre* host Earl Wrightson.

Despite his efforts, Preston was unable to completely disappear into his character. He was so memorable as Harold Hill that it was nearly impossible to see him as the familiar avuncular figure we know from the hundred-dollar bill. Of all the Founding Fathers, Franklin was probably the most interesting, but it would have taken a character actor with the status of a Burgess Meredith instead of one with Preston's leading-man looks to pull it off. Preston sang well and had a larger-than-life presence, but his miscasting made it impossible for audiences to suspend disbelief and imagine him as the famed statesman/inventor.

A secondary subplot has Franklin's teenaged grandson, Temple, played by Franklin Kiser, falling in love with a beautiful, but poor, Parisian girl named Janine Nicolet, played by Susan Watson (*The Fantasticks*, *Bye Bye Birdie*), who sells hot chocolate and is a member of the newly formed French Revolution Party.

The ponderous plot took a lot of detours, including some extraneous songs, and although the outcome is never in doubt (as in *1776*), *Ben Franklin in Paris* has none of that show's suspense. Critics noted that most of the characters were well-worn stereotypes, with Franklin dropping familiar names along the way that the audience would know, such as Paul Revere. The dialog featured a plethora of forced one-liners that would have been better suited in a television situation comedy than an eighteenth-century French court. Not all critics turned up their noses at the show, however. The *New York Daily News* thought it showed considerable charm while the *New York Post* also leaned on the word "charm" to describe its impressions.

Although *Ben Franklin in Paris* didn't portray Franklin as a fool, the lovably witty and cuddly character in *1776* was more likely to be closer to the real McCoy than the unremarkable braggart portrayed in this musical.

SCORE

The ultimate downfall of *Ben Franklin in Paris* was Jerry Herman's undistinguished score. Although "To Be Alone with You" was singled out by Howard Taubman in the *New York Times* as "an attractive Broadway number," the show failed to produce a bona fide hit song. *New York Herald Tribune* critic Walter Kerr suggested the music, which he compared to scores from stodgy operettas, would have been better had it been imbued with more size and sweep and less schmaltz. Case in point, the ridiculous "I am" song, "I Invented Myself," in which Franklin likens his body parts to tools of his trade, invented "out of odds and ends," using a repetitive phrase in the chorus, "The damn thing works like the devil!" And was there any more ridiculous premise for a song than "God Bless the Human Elbow"? The most embarrassing song of all was the boastful "I Love the Ladies," sung by Ben, Temple, Captain Wickes (Sam Greene), who commanded the USS *Reprisal*, and French polymath Pierre Caron de Beaumarchais (Bob Kaliban).

In the heavy-handed "Too Charming," Ben and Diane (Ulla Sallert) lay it on too thick by slathering sticky compliments upon each other like peanut butter, in an attempt to replicate the wistful and tenderhearted "I Remember It Well" from *Gigi*. Even the love song "When I Dance with the Person I Love," sweetly sung by Susan Watson, paled in comparison to *My Fair Lady*'s similar "I Could Have Danced All Night," and subsequently fell flatter than a French soufflé.

The composers also missed opportunity after opportunity to effectively convey the distinctive atmosphere of pre-Revolutionary Paris. The song "You're in Paris" shows none of the romance it proclaims in the lyrics, sounding more like a vaudevillian song-and-dance than what was heard at the *Opéra Comique* or other upper-crust salon gatherings.

Despite all this, Sidney Michaels and Mark Sandrich Jr.'s score was nominated for a Tony in 1965 but didn't stand a chance against the likes of *Fiddler On the Roof*. Sandrich, the namesake son of the famous film director Mark Sandrich (*Top Hat*, *Holiday Inn*), worked mainly as an assistant director in television situation comedies during the 1960s. *Ben Franklin in Paris* was his first and only musical to reach Broadway; he also wrote the 1962 play *Tchin-Tchin*, an adaptation of a French romantic comedy that earned him a Tony nomination for Best Play.

Hamilton

Historical context: The life of Alexander Hamilton
Time period: 1776–1804
Broadway run: August 6, 2015–still running (2,110 p. as of March 13, 2022)
Venue: Richard Rodgers Theatre
Book: Lin-Manuel Miranda
Score: Lin-Manuel Miranda
Cast album: Atlantic 552918-1 (2016)
Major characters: Alexander Hamilton (Lin-Manuel Miranda), Aaron Burr (Leslie Odom Jr.), George Washington (Christopher Jackson), Marquis de Lafayette/Thomas Jefferson (Daveed Diggs), King George III (Jonathan Groff), Eliza Hamilton (Phillipa Soo), Angelica Schuyler (Renée Elise Goldsberry)

HISTORICAL BACKGROUND

As the country's first secretary of the treasury and one of America's Founding Fathers, Alexander Hamilton (1755 or 1757–1804) established the economic policies of George Washington's administration, thus founding the nation's financial system. In addition, he established the US Coast Guard, the *New York Post*, the Bank of North America, and the First Bank of the United States; he also led the development of the Federalist Party, the new nation's first political party.

Born on the Caribbean Island of Nevis in 1755, Hamilton was an orphan who was adopted by a prosperous merchant and sent to New York to attend school. During the Revolutionary War, he served as an aide-de-camp to General George Washington (1732–1799). Elected to represent

New York in the Congress of the Confederation, Hamilton urged the convening of the Constitutional Convention in Philadelphia, which led to the drafting of the US Constitution, writing fifty-one of the eighty-five installments of the Federalist Papers.

Hamilton served as treasury secretary in President Washington's cabinet, stressing a strong central government that promoted economic growth and supported the financial efficacy of the original thirteen states. He controlled the Federalist Party from 1789 until 1801, when the party was defeated by the Democratic-Republicans, led by Thomas Jefferson (1743–1826) and James Madison (1751–1836).

A bitter rivalry developed between Hamilton and Aaron Burr (1756–1836), who had defeated Philip Schuyler, Hamilton's father-in-law, for a New York US Senate seat in 1791. Hamilton saw Burr, a Democratic-Republican, as a corrupt opportunist who, among other things, favored the Holland Land Company while serving in the New York legislature. In the presidential election of 1800, Burr and Jefferson finished in an electoral tie, but Hamilton exacted his revenge by taking measures to ensure that Jefferson was elected by the House of Representatives, with Burr becoming vice president, in accordance with the system of the Electoral College before the enacting of the twelfth Amendment to the Constitution.

Hamilton was also responsible for Burr losing another election, this time to Morgan Lewis for the governorship of New York, resulting in Burr challenging Hamilton to a duel. The duel took place on July 11, 1804, in Weehawken, New Jersey, with Burr shooting Hamilton, who died the next day.

PRODUCTION NOTES

Lin-Manuel Miranda became interested in writing a musical about Alexander Hamilton after his musical *In the Heights* completed its off Broadway run. While on vacation, he started reading Ron Chernow's 2004 biography of Hamilton and thought about how he could turn it into a musical. Initially, he considered using rap music to write a humorous song about the Hamilton/Burr duel, but then realized that since Hamilton's entire life was based on the power of words, he would use

Christopher Jackson (George Washington) and Lin-Manuel Miranda (Alexander Hamilton), from the 2020 Disney motion picture.
DISNEY + PHOTOFEST

hip-hop to relate the early development of the United States, a subject that had fascinated him since his father worked as a political advisor.

When *In the Heights* opened on Broadway, Miranda decided to turn his Hamilton idea into a "rap concept album." He would label Hamilton "as self destructive as he was brilliant and got into these epic fights with Thomas Jefferson, John Adams, and Aaron Burr, the last of which ended in him getting shot in Weehawken, New Jersey. And as I'm reading this, I'm thinking, 'This is Biggie, this is Tupac . . . this is hip-hop!'" The original project was titled *The Hamilton Mixtape*, a revue of rap-style songs that would eventually be developed into the musical.

On May 12, 2009, Miranda was invited to perform at the White House for President Barack Obama as part of an evening of poetry, music, and spoken word performances. Miranda was scheduled to perform songs from *In the Heights*, but instead, chose to premiere the opening number, "Hamilton," from the *Mixtape*, the first time any of the songs had ever been performed in public. The enthusiastic response by Obama and his guests gave Miranda the impetus to develop another number, "My Shot," followed by other songs from Act I.

By 2010, the *Mixtape* was now being called a "hip-hop song cycle," presented as part of Lincoln Center's "American Songbook" series and performed on Hamilton's 255th birthday. Three years later, it was finally transformed into a stage musical and presented in a workshop production at Vassar College, with Chernow serving as historical consultant. Miranda cast himself as Hamilton with Daveed Diggs playing Thomas Jefferson, the first of the cast members who would end up performing in the musical on Broadway.

A limited run was announced by the Public Theater for January 2015 but was extended to three months due to overwhelming popular demand and sold-out box offices. By this time, Leslie Odom Jr. had been cast as Aaron Burr and Act I was completed but only three songs from Act II had been written. By this time, Miranda had become completely obsessed with the history he was uncovering, especially Hamilton's relationship with Burr. Miranda saw Hamilton relentlessly charging forward while Burr, the more calculating of the two, waited for the right moment to strike. Some critics argued that Burr was the true central character of *Hamilton*, in the same way that the relentless policeman Javert could be considered the key figure in *Les Misèrables*.

At the end of February 2015, the producers announced a move to Broadway. In May, the off Broadway run ended and Miranda spent the next two months refining, cutting, and polishing the musical. On August 6, *Hamilton* opened on Broadway to a tumultuous reception and an unprecedented demand for tickets. By the time it opened, *Hamilton* had already taken in thirty million dollars in advance sales.

Hamilton was praised for its innovative use of hip-hop lyrics instead of spoken dialog as exposition, much as recitative is used in opera. Miranda had attempted this in *In the Heights*, but restricted its use only to the show's main character, Usnavi. In *Hamilton*, everyone raps, with the lyrics specifically designed to fit each character. Miranda elevated hip-hop by marrying it with traditional musical theater storytelling, in essence inventing a new way of integrating music and lyrics with plot, accented by Andy Blankenbuehler's scintillating choreography.

Miranda's decision to uses Black and brown-skinned actors to portray America's white Founding Fathers was the show's most visible innovation. Character breakdowns showcased the disparate cultural references of the show's historical figures. Alexander Hamilton was described as "part Sweeney Todd and part Eminem." His wife, Eliza Schuyler Hamilton (1757–1854), was "Alicia Keyes meets Elphaba"; Aaron Burr was "Javert meets Mos Def," etc. As a result, many of the major roles went to people of color. Although Miranda did not pioneer multicultural casting (Broadway was already moving in this direction with African Americans playing Belle in *Beauty and the Beast*), he was the first to do this throughout a cast, to convey the idea that *Hamilton*'s characters represented the American melting pot. In interviews, Miranda stressed that in casting the show, he looked for the best rappers, with racial disparities falling into place. Miranda's use of multicultural performers reversed traditional Broadway standards that had seen the Russian-born Yul Brynner playing a Siamese king in *The King and I*, and Carol Lawrence, who was of Italian heritage, playing the Puerto Rican heroine Maria in *West Side Story*.

In addition, Miranda paid homage to Broadway's classic shows by inserting references to them into his songs—some obvious, others more subtly—including *South Pacific*, *The Pirates of Penzance*, *The Last Five Years*, *Mamma Mia!*, *West Side* Story, and even *1776*. At the same time, *Hamilton* also referenced classic hip-hop, including Grandmaster Flash and the Furious Five's 1982 single, "The Message," one of the earliest hip-hop songs to provide social commentary, as well as lyrics from other songs by Notorious B.I.G., Eminem, and DMX.

As a chronicler of history, *Hamilton* is extremely accurate, in accordance with Miranda's careful research of Alexander Hamilton's life and times. Occasionally, he would condense storylines and veer off from history, such as in the depiction of Revolutionary War general Philip Schuyler and his three daughters. In actuality, Schuyler had fifteen children, including two sons, but these minor points did not detract from the overall story, which reflected Miranda's diligence in presenting as much factual information as possible, not a normal practice in Broadway.

SCORE
Hamilton begins with the stunning "Alexander Hamilton," which sets the tone for the musical by presenting Hamilton's backstory leading up

to 1776, when the action begins. Similar to the expository introductions to *Assassins* and *Ragtime*, *Hamilton*'s main characters relate how the orphaned and impoverished Hamilton arrived in New York, a nineteen-year-old immigrant who had suffered in his early life but excelled by becoming a self-starter, overcoming adversity through hard work, intelligence, and ingenuity.

Hamilton likened himself to the new nation: young, scrappy, and hungry, believing that his rhetorical eloquence would take him far ("My Shot"). (It's in this song that Miranda makes a reference to "Carefully Taught" from *South Pacific*.) The mantra of "My Shot" ("I am not throwing away my shot") becomes ironic when Hamilton does just that in his duel with Burr at the end of the musical.

One of the more popular songs in the score was King George III's solo, "You'll Be Back," whose sing-along "dat-da-da-da-da" chorus is reminiscent of hook-laden British pop songs of the 1960s. The song is reprised several times during the show whenever King George (1738–1820) comments on the state of the revolution. In "Right Hand Man," George Washington identifies himself as a "modern major-general," a reference to Gilbert and Sullivan's *The Pirates of Penzance* as well as a passing reference to events depicted in *Dearest Enemy* ("we're abandoning Kip's Bay").

Among Act I's important songs are "Helpless," Eliza Schuyler's love-at-first-sight song; "Wait for It," Aaron Burr's showstopping number that presents Burr as a tragic hero; and the tumultuous "Yorktown (The World Turned Upside Down)" about the climactic battle of the war.

Highlights of Act II include the boogie-woogie-flavored "What'd I Miss?" sung by Thomas Jefferson; "Say No to This," which includes a quotation from "Nobody Needs to Know" from the musical *The Last Five Years*; and the jazzy "The Room Where It Happens," the show's most exciting number, which relates the Compromise of 1790 (probably the first time a banjo was ever used in a hip-hop song).

Miranda's brilliant use of wordplay, contemporary cultural references, and rhythm are reasons that the score to *Hamilton* is considered brilliant. No word is misplaced, and the accents of the syllables all fall exactly where they are supposed to fall (unlike what is heard in many rap lyrics, where accents are shoehorned into lines, whether they fit the rhythm or not). Miranda painstakingly chose every single word in the score, keeping the rhythms of the hip-hop lyrics honest while still accurately telling the story. Many consider *Hamilton* to contain the most brilliant use of words and rhythm of any modern-day Broadway musical. One can imagine wordsmiths Cole Porter and Lorenz Hart nodding in approval after hearing Miranda's remarkable score.

Hamilton garnered a record-breaking sixteen Tony nominations, winning eleven, including Best Musical. In 2016 it received the Pulitzer Prize for drama. Today, *Hamilton* is being used by social studies teachers to instruct students about early American history and Alexander Hamilton's depiction as a person who combined ambition with a relentless work ethic in overcoming his lowly beginnings.

Bloody Bloody Andrew Jackson

Historical context: The life of Andrew Jackson
Time period: 1767–1833
Broadway run: October 13, 2010–January 2, 2011 (94 p.)
Venue: Bernard B. Jacobs Theatre
Book: Alex Timbers
Score: Michael Friedman
Cast album: Ghostlight 8-4443 (2010)
Major characters: Andrew Jackson (Benjamin Walker), Rachel Jackson
(Maria Elena Ramirez), James Monroe (Ben Steinfeld), John Quincy
Adams (Jeff Hiller), Martin Van Buren (Lucas Near-Verbrugghe),
Henry Clay (Bryce Pinkham), The Storyteller (Kristine Nielsen)

HISTORICAL BACKGROUND

Once deemed one of America's greatest presidents, Andrew Jackson
(1767–1845) has been the subject of revisionist thinking in recent years
among modern historians. There was a time when Jackson was seen as a
courageous war hero and an expansionist leader who spoke on behalf of
average Americans in strengthening the Union. Today, however, evidence
of Jackson's racist policies in brutally expelling Native Americans from
their homelands has resulted in a reevaluation of his previously exalted
status in history books.

Born in the Carolinas in 1767 (North and South Carolina had not
yet been separated), Jackson was the first natural-born child in his family
since his parents emigrated from Ulster, Ireland, in 1765. Jackson lost an
older brother in the Revolutionary War and was himself captured and
imprisoned by British troops, in the process nearly dying from smallpox

Andrew Jackson (1767–1845).

and starvation. The experience left him with a lifelong hatred of Great Britain.

In 1787, Jackson was admitted to the North Carolina bar and began practicing law. The following year, he met Rachel Donelson Robards (1767–1828), the daughter of a widow with whom he was boarding at the time. Rachel was in the throes of an unhappy marriage and was in the process of getting a divorce when she and Jackson decided to marry. Since she was not yet officially divorced, this made her marriage to Jackson bigamous. They would remarry legally in 1794.

After moving to Nashville, Jackson served as Tennessee's attorney general; and after it achieved statehood, he was subsequently elected as the state's sole US Representative to Congress. A member of the Democratic-Republican Party, Jackson opposed President Washington's signing of the Jay Treaty with Great Britain and fought for the rights of Tennesseans against Native American tribal interests.

In 1804, Jackson acquired the Hermitage, a sprawling plantation near Nashville, eventually owning as many as three hundred slaves during his lifetime. Jackson was not averse to whipping his slaves to ensure obedience and would offer rewards to people who captured runaway slaves who escaped from his plantation.

During the War of 1812, Jackson led an army of more than two thousand volunteers to defend New Orleans against attacks by British and Native Americans. Earning the nickname "Old Hickory" for his toughness, Jackson fought in the Creek War, defeating a confederacy between "Red Stick" factions of the Creek tribe and British and Spanish traders in the Southeast who were supporting them, adding Spain to his list of reviled foreign enemies.

In 1814, Jackson won fame for his defeat of the British in the Battle of New Orleans, even though the War of 1812 had already ended with the signing of the Treaty of Ghent. After the war, Jackson attempted to seize Florida from Spain after the Spanish promised freedom to fugitive slaves. In 1818 he invaded Florida, possibly against President James Monroe's orders, crushing Seminole and Spanish resistance, which resulted in the sale of Florida to the United States in 1819.

Jackson resigned from the army in 1821 to pursue a career in politics, serving first as territorial governor of Florida and then Tennessee senator. In 1824, he ran for president, winning a plurality of electoral votes, but not a majority. He subsequently lost to John Quincy Adams (1767–1848) in the House of Representatives after Adams received the endorsement of Speaker of the House Henry Clay (1777–1852). When

Adams appointed Clay his secretary of state, it only increased Jackson's already fervent resentment of the "Washington elite."

Opposing America's alliances with any foreign nation, Jackson immediately ran for president again, after being nominated in 1825 by the Tennessee legislature, a full three years before the next presidential election. Jackson ran a populist and often-contentious campaign against Adams, who was running for reelection. During the campaign, Jackson was the recipient of vicious slurs from the opposition, who labeled him a slave trader and even a cannibal. Pamphlets were handed out that attacked Jackson's late parents; his mother being called "a common prostitute" and his father a "mulatto man." Despite the personal attacks, Jackson won the 1828 election, but his victory was hollow; his already frail wife, Rachel, died of a heart attack before Jackson could even assume office.

As president, Jackson favored states' rights, agrarian sympathies, and the abolition of the Electoral College. He served two terms as a nationalistic-thinking president favoring a strong union and opposing corruption in government and abolitionists, who he believed were trying to destroy the Union. His term was marked by a series of treaties struck with Native American tribes that resulted in the Indian Removal Act, which resulted in the forced migration of major tribes westward along the Trail of Tears.

PRODUCTION NOTES

Bloody Bloody Andrew Jackson was a quirky off Broadway show that never should have been staged on Broadway. Its in-your-face style, profane language, and raucous rock score were not elements palatable to traditional theater audiences. Director Alex Timbers, who also wrote the book, was the artistic director of the theater company Les Fréres Corbusier, which he started with two other Yale graduates. The company's mission statement stressed productions that employed sophomoric humor and aggressive production methods to drive home its revisionist musical history lessons. Previous shows, such as *President Harding Is a Rock Star* and *Here's Hoover*, joyously stomped on the reputations of presidents with less than sterling accomplishments. Now it was Old Hickory's turn.

Timbers chose to take the more disreputable aspects of Andrew Jackson's biography and turn him into a potentate of populism, virulent in his hatred of Native Americans, the Spanish, and the British, all of which was drawn from his own personal experiences, the reasons for his racism only hinted at in the libretto. Representing Jackson as the champion of white, rural Americans who were fighting against an insurgency of foreigners predicted the presidency of Donald Trump five years before the bombastic businessman announced his presidential run in 2015. (Trump showed his affinity for Jackson by displaying a portrait of the seventh president in the Oval Office during his tenure.) In light of events that occurred during Trump's tumultuous term, with ubiquitous calls for a border wall and virulent anti-immigrant policies, the overriding theme in *Bloody, Bloody Andrew Jackson* of "let's take our country back" gives today's audiences a queasy feeling of "where have we heard this before?"

Bloody Bloody Andrew Jackson preceded *Hamilton*—another show that presented American history around a framework of modern musical styles, by five years, similarly employing contemporary language and depicting historical events with jaggedly cut, broad strokes. *Hamilton*, however, garbed its actors in era-appropriate costumes and incorporated language taken verbatim from historical documents. *Jackson* made no such pretense, choosing to use only minimal historical costuming, such as cheap headdresses with feathers sticking up to identify Native Americans, and having characters speak in twenty-first-century punk jargon. In the musical, Jackson is portrayed as a virulent revolutionary, fighting on behalf of his agrarian constituents, wearing a white T-shirt in various states of bloodiness throughout much of the show. The other historical figures in the cast, which include archrival John Quincy Adams, Southern stalwarts John C. Calhoun (1782–1850) and Henry Clay, and future president Martin Van Buren (1782–1862), are portrayed with monolithic uniformity, representing the corrupt Washington establishment that conspired to thwart Jackson in his campaign for the presidency in 1824.

The show's negative, racist image of Native Americans raised the hackles of the New Native Theatre, a Minneapolis company devoted to breaking down stereotypes and promoting Native American artists. Consequently, the company staged a protest, accusing the writers of being irresponsible toward Native Americans and making an antihero out of Jackson and his violent ethnic cleansing of tribes during his tenure as president.

Despite this, *Jackson* received mostly positive reviews from critics, who applauded the show for its representation of the ugly side of populism, its outrageous humor, and an overtly gory depiction of the seventh president. But with no character to root for, audiences stayed away in droves and the critics' plaudits proved to be insufficient to sustain a prolonged Broadway run. Only two weeks after its opening on October 10, 2010, nearly one-third of the 1,078-seat Bernard B. Jacobs Theatre was empty, and it stayed that way for most of the show's run; it shut down twelve weeks later, on January 2, 2011, after only ninety-four performances.

SCORE

Michael Friedman's score is similar to that of *Spring Awakening*, its closest musical relative, for its use of alternative rock—specifically, a subgenre known as emo, an outgrowth of grunge that is traditionally associated with socially oppressed, misanthropic points of view. Emo rose to popularity in the early 2000s, characterized by brief, dark, aggressive songs and screaming vocals. Bands that play emo often wear thrift store clothing, which carried over into the costumes for *Jackson*.

The show's introductory song, "Populism, Yea, Yea" summed up the raucous style, but Friedman's score also took some interesting musical turns. One of the score's best songs is "The Corrupt Bargain," a vaudeville-style number reminiscent of "He Reached for the Gun" from *Chicago* with its rapid-fire interchanging of lines and use of cynical humor. In the song, a female Greek chorus illustrates how Adams, Clay, and Calhoun conspired to keep Jackson from the presidency in 1824. The title directly refers to a phrase used by supporters of Jackson in denouncing what they deemed was a rigged election in the House of Representatives (another parallel with the Trump presidency), which resulted in John Quincy Adams being named America's sixth president after the election produced no clear-cut winner.

Comical cynicism and anger pervade many of the songs in the show. In her solo, "The Great Compromise," Jackson's wife complains of having no private life, wistfully saying that all she wanted was "a dog, two kids, and two slaves." In "The Saddest Song," there is no humor, just resentment and vitriol, as a vengeful Jackson threatens to "take on the world for America's sake," then take all the land and take back the country. The song is performed as a propulsive, angry waltz, disquieting in its fervor.

The show's final number, "The Hunters of Kentucky," comes from an actual song that was used in Jackson's 1824 and 1828 presidential campaigns. Written by Samuel Woodworth and first published in 1822, the song is sung by the entire company, employing two of Woodworth's original verses, adapted to the same frenetic emo style as the show's opening number, serving as fitting bookends for this controversial but intriguing musical.

Big River

Historical context: Mark Twain's America
Time period: 1840s
Broadway run: April 25, 1985–September 20, 1987 (1,005 p.)
Venue: Eugene O'Neill Theatre
Book: William Hauptman, adapted from *The Adventures of Huckleberry Finn* by Mark Twain
Score: Roger Miller
Cast album: MCA MCA-6147 (1985)
Major characters: Huckleberry Finn (Daniel H. Jenkins), Jim (Ron Richardson), Tom Sawyer (John Short), Pap Finn (John Goodman), The Duke (René Auberjonois), The King (Bob Gunton)

HISTORICAL BACKGROUND

Although *Big River* doesn't represent actual events in American history, it is a show that reflects the social history of a period that few musicals have covered. Like *The Music Man* and *Hair*, which we will discuss later, *Big River* explores the vernacular and cultural history of America at a specific time in history. Life in the nineteenth century was demonstrated by Mark Twain (1835–1910) in *The Adventures of Huckleberry Finn*. Twain's work described a Southern antebellum lifestyle that had already disappeared by the time he published his work in 1885, a scathing satire on slavery that had already embedded itself in American life, which would lead directly to the events of the Civil War.

Told from the point of view of Huck Finn, a barely literate teenager, the novel explored morality in the 1840s as it related to the hot-button issue of slavery. Societal mores during this period viewed slavery as a convention tolerated, even condoned, not only by the government but also by the church and the educational system. In the decades leading up to the Civil War, the United States maintained a tenuous balance of power between slave states and free states, thanks to the Missouri Compromise of 1820.

When Huck is faced with the decision to either harbor the escaped slave Jim or return him to his owners, he decides on the former, reconciling his decision by calling it "sinful." Huck goes through a transformation of character during the novel, becoming less impatient with Jim and more understanding of the fear and humiliation that Jim lived with from dawn until dusk of every day. At the end of the book, Huck declares he'd rather go to hell than return his friend to slavery. The character of Jim is presented as sympathetic but simple: an honest, dignified, and even heroic figure, but at the same time, ignorant and rebellious. Torn from his family, he has one overriding goal: to be reunited with his wife and child.

Twain's novel was marked by its vernacular language of Missouri Negroes, employing backwoods Southwestern and Pike County dialects.

Backstage shot of (L-R) René Auberjonois, Ron Richardson, Roger Miller, Daniel Jenkins, Bob Gunton.
PHOTOFEST

Frequent use of an epithet describing African Americans (the "N-word") is probably the most controversial element in the book today, although the word was used in the book by Jim to describe himself. Hauptman's adaptation doesn't sanitize the language, which is the main reason that many regional theater companies do not stage *Big River* anymore, despite the message Twain was trying to communicate in not removing the offensive word, an aspect that Hauptman wanted to retain.

The novel acts as a sequel to Twain's *The Adventures of Tom Sawyer*, a story of two friends (Tom Sawyer and Huck Finn) who live in St. Petersburg, a Missouri town on the banks of the Mississippi River. The musical begins with Huck addressing the audience and describing the events in *Tom Sawyer*, introducing its characters, including the Widow Douglas, who adopted him, her spinster sister Miss Watson, and Huck's abusive, drunken father, Pap Finn.

The story of the friendship between young Huck Finn and the slave Jim and their adventures together on a raft as they float down the Mississippi River is the central focus of the story, but what is important to students of history are the mores that drove the narrative, the language that was used, and the relationship between white and Black culture at this critical period in American history.

Another aspect of nineteenth-century culture that was dealt with in *Huckleberry Finn* involved the characters the Duke and the Dauphin, two grifters who survive by swindling unsuspecting, naive residents of the towns they pass through on their way down the Mississippi River. In the book, the disreputable pair pass themselves off as European royalty in order to make Huck and Jim obsequious, although Huck sees through their scheme fairly quickly. It is no coincidence that the novel took place during the 1830s or 1840s, a time when minstrel shows were beginning in the United States. The concept of combining lowbrow, racist entertainment with the hawking of phony cure-alls and other items of dubious quality began with characters like the Duke and the King, which would lead to the development of traveling medicine shows, vaudeville, and even today's infomercials on cable and local TV.

In the novel, the Duke and the Dauphin (whom Huck calls "The King") sell tickets to what they promote as a "Shakespearean play," *The*

Royal Nonesuch, gaining attention by announcing that they are refusing to sell tickets to women and children. This prompts curiosity among men who believe they are going to see something prurient. As it turns out, the "nonesuch" is merely the king, wearing nothing more than body paint and "wild" accouterments. The storyline of traveling con men fleecing residents out of their money would be used often in Broadway musicals such as *The Music Man* (1957), *110 in the Shade* (1963), *Sweeney Todd* (1979), and *Dirty Rotten Scoundrels* (2004).

PRODUCTION NOTES

Musicalizing *The Adventures of Huckleberry Finn* proved to be problematic from the very start because of the themes and language inherent throughout Twain's novel. *Big River* is set during a very dark time in American history, when the institution of slavery was in full force, several decades before the nation exploded into a civil war over the issue. Librettist William Hauptman's intent was to be faithful to Twain's story, taking key scenes directly from the book, incorporating regional dialect and, most controversially, usage of the racial slur, making any musical adaptation of the story a flashpoint for criticism. Hauptman recognized Twain's intent in exposing racism in otherwise "kind" people such as Huck, who is imbued with a basic goodness and struggles with his conscience throughout the play as his basically rebellious nature leads him to defy societal norms by harboring an escaped slave. "I don't care! I guess I'm a bad person," he proclaims. This is what makes Huck such a great character: his struggle to determine right from wrong.

For producer Rocco Landesman, only one person was suited to write the score for the show: country music maverick Roger Miller. During his career Miller's compositions were marked by their combination of whimsy, irony, and clever wordplay, all of which were also hallmarks of Twain's works. Miller, however, was totally ignorant of Broadway, having seen only two musicals in his life (*How to Succeed in Business Without Really Trying* and the film version of *Oklahoma!*) and was reluctant to take on such a daunting task. In addition to his unfamiliarity with musical theater, Miller was a notoriously undisciplined songwriter and after not having a hit for nearly two decades (his last Top 10 country single was "Little Green Apples" in 1968), and after recently dealing with substance abuse, he had lost confidence in his abilities, especially when Landesman told him he'd have to write an entire score all by himself with no collaborator.

As he often explained, Miller didn't write songs, he made them up, developed from clever throwaway lines or from other moments of inspiration. Songs virtually flew out of his head and onto sheets of music paper. His biggest hit, "King of the Road" was written while he was driving to Chicago to catch a plane when he saw a sign along the road that read "trailers for sale or rent." "Husbands and Wives" came to him while driving on the freeway in Los Angeles with his wife. Sometimes phrases popped into his head that became songs, such as "The Last Word in Lonesome Is Me." "Creative writing, to me, is a matter of allowing your imagination free rein," Miller told *Billboard* magazine. Being told to write songs about specific instances and characters was simply not in his nature.

With some cajoling, Landesman was able to convince Miller that he could refine and adapt some of his rejected or unfinished "trunk songs," scraps of words and music that he never had the discipline to complete. Ultimately, Miller agreed to write the score. After meeting the cast and crew, he relaxed and began to enjoy the process. Miller eventually recognized his kinship with other American literary wits like Twain and Will Rogers and developed his own form of creative discipline. "I sat and really took the writing seriously," he reflected, "and realized that I could dip into a bucket that I hadn't really dipped into before. I'd never written fiddle hoedowns before. Never wrote religious hymns or gospel music."

The first staging of *Big River* took place in February 1984, at the American Repertory Theater in Cambridge, Massachusetts. In June it opened the La Jolla Playhouse's second season, near San Diego, California. Critics raved, saying that Mark Twain would have approved of the score, citing Roger Miller's "oblique charm and shrewd rusticity," although a few of the trunk songs that he shoehorned into the show ("Hand for the Hog") didn't advance the story.

Musically, Miller produced songs that reflected musical Americana as it existed in the mid-nineteenth century: Christian hymns and rousing gospel, performed not as minstrel numbers but in the context of contemporary 1980s Nashville, performed by the Red Clay Ramblers, a six-piece North Carolina string band whose own repertoire reflected their roots in old-time mountain music, country rock, New Orleans jazz, and gospel.

Rehearsals for the New York production began on February 11, 1985. On March 26, it opened at the Shubert Theater in New Haven, Connecticut, and ran until April 7 before finally going on to Broadway. *Big River* became a huge hit, winning seven Tony Awards, including Best Musical, Best Score, Best Featured Actor (Ron Richardson), Best Adaptation (William Hauptman), and Best Director (Des McAnuff).

The show starred twenty-two-year-old Daniel H. Jenkins, making his Broadway debut as Huck with operatic baritone Ron Richardson as the slave Jim and John Short as Tom Sawyer. *Big River* also featured noted character actors John Goodman as Huck's abusive father Pap Finn and René Auberjonois as the Duke. During the initial New York run, Roger Miller played Pap Finn for a number of performances. Half the time he failed to remember his own lyrics and would instead blurt out hilarious ad-libs, to the delight of audiences.

SCORE

During his halcyon days, when amphetamines were part of his daily regimen, Roger Miller could write songs almost as fast as he could sing them. After procrastinating for weeks at a time, he finally delivered some of his trunk songs to Rocco Landesman, one of which was "Hand for the Hog," a throwaway song written in Miller's irreverent "Dang Me" style and sung in the show by Tom Sawyer. Struggling to come up with new material, Miller rejected a suggestion by his wife Mary, a former singer with Kenny Rogers and the First Edition, to go see some Broadway musicals to get ideas. But Miller refused, saying that he didn't want anything to influence his writing. By the time the cast was ready to begin rehearsals, Miller still had not come up with anything, so Mary and Landesman again pressured him. Miller snapped, "If you want Rembrandt, Rembrandt takes time. If you want Earl Scheib, you can have that in twenty minutes."

Forced to come up with songs, Miller thought about growing up in Texas during the Depression and his father raging about FDR's New Deal and wrote "Guv'ment," a witty patter song that showed elements of Miller's anger and frustration with the writing process.

Miller would later claim a kinship to the character of Huckleberry Finn. "The people who raised me, my aunt and uncle, were from Arkansas. Country people. We farmed, had cattle and this, that and the other. This particular book was my boyhood. All those things were stirred inside of me and it just started to flow."

Miller's strength fell in writing songs that grew from brief, nonsensical or whimsical ideas, like his hits "Chug-a-Lug" and "Dang Me." In order to adapt his writing style to Broadway, Miller was assisted by Des McAnuff, artistic director at the La Jolla Playhouse, who would go on to direct the New York production, and musical director Danny Troob, who helped fill out Miller's ideas to work within a Broadway framework. Two trunk songs that became part of the show were "Leavin's Not the Only Way to Go" and "You Ought to Be Here with Me." The song "Worlds Apart," which was written to characterize a broken relationship, worked perfectly within the show as Huck muses about how Black and white people experience the same natural phenomena (the sun and the stars), but remain different because of how they are treated. Sung as a gentle waltz, "Worlds Apart" uses a theme of regret to make a powerful statement about prejudice that summed up Huck's conflicting thoughts about Jim's humanity and, ultimately, the humanity of all Black Americans.

Two songs stand out in *Big River*: "River in the Rain" and "Muddy Water," both numbers written specifically for the show. "River in the Rain" is one of Roger Miller's most beautifully crafted songs, which uses the raft on which Huck and Jim are floating down the Mississippi as a metaphor for a utopian sanctuary where the two are equals. "Muddy Water," sung as a rousing gospel shout, is a statement of fervent fortitude that embraces the spirit of adventure that is a central theme in the musical.

At the initial rehearsals in Cambridge, Miller played his songs on guitar for the cast. After Miller sang the hymnlike "Free at Last," whose title he took from Martin Luther King Jr.'s "I Have a Dream" speech,

Landesman recalled, "everyone's jaw dropped to the floor. Everyone was so moved by this song they'd never heard before. He was doing some incredible songs." Miller knew that he was compiling a score of singular beauty, noting, "I've written the greatest music I've ever written for this. It's just been flowing out of me. And to see a whole company of actors doing it is a thrill I can't describe."

Bloomer Girl

Historical context: The women's reform movement and the Underground Railroad at the dawn of the Civil War
Time period: Spring 1861
Broadway run: October 5, 1944–April 27, 1946 (654 p.)
Venue: Shubert Theatre
Book: S. M. Herzig and Fred Saidy, based on Lilith and Dan James's unpublished play, *Bloomer Girl*
Score: Harold Arlen (music), E. Y. Harburg (lyrics)
Cast album: Decca DA-381 (8-disc 78 rpm album) (1944)
Major characters: Evelina Applegate (Celeste Holm), Jeff Calhoun (David Brooks), Dolly (Margaret Douglass), Pompey (Dooley Wilson), Daisy (Joan McCracken), Alexander (Richard Huey), Augustus (Hubert Dilworth), Unnamed soloist on "Man for Sale" (Harold Arlen)

HISTORICAL BACKGROUND

In 1849, thirty-year-old Amelia Jenks "Dolly" Bloomer (1818–1894) created *The Lily*, a newspaper published specifically for women that addressed the temperance movement, Bloomer's most fervent cause. The paper would soon feature articles devoted to women's rights. In accordance with this, Bloomer decided to promote a new kind of women's fashion to supplant the use of hoopskirts and corsets, which were perceived as not only restricting but unhealthy, resulting in lung infections as well as constipation. Bloomer's solution was short, baggy pantaloons gathered at the ankle, an idea that was originally designed by Elizabeth Smith Miller. Bloomer's "fashion rebellion" became a symbol for the fight for women's rights, and a metaphor for the loosening of the bonds in which women were constrained. Leaders of the women's rights movement began wearing the garment as a sign of defiance, and the trousers were eventually given a new name in honor of its chief proponent, becoming known as "bloomers."

Dolly Bloomer was responsible for introducing Elizabeth Smith Miller's cousin, Elizabeth Cady Stanton, author and chief philosopher of the women's rights movement in the mid-nineteenth century, to activist Susan B. Anthony, forming a formidable partnership. During the 1850s, Dolly Bloomer continued her advocacy by giving temperance lectures at various towns in the Midwest. She eventually settled in Council Bluffs, Iowa, where during the Civil War she founded the Soldier's Aid Society, benefiting Union soldiers.

Bloomer Girl also dealt with the emancipation of slaves through the Underground Railroad, a network of secret routes and safe houses established to smuggle escaped slaves out of the South and into free states. In the years prior to the Civil War, abolitionists such as William Still and Harriet Tubman helped hundreds of slaves escape to freedom. *Bloomer Girl*'s climax takes place at the beginning of the Civil War, when young men joined Zouave regiments, so named for the bold, agile soldiers who fought for the French in North Africa beginning in 1830.

PRODUCTION NOTES

Composer Harold Arlen wore many hats in his career as a prominent composer. Not only did he write for the screen and Broadway; in the 1920s he sang and played piano in his own dance band. In 1937 Arlen teamed up with lyricist E. Y. "Yip" Harburg for the first time to write the score for the antiwar satire *Hooray for What!* It would be seven years before they would write another musical, instigated when theatrical agent Nat Goldstone presented Arlen with the unproduced play version of *Bloomer Girl*, which had been written by Lilith and Dan James. He presented the idea to Harburg, who thought the play was funny but needed more heft, and as a political activist with leftist leanings, he brought in playwrights Sig Herzig and Fred Saidy to flesh out the story by putting a greater emphasis on women's rights and the emancipation of slaves.

Yip Harburg believed that Dolly Bloomer's acts of rebellion in the 1850s would strike a chord with World War II audiences. Women had begun wearing slacks instead of dresses while working in defense plants, and the show's advocacy for bloomers represented the increasing trend toward women's equality and individuality, not to mention the war's struggle for freedom.

Celeste Holm as Evelina Applegate in *Bloomer Girl*.
PHOTOFEST

Co-producer John C. Wilson saw in *Bloomer Girl* the potential of another *Oklahoma!* and brought in veterans from that show's creative team, including actresses Celeste Holm and Joan McCracken, choreographer Agnes de Mille, orchestrator Robert Russell Bennett, scenic designer Lemuel Ayers, and costumer Miles White.

The expanded story focused on Evelina Applegate, the only unmarried daughter of hoopskirt magnate Horatio Applegate, set in the fictional town of Cicero Falls, New York. Evelina is the rebel of the Applegate family whose aunt happens to be Dolly Bloomer. Horatio is concerned about Evelina's future and arranges a match for her with Jeff Calhoun, scion of a formerly wealthy Southern family. The two hit it off immediately and fall in love, but Horatio's machinations prove fruitless when Jeff, instead of defusing Evelina's rebellious instincts, assists her in securing the freedom of his own slave Pompey through the Underground Railroad. At a garden party meant to show off Horatio's latest hoopskirt model, Evelina whips off her own skirt, showing the stunned guests her newly designed bloomers.

Pompey's presence is discovered by Jeff's brother Hamilton, who promptly files charges against Aunt Dolly for heading up Cicero Falls' chapter of the Underground Railroad; as a result, Evelina and all of the freed slaves end up in jail. The group is eventually released by New York's sympathetic governor and a performance of *Uncle Tom's Cabin* is staged at the local opera house.

In the middle of the performance of the play, word arrives that Fort Sumter has been fired upon and Jeff leaves to join the Confederate army. The governor announces that he has taken over Horatio's hoopskirt factory, which will now be used to manufacture not only uniforms for Union soldiers but also bloomers, with Dolly put in charge of production. The story ends as Jeff Calhoun is swayed to the Union cause after hearing President Lincoln speak in Washington and fails to report for duty with the Confederate army.

Celeste Holm, the original Ado Annie from *Oklahoma!* who played the part of Evelina, was replaced after the first year by Nanette Fabray, who continued in the show's return engagement at City Center at the beginning of 1947. The other *Oklahoma!* cast member added to *Bloomer*

Girl was Joan McCracken, an exceptional dancer who specialized in comic dance and played the part of Daisy, singing two solos: "T'Morra', T'Morra'" and "I Never Was Born."

Playing Jeff Calhoun was David Brooks, making his Broadway debut. The show launched his career as an actor and later a director and producer of stage plays. Brooks would originate the role of Tommy Albright in the 1947 production of *Brigadoon*.

Dooley Wilson, already famous for playing Little Joe in *Cabin in the Sky* and for singing "As Time Goes By" in the film *Casablanca*, was praised for his performance as the slave Pompey. Also in the cast were 297-pound Richard Huey, a singer, booking agent, and part-time restaurateur who played the slave Alexander, and Margaret Douglass, playing the non-singing role of Dolly Bloomer, the only historical character in the show. At the time *Bloomer Girl* took place, Edwin D. Morgan, soon to be a general in the Union army, was governor of New York, but the writers decided to invent the fictional Governor Newton instead.

Choreographer Agnes de Mille was entrusted with creating a ballet to bridge a gap in the second act representing scenes from the Civil War. De Mille's sequence starts with young ladies saying goodbye to their men, who are heading off to battle. At the end of the sequence, a widow is seen standing over the body of a dead soldier. After showing her work to Harburg, de Mille was dismayed when he told her that the scene was too stark for musical comedy, especially at a time when such a scene was very real for women in the wartime audience who may have been waiting for their own husbands to return from European battlefields. When de Mille retorted that she wasn't about to create an *Oklahoma!*-style barn dance about the Civil War, Harburg calmed her down and told her to remove the dead soldier and replace it with the ringing of victory bells. This compromise resulted in de Mille's "Civil War Ballet," singled out by some critics as the best scene in the musical.

Bloomer Girl was a popular attraction with wartime audiences, although it didn't come close to achieving the fame of *Oklahoma!*, running for 654 performances before closing on April 27, 1946.

Score

Harold Arlen's music evoked the simple folk melodies and spirituals that were sung in antebellum America prior to the Civil War. E. Y. Harburg infused the lyrics with his own philosophical principles, a trademark of much of his work, especially with regard to human freedom, the central theme in the sprightly "The Eagle and Me," sung by Dooley Wilson, in which Harburg uses elements of nature such as possums, bumblebees, and even ivy as metaphors to represent the natural tendency of all living things to be free.

One of the showstoppers in *Bloomer Girl* was "I Got a Song," performed by the mammoth figure of Richard Huey, who contributed to the popularity of gospel music in the 1940s with songs like "Hurry Sundown (See What Tomorrow Brings)" and "Rock My Soul (In the Bosom of Abraham)." Huey's theatrical work included roles in the play *In Abraham's Bosom* and the original 1935 production of *Porgy and Bess*. His income was bolstered by working as a redcap in Grand Central Station and as the proprietor of Aunt Dinah's Kitchen, a popular Harlem restaurant. Huey's celebrity turn in *Bloomer Girl* resulted in him being named "The 'I Got a Song' Man" in a feature in the *New York Times*.

Although *Bloomer Girl* didn't have any lasting hits, the love duet "Right as the Rain," sung by Celeste Holm and David Brooks, came close to becoming a classic. Brooks and Holm also sang the breezy "Evelina," in which Harburg playfully rhymed Evelina with phrases like "take a shine-a" and "pay a little mind-a me."

As in a later show, *Finian's Rainbow*, Harburg used humor to make a point, in this case, women's rights, in the clever "It Was Good Enough for Grandma," with Holm leading the female ensemble in declaring a revolt against men, calling them tyrants who believed a woman's place is the space around a frying pan.

Arlen's lighthearted melodies disguised the serious message behind Harburg's lyrics, with the composer himself singing "Man for Sale," a brief but chilling representation of a slave auctioneer enticing buyers with descriptions of cotton-picking, rock-busting hands as strong as forty mules, and broad shoulders that can hold up the sky.

Arlen wrote most of the score while he was in Hollywood, coming to New York for rehearsals. An exception was "Sunday in Cicero Falls," a waltz that he wrote in twenty minutes, on a sweltering summer day after arriving in New York. The song featured more of Harburg's ingenious wordplay, rhyming "whiskers" with "hibiscus" and coming up with the slyly worded line, "even the rabbits inhibit their habits" (merrily chirped by Holm), which even W. S. Gilbert, a wordsmith whom Harburg held in high regard, would no doubt have admired.

Shenandoah

Historical context: The Civil War
Time period: 1864
Broadway run: January 7, 1975–August 7, 1977 (1,050 p.)
Venue: Alvin Theatre (January 7, 1975–March 27, 1977); Mark Hellinger Theatre (March 30, 1975–August 7, 1977)
Book: James Lee Barrett, Peter Udell, and Philips Rose, based on an original screenplay by James Lee Barrett
Score: Gary Geld (music), Peter Udell (lyrics)
Cast album: RCA Victor Red Seal ARL 1-1019 (1975)
Major characters: Charlie Anderson (John Cullum), Jacob Anderson (Ted Agress), Robert Anderson (Joseph Shapiro), Ann (Donna Theodore), Jenny (Penelope Milford), Gabriel (Chip Ford)

HISTORICAL BACKGROUND

Shenandoah was based on a 1965 motion picture starring James Stewart as Charlie Anderson, a Virginia widower during the Civil War with six sons and a daughter who run their family farm but have no slaves. Charlie attends church but blames God for the death of his wife and will not permit any of his sons to enter the war unless it concerns them directly. Although there are no historical characters in the story, *Shenandoah* serves as a parallel to the national dilemma faced by American families at the time the film came out a century later, just as the war in Vietnam was escalating. In the story, Charlie, who is opposed to the war on moral grounds, is forced to become involved when his youngest son is taken prisoner by Union soldiers.

John Cullum in *Shenandoah*.
Photofest

A prolific writer for film and television, James Lee Barrett (1929–1989) was a North Carolina native who wrote screenplays for such films as *The Greatest Story Ever Told*, *Smokey and the Bandit*, and *The Green Berets*, the latter a movie about the US Army Special Forces during the Vietnam War that was especially pro-military, the antithesis of the themes displayed in *Shenandoah*. Barrett also wrote a number of made-for-television films, pilots, series, and miniseries and was used to write for a variety of projects of varying lengths. *Shenandoah* was Barrett's only work for the Broadway stage, which he adapted from his own screenplay. Near the end of his career, Barrett would say about his work, "I've told mostly about people, and that, really, is what makes a good motion picture, the people and how real they are. Always the people." *Shenandoah* is very much a story about people—specifically, the Anderson family and how Charlie Anderson is able to keep them together, in spite of being torn apart by the conflict that divided America into two warring factions.

Production Notes

The original stage production took place in 1974 at the Goodspeed Opera House in East Haddam, Connecticut. It was then transferred to the Alvin Theatre on Broadway where it made its debut on January 7, 1975. The cast featured John Cullum, in a career-defining role, as Charlie Anderson. Cullum would win a Tony for Best Actor in a Musical for his characterization. Of the six nominations it garnered, it won two: one for Cullum and the other to Barrett and his writing partners Peter Udell (who also wrote the show's lyrics) and Philip Rose for the adaptation.

The plot follows the film version closely with a few minor deviations. Although the film version takes place in 1864, in the stage musical it is two years earlier. The main story arcs involve the wedding of Charlie's daughter Jenny (spelled Jennie in the film) to Sam, a lieutenant in the Confederate army, and the disappearance of Boy, Charlie's youngest son, who is given the name Robert in the musical but is still referred to as "Boy." While wearing a gray cap he had found, Boy is mistaken for a rebel soldier and captured. Charlie and his family spend the bulk of the play looking for him.

Score

The major difference between the film and the stage musical was the addition of a score, with music by Gary Geld and lyrics by Peter Udell. In the prologue, the opening song, "Raise the Flag of Dixie" is full of vim, vigor, and jingoistic zealotry, sung by a men's ensemble representing each side of the conflict. Cullum's first solo, "I've Heard It All Before," shows Charlie's philosophical musings about war and why he is intent on staying out of it. "They've always got a holy cause," he snarls in defiance, "but always the ending is the same."

Charlie's sons share their father's pacifist convictions but are fiercely devoted to defense of their land, especially when a Confederate patrol arrives with orders to draft them. They celebrate their resistance with "Next to Lovin' (I Like Fightin')," a rollicking country-flavored hoedown dance number. Meanwhile, Charlie is worried that his attractive daughter Jenny will soon be courted by suitors, likening her to ripening crops ready to be harvested in the wistful "The Pickers Are Comin'."

Jenny and Sam's wedding arrives and Jenny and Charlie's daughter-in-law Ann, who is about to give birth, sing one of the show's best songs, the lyrical "We Make a Beautiful Pair," about the men in their life, sung in the style of a heartfelt country-western ballad. The brief wedding vow, "Violets and Silverbells," sung by Jenny and Sam, was written to sound like a generation-spanning folk song.

"Freedom" is a catchy, sing-along anthem sung by Ann and Gabriel, Boy's young African American friend whose plantation had been burned down by Union forces. He subsequently declares himself free, likening freedom to a state without borders ("Freedom's in the state of mind"). In the most emotional sequence in the show, Charlie sings the moving, exquisite "Meditation II," which sums up the show's major theme about the horrors of war as he mourns the death of those who fall in battle, wondering "what for?"

Shenandoah's homespun songs are fully integrated into the story in the best tradition of the example set by Rodgers and Hammerstein's *Oklahoma!* The enigma about *Shenandoah* is why its very personal story about a family struggling to stay together hasn't become a staple of regional theater. It's only been revived once, in a brief thirty-two-performance run in 1989, despite Cullum returning to reprise his Tony-winning performance as Charlie Anderson. Hopefully this will be rectified as future generations discover this moving, emotionally rich, and timeless musical.

The Civil War

Historical context: The Civil War
Time period: 1861–1865
Broadway run: April 22, 1999–June 13, 1999 (61 p.)
Venue: St. James Theatre
Book: Frank Wildhorn and Gregory Boyd
Score: Frank Wildhorn (music), Jack Murphy (lyrics)
Cast album: Atlantic Theatre 83091-2 (1999)
Major characters: Lydia Bixby (Beth Leavel), Frederick Douglass (Keith Byron Kirk), Private Sam Taylor (Matt Bogart), Corporal William McEwen (Gilles Chiasson), Harriet Jackson (Capathia Jenkins), Sarah McEwen (Irene Molloy), Captain Emmett Lochran (Michael Lanning)

HISTORICAL BACKGROUND

How does one encapsulate a war as sweeping as the Civil War in the span of a two-hour musical? Gregory Boyd, the creator of this 1999 flop, tried a novel approach: a bookless song cycle with no plot and no continuity to connect one scene to another. The show was instead a pastiche of self-contained vignettes in what was essentially a theatrical concert, designed to invoke a whole that was the sum of its individual parts. Without central characters to bind the story or references to specific battles, the musical ended up having no soul, no momentum, no one to root for, and no one to root against. In essence, *The Civil War* rendered the most tragic event in American history emotionally inert.

The production, which was directed by Jerry Zaks, drew on primary documents for some of its source material: letters, diaries, firsthand accounts, and the written words of Abraham Lincoln, Frederick Douglass, Sojourner Truth, and Walt Whitman, among others, in an attempt to do for the Broadway stage what Ken Burns's acclaimed documentary on the war did for television. Described as a "dramatic theatrical concert," *The Civil War* attempted to put a human face on the war by telling its story through the voices of soldiers in both armies, political leaders, and the slaves whose freedom was at stake. But the lack of developed characters drained the drama out of what was the most dramatic period in American history. Burns's documentary, however, vividly humanized the participants of the war through their own words, not just in one scene, but throughout the series. The musical turned its stories into abstracts, with penciled-in fictitious characters representing large swaths of people: husbands and wives, siblings, underage soldiers, and, of course, slaves. What was left were clichés about the war that every schoolchild already knew.

The show's more than two dozen vignettes presented general attitudes prevalent throughout the war: the initial rush of patriotic fervor and confidence from each side followed by despair as the war dragged on, year after year; enslaved Blacks praying for salvation; families divided when brothers enlisted in opposing armies (something that, in reality, rarely occurred); and fictional husbands and wives wondering when they would be reunited.

The depiction of Union and Confederate armies as unified forces proudly defending their ways of life was simplistic at best. There were many differences between the soldiers from each side other than the color of their uniforms, but the musical treated them as if they were interchangeable. Many of the events of the war were either simplified or compressed in time, such as Lincoln's assassination; it occurred in April 1865 but is depicted as taking place less than a month after the Battle of Gettysburg, which was fought in July 1863.

Historical characters in the musical were limited to Abraham Lincoln (1809–1865) (whose words are read by an off-stage voice) and Frederick Douglass (1818–1895). Only one other character represented a real person: Lydia Bixby (18??–1878), a Boston widow who lost five sons during the war and received a brief but eloquent letter of condolence from President Lincoln. The letter, which Mrs. Bixby received in November 1864, is viewed as one of Lincoln's finest written works and is often quoted in memorials.

Shenandoah was a success because it zeroed in on a specific family and how its members dealt with the war as a framework for the narrative. Because *The Civil War* treated the war in broad strokes, the canvas was too large to fill, and the musical, for all of its technical glitter and bravura singing talent, just didn't resonate with audiences.

PRODUCTION NOTES

The Civil War made its debut on September 16, 1998 at the Alley Theatre in Houston, where its coauthor Gregory Boyd had served as artistic director since 1989. Critics of the original production complained about the lack of a narrative structure and the songs' grandeur without gravity, but despite this, the Houston production did well at the box office, resulting in enough backing to move it to Broadway the following April. By this time, there had been major revisions made to the show's structure, but it still retained the theatrical concert setting. This time, New York critics were even more merciless in their attacks on the show's concept, pointing out its clichéd themes and simplistic messages.

The show's Broadway run was brief; it closed after only sixty-one performances, despite garnering Tony nominations for Best Musical and Best Original Score, with Boyd's book glaring in the absence of its recognition. In 2000, it toured the United States with a cast whittled down from twenty-eight to fifteen, receiving somewhat more favorable notices, especially after the 9/11 attacks the following year, when heightened patriotism softened criticism. In 2009, a new production was mounted at Ford's Theatre in Washington, DC to commemorate the bicentennial of Abraham Lincoln's birth, featuring the recorded voice of Hal Holbrook as Lincoln. The concert setting was actually better suited for a museum theater than on Broadway, where storytelling is paramount to a show's success. One can envision the segments playing on a video screen in which museum visitors shuffle in and out in groups of ten or fifteen at a time, but none staying to watch the entire show.

SCORE

With no stories to tell, the songs in *The Civil War* served as empty emotional statements: armies defiantly raising their swords and rifles, proud slaves defiantly protesting their forced captivity by proclaiming with rousing gospel fervor that "someday we'll all be free," and the audience expected to clap along in exuberant reverence. Ben Brantley of the *New York Times* merely yawned at the score, calling the songs "a jukebox stocked entirely with B-side selections."

The show's musical style was a pastiche of power ballads with shades of roots-oriented genres like country and gospel, watered down for Broadway consumption. Occasionally one would hear a fiddle, banjo, recorder, or thumb piano in the background, but these were used merely as token accents instead of a stylistic representation of the times. Added to this was a succession of soaring showstoppers looking for a show to stop. With no narrative framework to hang the songs on, few of the score's two dozen songs came off as either original or memorable. Many were pale copies of similar songs from other shows: "The Glory" paralleling "One Day More" from *Les Misèrables*, "Freedom's Child" recalling "Make Them Hear You" from *Ragtime*. "Greenback," a colorful change-of-pace number, was sung by Leo Burmester as Autolycus Fell, whose first name references a legendary thief in Greek mythology. The spoken introduction to the song implies that Autolycus is a pimp selling "horizontal refreshment" to naive soldiers, but the song then morphs into a boastful song about his accumulation of wealth, like "Master of the House" from *Les Misèrables* but not half as funny. After a while, too much weighty nobility becomes tiresome, and *The Civil War* overflows with it. It was as if Wildhorn and Murphy were putting together an entire musical of 11:00 numbers.

In a season in which formless scores abounded (*Passion*, *Parade*), audiences were looking for something they could whistle after leaving the theater. The score's abundance of soaring ballads, aimed squarely at pop audiences, just didn't register, due to the lack of context and a meaningful story arc.

Miss Liberty

Historical context: The construction of the Statue of Liberty
Time period: 1885–1886
Broadway run: July 15, 1949–April 8, 1950 (308 p.)
Venue: Imperial Theatre
Book: Robert E. Sherwood
Score: Irving Berlin
Cast album: Columbia Records MM-860 (78 rpm) (1949)
Major characters: Horace Miller (Eddie Albert), Maisie Doll (Mary McCarty), Monique DuPont (Allyn McLerie), James Gordon Bennett (Charles Dingle), Joseph Pulitzer (Philip Bourneuf), Auguste Bartholdi (Herbert Berghof)

HISTORICAL BACKGROUND

The idea behind constructing the Statue of Liberty began with Edouard de Laboulaye, a French abolitionist who wanted to have a statue built to honor the United States in its centennial year of 1876 and also to commemorate its long-standing friendship with France. Five years later, French sculptor Frédéric Auguste Bartholdi (1834–1904) began work designing the statue, which was tentatively called "Liberty Enlightening the World." Bartholdi reportedly based the image of the proud lady with the lamp, beckoning to the world's bedraggled, on that of his own mother. On a trip to the United States in 1871, Bartholdi selected tiny Bedloe's Island in New York Harbor as the site where the statue would stand, selected for its ability to be seen by every ship entering the harbor.

The first segment of the statue to be completed was the arm holding the torch, which was presented and displayed at Philadelphia's Centennial

Exposition in 1876. By 1878, the head and shoulders were completed and displayed at the Paris Universal Exposition. It took three years, from 1881 to 1884, for the entire statue to be completed.

On July 4, 1884, the statue was presented to Levi P. Morton, the US minister to France, and then disassembled and shipped to the United

Allyn McLerie in *Miss Liberty*.
PHOTOFEST

States aboard the French naval ship, the *Isère*. On July 17, 1885, the ship with the crates containing the statue's numerous parts arrived, but $250,000 was still needed to build the granite pedestal on which it would stand. New York governor Grover Cleveland refused to take money from city coffers to fund construction of the pedestal, and when Congress was also unwilling to come up with the money, four US cities—Baltimore, Boston, Philadelphia, and San Francisco—offered to put up the remaining funds under the stipulation that the statue be relocated to their city.

In 1883, American poet Emma Lazarus was asked to write a poem to help inspire donors to contribute to the building of the pedestal. The result was "The New Colossus," a sonnet that included the memorable sentence, "Give me your tired, your poor, your huddled masses, yearning to breathe free, the wretched refuse of your teeming shore."

Ultimately, it fell to Joseph Pulitzer (1847–1911), publisher of the *New York World*, to secure the statue for New York. In March 1885, Pulitzer exercised the power of the press and made a plea in the *World* for its readers to help fund the building of the pedestal. The result was a massive response from the city's citizenry, a nineteenth-century version of a GoFundMe drive, with the newspaper's crack team of journalists contributing to the cause by writing emotionally charged articles about the significance of the statue. As money started pouring in, the *World* chronicled each and every donation sent to the paper. No amount was too small to print, and families' donations, in the amount of pennies, nickels, and dimes, were all noted in the paper's regularly updated tally. On March 22, the *World* reported that the Philip Bender family of Jersey City, New Jersey, had donated a grand total of $2.65 to the effort, with parents Philip and Eliza Bender giving fifty cents each and their eight children contributing amounts in nickels, dimes, and quarters.

Momentum grew with each day. On May 30, Jonathan Sooville, the mayor of Buffalo, donated his entire annual salary, a sum of $230.00, to the cause. Forty-three of New York City's wealthiest citizens gave $250.00 each. The *World* offered rewards, such as a gold coin to the donor who contributed the largest amount. In August, after five months of pleading, $101,091 had been raised, more than enough to complete the job.

When the granite slab was finally installed on Bedloe's Island, the statue, now called the Statue of Liberty, was reassembled in place. On October 28, 1886, the same Grover Cleveland, who as governor had refused to allocate money from city funds to support the pedestal's construction, was now the twenty-second president of the United States and presided over the dedication ceremony. In 1903, Emma Lazarus's poem, "The New Colossus," was cast in bronze on a plaque that was mounted inside the pedestal's lower level.

The true story of the creation of the Statue of Liberty is a remarkable example of a rainbow coalition of rich and poor citizens coming together for a common cause. It was a Herculean effort that resulted in one of the proudest accomplishments of Joseph Pulitzer's life; however, when the musical that would become *Miss Liberty* came into being, this amazing, dramatic, uplifting story was almost totally ignored.

PRODUCTION NOTES

At the end of World War II, playwright Robert E. Sherwood (1896–1955) was crossing the Atlantic aboard the *Queen Mary* on his way to his new home in Surrey, thirty miles from London. On board were thousands of soldiers being transported to Europe for active duty. Noticing the emotional reactions of the GIs upon passing the Statue of Liberty, Sherwood got an idea for doing a musical about the construction of the statue. When he arrived in England, he met with Irving Berlin (1888–1989), who was visiting his English publishing office, and invited him to write the score. Sherwood had done his research and was aware of the Pulitzer-led fundraising campaign, but decided to go in a different direction. Sherwood, ironically a Pulitzer Prize winner himself, decided instead to focus on the competitive atmosphere between Pulitzer's *World* and the *New York Herald*, whose own publisher, James Gordon Bennett (1841–1918), assigns rookie reporter Horace Miller to document the ceremony in which Pulitzer hands over the check for the construction of the pedestal.

Horace bungles the assignment by taking photos of the packing cases containing the pieces of the statue instead of documenting the ceremony and is fired, but his girlfriend talks him into going to Paris to find the model who posed for Bartholdi's statue, hoping to make amends by delivering the scoop of all scoops to the *Herald*. In Bartholdi's Paris studio, Horace meets penniless model Monique duPont, who lives under a bridge with a daffy elderly flower seller known only as "The Countess." When Horace first sees Monique, she is assuming the pose of the Statue of Liberty, leading Horace to believe she was the model he was looking for. Horace brings the unsuspecting Monique to America to great acclaim; she is deemed the living symbol of Liberty herself with Horace ultimately falling in love with her.

Berlin, however, conducted his own research on the history of the statue and told Sherwood that the inspiration for Lady Liberty wasn't a bedraggled gypsy music hall girl but the sculptor's own sainted mother, throwing a monkey wrench into Sherwood's story. Sherwood then changed the plot so that it focused on a competitive battle between Pulitzer and Bennett for circulation supremacy. When the true inspiration for the statue is revealed, Horace is thrown in jail and Monique threatened with deportation.

With Moss Hart coming on board to direct and Jerome Robbins to choreograph, it appeared that all elements were in place for a sure-fire hit. Berlin was coming off the massively popular *Annie Get Your Gun* and Broadway patrons were eagerly looking forward to the premiere of the show, now called *Miss Liberty*, to the tune of $50,000 in advance sales. Berlin and Sherwood were so sure they had a hit on their hands that they decided to produce the show themselves. *Miss Liberty* would premiere at a perfect time in New York history, fresh from the Allies' triumph over Nazism and resplendent as the center for world culture.

Problems began when Berlin delivered the score even before Sherwood finished his libretto, hoping to have the musical open on the Fourth of July. Berlin had always had difficulty integrating music into his shows; wise overseers like Richard Rodgers and Oscar Hammerstein would certainly have improved *Miss Liberty*, but Berlin and Sherwood had their heads in the clouds and pressed on. Sherwood proved to be obdurately recalcitrant and refused to alter the book, leading Moss Hart to threaten to quit the production altogether. The notoriously frugal Berlin decided against hiring high-priced Broadway talent, preferring to use less experienced actors. As rehearsals dragged on through the spring of 1949, Rodgers and Hammerstein's *South Pacific* opened to universal acclaim with the biggest advance ticket sales in Broadway history.

With rewrites persisting almost until opening night, *Miss Liberty* was the first show to make its debut in the 1949–1950 Broadway season, but *New York Times* critic Brooks Atkinson threw cold water into *Miss Liberty's* face with a scathing review, labeling the show "old fashioned" and "disappointing." Atkinson gave mild praise to Berlin's score but saved his ire for Sherwood's wooden, routine book. With *South Pacific*, *Kiss Me, Kate*, and *High Button Shoes* garnering raves, along with other plays such as *Death of a Salesman* and *Anne of a Thousand Days* drawing big crowds, there was no room for *Miss Liberty*. A follow-up article by Atkinson, in which the critic labeled the show a "missed opportunity" to capitalize on the wave of patriotic fever Americans were experiencing after the world war's successful conclusion, sealed its coffin.

Despite critics' lukewarm response to the show, praise was reserved for its two stars: Eddie Albert, who played Horace, and Allyn McLerie as Monique. In addition, critics gave raves to seventy-two-year-old Ethel Griffies as the Countess and ensemble dancer Tommy Rall, saving *Miss Liberty* from being a total disaster.

As far as history is concerned, although the *World* and the *Herald* were rival newspapers, the fabricated story about the fraudulent model who inspired the statue's creation became the show's downfall. No one cared about its characters, all of whom seemed to have avaricious motives. Despite writing actual historical figures into the story, including newspaper moguls Pulitzer and Bennett and sculptor Bartholdi, *Miss Liberty* took a truly heartwarming story and turned it into a cynical mess.

SCORE

After the success of *Annie Get Your Gun*, Irving Berlin had become confident to the point of arrogance with his abilities as a songwriter and was fully anticipating every song in *Miss Liberty* to become a hit. This proved to be his undoing because ever since *Oklahoma!* made its debut in 1943, Broadway musicals had changed, with songs now being routinely integrated into story lines and relevance to plot now superseding any ideas of a song becoming popular on the Hit Parade. *Annie Get Your Gun*, with its bevy of hits, convinced Berlin that he could do it again, but the songs in *Miss Liberty* proved to be a drag on the show's literary momentum.

Berlin was most enthusiastic about "Give Me Your Tired, Your Poor," the only song he ever composed with words written by someone else, in this case, taking them directly from Emma Lazarus's sonnet. When he invited songwriter/arranger Gordon Jenkins to come to his office to hear his song, Berlin proudly predicted it would become an anthem comparable to his previous hit, "God Bless America" and was already planning to establish a Give Me Your Tired, Your Poor Foundation, but when Jenkins blithely informed Berlin that he himself had used the poem in his own 1946 cantata called *Manhattan Tower*, Berlin cursed Jenkins and threw him out of his office, refusing to believe it.

"Give Me Your Tired, Your Poor" ended up having a life after *Miss Liberty* after all, although it never ascended to the heights reached by "God Bless America." An arrangement by Roy Ringwald for a choral series published for Fred Waring's publishing company became a staple in the repertoire of high school, college, and amateur choirs and was performed often by Waring's own vocal glee unit. During the dark, pessimistic days of the Cold War, the song was often programmed at patriotic civic ceremonies to showcase pride in American liberty.

As for the other songs in the score, only a few became popular outside of the musical, the best known being "Let's Take an Old-Fashioned Walk," which became a pop hit for Perry Como and was also recorded by Sarah Vaughan and as a duet by Frank Sinatra and Doris Day. Of the other songs, only "The Most Expensive Statue in the World," which was mostly spoken rather than sung, had anything to do with the construction of the statue. Most dealt with the show's fictional romantic entanglement, with a few, such as "Little Fish in a Big Pond," becoming a total embarrassment.

Annie Get Your Gun

Historical context: The life of Annie Oakley
Time period: 1885
Broadway run: May 16, 1946–February 12, 1949 (1,147 p.)
Venue: Imperial Theatre
Book: Herbert Fields and Dorothy Fields
Score: Irving Berlin
Cast album: Decca DL-9018 (1946)
Major characters: Annie Oakley (Ethel Merman), Frank Butler (Ray Middleton), Charlie Davenport (Marty May), William F. "Buffalo Bill" Cody (William O'Neal), Winnie Tate (Betty Anne Nyman), Tommy Keeler (Kenny Bowers)

HISTORICAL BACKGROUND

William F. "Buffalo Bill" Cody (1846–1917) worked as a cattle herder, wagon train driver, gold miner, and Pony Express rider before ever getting into show business. He became known for killing 4,282 buffalo in eighteen months between 1867 and 1868, earning his nickname while supplying Kansas Pacific Railroad workers with American bison meat. In December 1872, at the age of twenty-six, Cody made his first acting appearance, in *Scouts of the Prairie*, a drama created by dime novelist Ned Buntline. The following year he organized his own show, the Buffalo Bill Combination, which featured frontier-scout-turned-actor "Texas Jack" Omohundro, noted for performing the first roping act on an American stage. A succeeding play, *Scouts of the Plains*, featured, for a brief period, famed gunfighter "Wild Bill" Hickok, who hated acting and once pulled a gun and shot out a spotlight that was focused on him.

Cody continued staging plays until 1882, when he created his Wild West show, an outdoor spectacle in which he utilized the talents of authentic working cowboys and cowgirls to demonstrate such ranch activities as bronco riding, calf roping, and other skills that would become popular at rodeos.

Along with minstrel shows, which began during the 1830s, Wild West shows became a popular aspect of traveling entertainment during the nineteenth century, forerunners of what would become vaudeville in the United States. Buffalo Bill's Wild West led the way as the first of these traveling shows, which featured historical tableaux, exhibitions of marksmanship, foot races, and rodeo-style events. Native Americans from the Pawnee and Lakota tribes, called "Show Indians," were also hired, presented in sensationalist demonstrations as curious and threatening savages adept at archery and showcased as skilled equestrians. The Wild West shows influenced the influx of Western films, rodeos, and circuses that are still in evidence today.

Cody was unusual in his respectful, benevolent treatment of Native Americans; he gave them the opportunity to share their culture with his audiences. In addition, Cody had a great affection for children and would distribute free passes to his Wild West shows at orphanages when he came to town. Thirty years before the suffragette movement, Cody was championing women's rights, advocating equal rights and women's suffrage. Women performers hired by Cody received equal pay for equal work and often out-rode and out-shot their male counterparts.

It was into this realm, in 1885, that Annie Oakley (1860–1926) joined Buffalo Bill's Wild West. Born Phoebe Ann Mosey, Oakley demonstrated her remarkable shooting abilities when she was still a child. At the age of fifteen, she defeated expert marksman Frank E. Butler (1847–1926) in a shooting contest, beginning a friendship that would culminate in their marriage in 1876. When they began their professional partnership, she assumed her stage surname "Oakley," ostensibly named after the Cincinnati neighborhood where the couple had taken up residence.

Oakley's performances in Buffalo Bill's Wild West included such stunts as hitting dimes tossed into the air, shooting over her shoulder while holding a hand mirror, riddling a tossed playing card with bullets before it hit the ground, and shooting off the end of a lit cigar from her husband's lips. In time, Oakley became so good at her craft that Frank Butler gave up shooting altogether and became her manager.

Buffalo Bill's Wild West made Annie Oakley a star. The Hunkpapa Lakota leader Chief Sitting Bull (c. 1831–1890), who had massacred the forces of General William Armstrong Custer at the Battle of Little Big Horn, started his own show business career in 1884 with his show, Sitting Bull Connection. It was at an appearance in Minnesota that Sitting Bull first met Annie Oakley. The two developed a close friendship, with Sitting Bull symbolically adopting her later that year and giving her

Annie Oakley (1860–1926).
PHOTOFEST

the name Little Sure Shot, inspired by her slight, five-foot-tall frame. Oakley would use the name throughout her career. In 1885, Sitting Bull and Oakley joined Buffalo Bill's Wild West. Sitting Bull would appear in the show for the next four months, earning fifty dollars a week signing autographs and posing for pictures.

PRODUCTION NOTES

The idea to create a musical around the life of Annie Oakley is credited to Dorothy Fields (1904–1974), a lyricist who had written words with composer Jimmy McHugh for such Tin Pan Alley standards as "On the Sunny Side of the Street" and "I Can't Give You Anything But Love." Teaming up with her brother Herbert, she helped write the books for three Cole Porter shows, including *Let's Face It* (1941), which made a star of Danny Kaye, and *Mexican Hayride* (1944), featuring Bobby Clark and June Havoc. During World War II, Fields, a regular patron of New York's ritzy 21 Club, was listening to someone from the Travelers Aid Society talking about seeing a sharpshooter win every contest he entered at Coney Island when, out of the blue, she got a brainstorm for a new musical, envisioning Ethel Merman playing Annie Oakley.

After she shared her idea with her brother Herbert, the pair approached impresario Michael Todd, producer of the extravagant *Mexican Hayride*, reasoning that a woman with a gun would resonate with wartime audiences, in which women had been an important part of the war effort. Todd didn't buy it, so the Fieldses went to Richard Rodgers and Oscar Hammerstein II, who agreed to produce the show, now titled *Annie Get Your Gun*, but not to write the score. Instead, they recommended Jerome Kern, composer of *Show Boat*, who hadn't had a Broadway hit since *Roberta* in 1933 and was now writing for motion pictures. Kern was reluctant to return to the East because his doctor had advised him to avoid stress due to his high blood pressure; the last thing he needed was the risk of another stage flop. Eventually, Rodgers and Hammerstein talked Kern into doing the score, with Dorothy Fields taking on the task of lyricist. On November 4, 1945, the day after Kern returned to New York from California, he was walking in Midtown Manhattan when he suffered a sudden cerebral hemorrhage and collapsed, at the corner of Park Avenue and Fifty-Seventh Street. He died a week later at the age of sixty.

After Kern's funeral, Rodgers and the Fieldses got together at a restaurant to decide what composer of Kern's status they could get to write the show. The only two names that came to mind were Cole Porter and Irving Berlin. They immediately dismissed the idea of asking Porter, whose sophisticated wit just didn't work for a show about the Wild West. Eventually, they approached Berlin, whose last two Broadway shows, *Louisiana Purchase* (1940) and *This Is the Army* (1942) had seen moderate success. Berlin had donated nearly ten million dollars of his earnings from his wartime revue to the US Army and thought that returning to Broadway in a production produced by Rodgers and Hammerstein and written by Dorothy and Herbert Fields would be a can't-miss opportunity. Although his productions customarily included his name in front of the title of a show (*Irving Berlin's This Is the Army*), Berlin agreed to relinquish the billing in exchange for a 30 percent cut of the box office and began work on what he called "hillbilly stuff." Berlin soon realized that *Annie Get Your Gun* wasn't about hillbillies; it was about show business, something with which he was quite familiar. He would write the score in a matter of a few months, later saying that it was the most pleasant job he ever had.

Ethel Merman was recovering from a Caesarian section birth of her son, Bobby, when Dorothy Fields called her at the hospital and told her about her idea. Merman agreed to play the part of Annie Oakley and rehearsals for the show began in February 1946. Robust-voiced Ray Middleton was cast as Frank Butler while William O'Neal played Buffalo Bill.

The show begins as Buffalo Bill's Wild West arrives in Cincinnati, with Butler challenging anyone in town to a shooting match. When Annie, a plain-looking teenager in ragged clothes who is good with a gun, beats him, she is invited to join the troupe. She falls in love with Butler but eventually replaces him as the show's chief attraction, resulting in tension between the two (shades of *A Star Is Born*). When the show falls on hard times, Buffalo Bill decides to merge his Wild West with another Western show led by his rival, Pawnee Bill.

The fictionalized story changes some of the chronology in the lives of the show's characters. In reality, Annie Oakley and Frank Butler married in 1876, nine years before the action in the musical takes place. The resentment Butler felt after being bested by Oakley was fabricated to create the main conflict of the story. It is also unlikely that Annie ever deliberately threw a match in order to appease Frank's masculine ego. In reality, the fact that Annie was a better shot than Frank was one thing he loved about her.

The story could have been more compelling had Annie Oakley's real role as a champion of women's rights been more pronounced. Her innate talent for sharpshooting helped her overcome poverty, prejudice against women in show business, and her own modesty about her talents. Her fight to secure equal rights for women would have certainly resonated, except this was the 1940s, when women's roles in society were still considered subservient to men. Today's audiences cringe when they see Annie deliberately losing to Butler in their final challenge just to appease his ego.

According to Bess Edwards, Oakley's grandniece, Annie Oakley got her stage name not after the Ohio town where she and Frank Butler lived but from a man who rescued the teenaged Annie from an oppressive county poor farm where she was living with a local family that abused her, both mentally and physically. Annie had run away from the family, and the man, whose name was Oakley, gave her train fare to complete her escape. Edwards objected vehemently to many aspects of the show, including the representation of Annie at the beginning of the show as an ignorant, illiterate, disheveled girl. In reality, she was far from the brash persona imbued in Ethel Merman's performance; her grandniece said that during breaks in shows, she would sit quietly in her dressing room, knitting. One aspect of the show that was correct was the depiction of the warmth and respect Sitting Bull felt for Annie, as an outgrowth of his admiration of her skills with firearms.

Merman enjoyed playing the part of Annie Oakley because it enabled her to flesh out her "brassy dame" persona into a character that had more depth and a soft side. The role ended up being, along with Mama Rose in *Gypsy*, one of the two defining performances of her career. *Annie Get Your Gun* ended up being a smash hit, running for nearly three years on Broadway. A popular motion picture version starring Betty Hutton and Howard Keel was released in 1950. Merman reprised her role in a 1966

Broadway revival, with Bruce Yarnell playing Frank. A second revival in 1999 starred Bernadette Peters and Tom Wopat, with a revised book that had the final shooting match between Annie and Frank ending in a tie.

SCORE

Irving Berlin's score to *Annie Get Your Gun* featured a bevy of some of his best-loved songs, most notably "There's No Business Like Show Business," which had nothing to do with the plot, but nevertheless became an anthem of Berlin's career, taking a place of honor beside "God Bless America" and "White Christmas." Berlin auditioned his songs before an audience consisting of producers Richard Rodgers and Oscar Hammerstein, librettist Dorothy Fields, and director Joshua Logan. Berlin had a quaint manner of performing but was keenly attuned to any reactions from his esteemed audience. When Rodgers didn't bat an eye after Berlin croaked out "There's No Business Like Show Business," the sensitive composer put the song away, thinking Rodgers didn't like it. At the next run-through, Rodgers asked him what had happened to the song, which he said he was crazy about. After a panic-stricken search of Berlin's office, they finally found the manuscript neatly placed underneath a telephone book and it was reinserted into the score.

Most of the numbers were character songs (Annie's "I am" song, "Doin' What Comes Natur'lly," and Frank's "I'm a Bad, Bad Man"). The show's two love duets, "The Girl That I Marry" and "They Say It's Wonderful" became enduring standards. Removed from the score for the 1999 revival were "Colonel Buffalo Bill" and "I'm an Indian, Too," both deemed insensitive to Native Americans.

The last song to be added was "Anything You Can Do," the result of Joshua Logan's request for a second-act duet for Merman and Ray Middleton. Since Annie and Frank were at odds with one another and not speaking at this point in the story, Rodgers suggested some kind of a challenge song. Berlin's eyes lit up; he went home, and wrote "Anything You Can Do" in a matter of fifteen minutes. Berlin's biographer, Laurence Bergreen, suggested that the song reflected the competitive Berlin's obsession with Rodgers's own successes as a songwriter and he enjoyed rubbing it into Rodgers's face at every opportunity.

Show Boat

Historical context: The era of floating theaters in the American frontier
Time period: 1887–1927
Broadway run: December 27, 1927–May 4, 1929 (575 p.)
Venue: Ziegfeld Theatre
Book: Oscar Hammerstein II, based on *Show Boat* by Edna Ferber
Score: Jerome Kern (music), Oscar Hammerstein II (lyrics);
lyrics for "Bill" by P. G. Wodehouse; music and lyrics for "Goodbye,
My Lady Love" by Joseph E. Howard; music and lyrics for "After
the Ball" by Charles K. Harris
Cast album: Brunswick 20114–20117 (78 rpm album) (1932)
Major characters: Gaylord Ravenal (Howard Marsh), Magnolia
(Norma Terris), Julie (Helen Morgan), Steve (Charles Ellis), Cap'n
Andy (Charles Winninger), Parthy (Edna May Oliver), Joe (Jules
Bledsoe), Queenie (Tess Gardella, aka "Aunt Jemima"), Frank
(Sammy White), Ellie (Eva Puck)

HISTORICAL BACKGROUND

Edna Ferber's (1885–1968) 1926 novel chronicled the lives of three generations of performers on the *Cotton Blossom*, a steamboat that traveled on the Mississippi River, giving performances to residents in small towns along its banks. The tradition of theatrical showboats dates to 1816, when keelboats were repurposed as floating theaters, bringing valued entertainment to frontier communities along America's rivers. Before the advent of the railroad, this became the main method for what served as national tours, but showboats were also ancestral precedents for what would become vaudeville by the turn of the twentieth century.

The first showboat built solely for the purpose of presenting traveling entertainment was the *Floating Theater*, launched in 1831 by a British-born actor named William Chapman Sr., whose cast included himself and his family of nine. Beginning in Pittsburgh, Chapman and his family floated from town to town, performing plays such as Shakespeare's *The Taming*

Charles Winninger as Cap'n Andy in *Show Boat* (1927).
PHOTOFEST

of the Shrew, adding music and dance numbers as sidelights. When they reached New Orleans, they junked the boat, returned to Pittsburgh by steamer, and started again the next year with another vessel. The practice proved popular and successful; and subsequently, grander showboats were built to feature not just plays, but equestrian shows, wax museums, and other kinds of attractions, with seating capacity reaching as high as 3,400.

Disrupted by the Civil War, the showboat tradition vanished until 1878, when it was revived, including vaudeville revues and melodramas. Steam-powered calliopes, first patented in 1855, were used on river excursions as well as on showboats, their powerful clarion calls alerting towns of a boat's presence from miles away.

Destined to extinction with the advent of railroads and automobiles, which allowed Americans to more easily travel to cities that featured regular entertainment venues, showboats became grander and more ornately decorated over the years. (The term "showboating" was derived from this practice, meant to describe the actions of someone behaving ostentatiously.) After 1900, most showboats featured exclusively melodramas, with seating topping out at 1,400 on the *Golden Rod*, the last traveling showboat, which ended operations in 1943.

Edna Ferber gathered material for her novel by doing extensive research on the showboat tradition, eventually spending four days on the *James Adams Floating Palace Theatre* in Bath, North Carolina. The *Cotton Blossom*, the boat featured in Ferber's novel as well as the Broadway musical, was the name of an actual showboat, whose history dates to 1891, when Ellsworth Eugene Eisenbarth, a twenty-six-year-old budding impresario, bought a floating store that he retrofitted as a showboat, naming it *The Eisenbarth Wild West and Floating Opera*. In addition to his showboat, Eisenbarth and his wife also inaugurated a traveling railway show, which featured a calliope and a full-sized orchestra, traveling throughout the Midwest by rail.

In February 1900, the Eisenbarths converted a glass barge into the *Eisenbarth-Henderson Floating Theatre*, promoted as "The New Great Modern Temple of Amusement," bringing performances of Shakespeare and other classic plays to towns along the Mississippi and Ohio rivers, with advertisements boasting "the largest seating capacity of any marine theater ever constructed." In 1909, Eisenbarth sold his floating theater to the Needham-Steiner Amusement Company of Chicago, which remodeled it and renamed the boat the *Cotton Blossom*. The *Cotton Blossom* was painted white and gold, with red velour seats and matching curtains with strings of electric lights illuminating its decks. Programs were changed to more mainstream melodramas and vaudeville revues, but after a year of operation, the *Cotton Blossom* was sold again, this time to Ralph Emerson, "The Showboat King," who owned a fleet of nine similar vessels that sailed on America's rivers from Pittsburgh to New Orleans. The *Cotton Blossom* flourished until 1917, when it was crushed by ice while tied up at Mount Vernon, Indiana, marking the beginning of the end for the showboat industry. Motion pictures were capturing the attention of America's entertainment industry, and in the next decade, showboats began vanishing from the scene.

PRODUCTION NOTES

Composer Jerome Kern (1885–1945) got the idea to make a musical out of Edna Ferber's novel in October 1926, a month after the book was published. He contacted his friend and fellow Algonquin Hotel habitué, Alexander Woollcott, theater critic for the *New York World*, asking if he had read the book. When Woollcott said that he had, Kern asked him if he knew Ferber personally. Woollcott, whose expansive personality made him thrive in instances where he was the center of attention, agreed to introduce Kern to Ferber and did so, at the opening of *Criss Cross*, a musical Kern had recently written.

Ferber was reluctant about Kern's proposed adaptation for several reasons. First was the sweeping, fifty-year time span of the novel. Then there were the matters of key plot devices involving miscegenation, alcoholism, and spousal desertion, all of which were totally alien to Broadway's usual fare of lighthearted musical comedies featuring the well-to-do in carefree, upscale locales such as colleges, country clubs, and fancy estates. Even more importantly, the musical would have to combine white and Black actors and singers, an unheard of practice for its time.

Kern had already decided that thirty-one-year-old Oscar Hammerstein II (1895–1960) would write the musical's libretto. Hammerstein was a forward-thinking lyricist and writer who had been working with such composers as Otto Harbach, Rudolf Friml, and Sigmund Romberg. On November 17, Ferber agreed to sign over the dramatico-musical rights to Kern and Hammerstein, with a promise to deliver the finished adaptation by January 1, 1927, a matter of only six weeks.

Nine days after signing the contract, Kern and Hammerstein presented parts of their proposed score to Florenz Ziegfeld, who they had selected to produce the play. Ziegfeld was currently beginning construction on a new theater bearing his name, which opened on February 2, 1927, with the musical comedy *Rio Rita*, starring the vaudeville comedy team Bert Wheeler and Robert Woolsey.

Hammerstein, known as a workmanlike writer of light opera and musical comedy, was devoted to Ferber's book, which resulted in him dramatizing nearly every key scene in the story. This frustrated the notoriously impatient Ziegfeld, who expected the play to be produced before the first day of April. Hammerstein would make many changes to the novel, tightening the chronology of the story arc, eliminating minor characters, combining others, and, in adhering to theatrical conventions of the day, ensuring that no characters died.

The story focused on two white couples: riverboat gambler Gaylord Ravenal, who falls in love with Magnolia, the eighteen-year-old daughter of the *Cotton Blossom*'s Cap'n Andy; and Julie Dozier, the boat's reigning star, and Steve Baker, her leading man. When it is revealed that Julie is a mulatto (born of mixed ethnic parents), she is banished from the boat and begins a steady, downward spiral, resulting in her becoming an alcoholic and singing in cheap Chicago dance halls. Miscegenation, the interbreeding of mixed races, was against the law in thirty-eight states in the late 1800s, and even by 1924, the ban was still on the books in twenty-nine states. Julie's fall from grace was seen as an implicit indictment of her ancestry, whereas Magnolia, who is deserted by Ravenal, a compulsive gambler, is seen as a heroic figure for surviving as a single mother after Ravenal abandons his wife and young child in shame.

Show Boat opened at the National Theatre on November 15, 1927, the epic production beginning at 8:30 p.m. and concluding more than four hours later, at 12:40 a.m. The opening night audience was shocked by a show that was unlike any Ziegfeld production they had seen. In addition to the mixed cast, there were no showy Ziegfeld production numbers, no light comedy scenes, and no frivolous songs, even though Ziegfeld advertised *Show Boat* as a "musical comedy."

Although today, the themes touched on in *Show Boat* are commonplace, in 1927 they were unheard of. For the first time, Black characters were given a sense of humanity and depth and were treated seriously. Dramatizing the other taboo subjects was just as daring.

The opening night audience was thunderstruck and did not know how to react. When they walked into the theater, they expected the usual Ziegfeld showcase: beautifully coiffed chorus girls and lighthearted subject matter. On that first night there was no applause, not even after Bledsoe's affecting solo on "Ol' Man River." Except for some polite clapping at the end of each act, the audience remained silent. At intermission, patrons chatted about trivialities, discussing any subject other than the show's content. Ziegfeld was devastated, believing he had made a tragic mistake in staging *Show Boat*. He cringed whenever "Ol' Man River" was sung. "Goldie" Stanton Clough, Ziegfeld's longtime secretary, actually saw the impresario crying while sitting on steps leading to the balcony.

Things changed for the better after critics raved about the production in the morning newspapers. Immediately, lines started forming at the box office and on the second night, it was as if a giant switch had been turned on. Suddenly, the audience's reaction changed. Huge ovations were given after every number. At intermission, cries of "wonderful!" "beautiful story!" and "the best thing I ever saw" flooded the theater and the lobby. By the end of the year, *Show Boat* was transferred to Ziegfeld's grand new theater, where it remained throughout the rest of its 575-performance run.

Show Boat is noteworthy in Broadway history as being the first musical to fully integrate story and song, an aspect that would not be solidified for another sixteen years, when *Oklahoma!* revolutionized Broadway musicals by integrating not just music but dance into its story. In addition, *Show Boat* daringly brought Black and white performers, both actors and ensemble singers, together on the stage. Oscar Hammerstein insisted on retaining a racial epithet used in dialog as an indictment of the times and conditions Black Americans were experiencing. Hammerstein's fervent stand against racism would be reflected by a later show, *South Pacific*, which featured his most famous statement on the matter, the song "You've Got to Be Carefully Taught."

Another innovation pioneered by *Show Boat* involved actual character development and growth. Characters in Broadway musicals in 1927 remained exactly the same at the final curtain as they appeared when they were introduced. In *Show Boat*, Magnolia, played by Norma Terris, goes through a marked transformation, surviving and even flourishing as a single parent after her "no-account" gambling husband deserts her and her young child.

The show's Black couple, Joe the stevedore and his wife Queenie, the *Cotton Blossom*'s cook, represent stability to contrast with the two troubled white couples. (Ironically, Queenie was played not by a Black actress, but by Tess Gardella, a white entertainer who performed in blackface so often, her stage name "Aunt Jemima" was used in the show's program. When Gardella reprised her role in the 1932 revival, credit was restored to her real name.)

The play's second act begins at the Midway Plaisance, at the 1893 World's Columbian Exposition in Chicago, which celebrated the four hundredth anniversary of Columbus's arrival in the New World. The scene featured backdrop images of many of the fair's famous exhibits, including the original Ferris wheel, the MacMonnies Fountain, and Hagenback's wild animal arena. A song, "At the Chicago World's Fair," was featured in the original 1927 production but was omitted from all subsequent film versions. Hammerstein and Kern added the song "In Dahomey" after learning about the employing of African natives in exhibits at world's fairs; the Chicago exposition's Dahomey Village documented life in the West African kingdom. The song was used up until the 1946 revival but was cut from future productions.

Two other real-life locations showed up as settings in the original 1927 production. One was the Trocadero Theatre, one of Chicago's best-known burlesque houses, which opened in September 1899 and was especially known for its decadent entertainment. The other was St. Agatha's Catholic Church, founded in 1893 and located on Chicago's

West Side. St. Agatha's convent is where Magnolia leaves her eight-year-old daughter Kim and also where Ravenal bids her a final farewell.

Hammerstein's devotion to Ferber's original story resulted in an honest depiction of the lives of entertainers aboard showboats in the early part of the twentieth century, with real-life situations and dilemmas experienced by its characters. It continues to be, stylistically as well as historically, a milestone in the history of musical theater.

The much-vaunted 1951 MGM motion picture version, which starred Howard Keel, Kathryn Grayson, and Ava Gardner, followed the general storyline in Ferber's novel, but was stripped nearly completely of Hammerstein's dialog, as well as scenes and songs dealing with the show's secondary and peripheral characters (especially Joe and Queenie). All racial epithets were removed from the dialog, although a key scene remained in which Steve cuts Julie's hand and swallows some of her blood so that he can declare that he, too had "Negro blood" in him, thus avoiding the miscegenation charge.

Score

Show Boat's sumptuous score went through many changes over the years. Its most famous song, "Ol' Man River," was sung by the stevedore Joe, played in the original production by Jules Bledsoe. But it was Paul Robeson's memorable portrayal of Joe and especially his stirring performance of the song, first in the 1928 London production, then in the first Broadway revival in 1932, and finally in the 1936 motion picture, that resulted in the song becoming a classic. Robeson was Kern and Hammerstein's first choice to play Joe, but in October 1927, Robeson and his pianist-accompanist Lawrence Brown signed a contract for a one-year tour of Europe, where he had had significant success singing spirituals in 1922 and 1925. Robeson had reservations about playing Joe, a subservient Negro stevedore, but changed his mind and played the part when the London production was cast in 1928. In the 1936 film, Joe and Queenie, now played by Robeson and Hattie McDaniel, were given a new song, one of three written specifically for the film by Kern and Hammerstein, the charming "Ah Still Suits Me," which humanized their relationship.

Hammerstein didn't blanch at using the offensive epithet in the musical's introductory scene, in which an ensemble of stevedores begins the song's introductory quatrain, "N------ all work on de Mississippi." Over the years, the quatrain was gradually sanitized, changed to "Darkies all work on de Mississippi" in the 1936 film version (and on Robeson's initial recording), then to "colored folks" in the 1946 Broadway revival, and finally, "here we all work on the Mississippi," in the Jerome Kern film biography *Till the Clouds Roll By*. For the 1951 film, the quatrain was removed completely, with William Warfield beginning his rendering of the song with "Dere's an old man called the Mississippi," focusing on humanizing the spirit of the river. Through all of its permutations, "Ol' Man River" remained a powerful commentary using the Mississippi River to represent society's discrimination against Blacks, such as those who worked on board the *Cotton Blossom*, and, implicitly, how that discrimination carried over to the fate of Julie, a white person "infected" by Black blood, leading to her ultimate downfall.

In addition to "Ol' Man River," *Show Boat* featured other songs of lasting beauty and influence, including "Can't Help Lovin' Dat Man" and the torch song "Bill" (a Kern song from 1918 with lyrics by P. G. Wodehouse), both sung in the original production by Helen Morgan, and "Make Believe," the recurring love song sung by Howard Marsh and Norma Terris.

In addition to its importance as musical theater's first integrated musical (in structure as well as in casting), *Show Boat* also resulted in what could be considered the first Broadway "cast album." In 1932, Brunswick Records recorded eight sides of selections from the show's revival, featuring performances by Paul Robeson and Helen Morgan, and including the musical's overture and finale, played by a studio orchestra conducted by Victor Young. It was released as a sumptuous four-record, 78 rpm set, complete with elaborate artwork and liner notes, the first attempt to re-create a Broadway performance for listeners to experience in their own homes.

Newsies

Historical context: The newsboys' strike of 1899
Time period: 1899
Broadway run: March 29, 2012–August 24, 2014 (1004 p.)
Venue: Nederlander Theatre
Book: Harvey Fierstein, based on the Disney film, written by Bob Tzudiker and Noni White
Score: Alan Menken (music), Jack Feldman (lyrics)
Cast album: Ghostlight Records 8-4457 (2012)
Major characters: Jack Kelly (Jeremy Jordan), Crutchie (Andre Keenan-Bolger), Joseph Pulitzer (John Dossett), Katherine (Kara Lindsay), Davey (Ben Fankhauser), Spot Conlon (Tommy Bracco)

HISTORICAL BACKGROUND

There is nothing like a grassroots uprising pitting a group of idealistic oppressed underdogs against wealthy corporate magnates to inspire a Broadway musical. *Newsies* was the story of one such encounter, based on an actual 1899 strike by teenaged newspaper carriers against two powerful New York publishers.

In the years before modern communication (radio, television, computers), newspapers were the only way news could be disseminated to the masses. In New York City, newspapers were delivered by underage street urchins—teenaged orphans and runaways who had no other means of support. Sleeping on the streets and getting by on their wits and survival instinct, newsboys would pay fifty cents for a stack of one hundred newspapers and then sell them for a penny apiece. They earned their money by aggressive street sales tactics, but in order to make any money, they had to sell their entire lot of one hundred papers in order to earn just a fifty-cent profit. In the years before child labor laws were enacted, employers exploited children as cheap labor, paying low wages without benefits and forcing them to work long hours for no extra pay. In 1904, the National Child Labor Committee led the charge in restricting forced child labor, which met with fierce resistance, especially in Southern states. It wasn't until 1938, after the passage of the Fair Labor Standards Act, that a national minimum wage was established and limitations were placed on child labor.

All of that was in the future at the time newspaper tycoons Joseph Pulitzer (1847–1911) of the *New York World* and William Randolph Hearst of the *New York Journal* took advantage of the increased demand for newspapers, sparked by interest in the Spanish-American War, by raising the amount their young distributors had to pay from fifty to sixty cents per bundle of one hundred newspapers. When Pulitzer and Hearst failed to reduce prices after the end of the war, the newsboys, known as "newsies," formed a union and went on strike. For two weeks, beginning on July 18, 1899, angry newsboys (and some girls), marched in protest through the streets of Manhattan and across the Brooklyn Bridge, bringing traffic and businesses to a standstill.

The leader of the strike was eighteen-year-old Louis Balletti (1881–1913), who wore an eye patch because he was blind in one eye, prompting his nickname, Kid Blink. Balletti, however, was not an orphan like other newsies. The 1900 census showed he was living with his Italian immigrant parents and three siblings and was employed as a driver. Balletti and Newsboys Union president David Simmons organized the strike, staging rallies supporting their fellow newsies across the city, paralyzing the publishing magnates' businesses. Kid Blink's army included boys with equally colorful nicknames including Michael "Boots" McAleenan, Nick "Mush" Myers, "Crutchie" Morris, Ed "Racetrack" Higgins, and Bob "Indian" Stone. The rallies culminated with a giant gathering at Irving Hall, in the Union Square neighborhood of Midtown Manhattan, sponsored by state senator Timothy D. Sullivan and attended by five thousand newsies.

On July 27, several newspapers reported that Kid Blink and David Simmons had betrayed the strike by selling newspapers, purportedly after being bribed by newspaper executives. As a result, Blink was chased through the streets by an angry mob of newsies, resulting in his arrest for disorderly conduct. The accusations were suspicious since the *New York Tribune* was reporting that Kid Blink was negotiating with the publishers. The pair removed themselves from their leadership roles but no one with Kid Blink's charisma could step up to lead the strikers.

The strike lasted two weeks, during which time the *World*'s circulation dropped from 360,000 papers sold to 125,000. The end came on August 2, when Pulitzer offered a compromise by guaranteeing to buy back any unsold newspapers at the end of each day at full price, although the sixty-cent wholesale price per hundred remained in force.

After the strike, Kid Blink worked as a coach driver, a Chinatown guide, and a barkeeper. In 1912 he was arrested and held on $1,000 bond for possession of dynamite. He died in May 1913 of tuberculosis at the age of thirty-one.

PRODUCTION NOTES

The 2012 stage musical *Newsies* was based on a 1992 film produced by Walt Disney Pictures with twelve songs written by Alan Menken. Although the movie failed at the box office, it has since become a cult favorite, leading to its successful stage adaptation.

In the film, Kid Blink was renamed Jack "Cowboy" Kelly, played by Christian Bale. Kid Blink was retained as a minor character, along with others based on real-life newsboys from the 1899 strike, including Mush Meyers, Racetrack Higgins, and Crutchie Morris, the latter getting his nickname from being disabled and using crutches to get around. Newsies union president David Simmons was renamed David Jacobs, played by David Moscow, and esteemed actor Robert Duvall portrayed *New York World* publisher Joseph Pulitzer. Six of Alan Menken's songs were carried over to the stage musical. Menken had been scheduled to write the songs with his partner Howard Ashman, but Ashman was dying of AIDS and Menken ended up writing most of the music himself, with help from lyricist Jack Feldman.

In conducting research for the film, first-time screenwriters Bob Tzudiker and Noni White enlisted Tzudiker's parents, who lived in the

Washington, DC area, to go to the Library of Congress archives and photocopy period newspapers from 1899. At the outset, Tzudiker and White also planned on producing a musical, but the film's disappointing reception threatened to dash those plans.

The film's quick demise did not discourage its fervent fan base, which resulted in Disney Theatricals agreeing to produce a stage adaptation, intended for stock and amateur productions. Menken and Feldman returned to write new material to go with the five songs retained from the 1992 movie. Librettist Harvey Fierstein added a new character, Katherine Plumber, a spunky journalist representing a feminist point of view and a potential love interest for the show's brash hero, Jack Kelly.

The musical made its debut at the Paper Mill Playhouse in 2011 and was a hit during its three-week run. The Broadway version, which opened on March 29, 2012, was initially listed as being an "open-ended" engagement, which was extended after promising previews. Jeremy Jordan, who played Jack in the Paper Mill Playhouse tryout, went on to play the role on Broadway, with Kara Lindsay playing Katherine and Ben Fankhauser as Jack's best buddy, Davey Jacobs. The musical was a hit, thanks to Christopher Gattelli's energetic choreography and Jeff Calhoun's vibrant direction. The musical played an impressive 1,004 performances in a run that lasted for nearly two and a half years, winning Tony Awards for Gattelli's choreography and for Menken and Feldman's score.

In addition to the life-based principal characters, the musical added then–New York governor Theodore Roosevelt (1858–1919) to the cast, providing an additional element of historical authenticity to the story. In the musical, Roosevelt helps Jack and the newsies by forcing Pulitzer to concede to Jack's demands, although in actuality, Roosevelt, who would become William McKinley's vice president in 1900 and then president after McKinley was assassinated in 1901, did nothing to assist either side in settling the strike. Roosevelt did, however, champion child labor reform when he became president, addressing the issue in his annual State of the Union addresses. Although Roosevelt would not support a federal law restricting child labor, he did order the Department of Commerce and Labor to direct their attention to the "conditions of child labor and child labor legislation" in several states.

SCORE

Newsies was only the fourth score written by composer Alan Menken for Disney, but his work was already falling into musical formulas. Jack Kelly's "I wish" song, "Santa Fe," is reminiscent of a similar song Menken wrote for *The Little Mermaid*, "Part of Your World," sung by Ariel, the mermaid who yearns to explore the wonders of dry land. In filling out Jack's character, screenwriters Bob Tzudiker and Noni White invented an alternate goal for Jack, who yearned to leave the dirty city and move to New Mexico. The song summoned an idealized fantasy world, not unlike the one dreamed about by Dorothy in "Over the Rainbow" from *The Wizard of Oz*.

Five other songs were carried over from the film to the stage version. In "Carrying the Banner," the newsies exhibit pride and exuberance in flinging "papes" around the city. The song bears a musical resemblance to "Birdland," written by Joe Zawinul for the jazz fusion band Weather Report.

"Seize the Day" is the newsies' rallying cry, a protest song in support of the strike, which sets off one in a series of exuberantly choreographed production numbers in the show. Another is "King of New York," in which Davey appears to be more thrilled getting his picture in the paper then having the Brooklyn newsies join the strike.

Of the new songs added to the show by Menken and lyricist Jack Feldman, the best was "Watch What Happens," sung by Katherine, a humorously wordy patter song reminiscent of Stephen Sondheim's "Not Getting Married" from *Company*. The show's antagonist, publisher Joseph Pulitzer, also got a song, "The Bottom Line," in which he and his newspaper cronies come up with the scheme to maximize their profits while victimizing the already strapped newsies, convincing themselves that they are doing a good thing by giving the newsies a "lesson in economics." Pulitzer's character was simplified to the point that he had become just another avaricious corporate villain, ignoring positive aspects of his life, such as his crusades against corruption and his numerous innovations in publishing.

Menken and Feldman also added "Brooklyn's Here," a variation on "Carrying the Banner," sung by the Brooklyn newsies, and "I Never

Planned On You," sung by Jack and Katherine, which harkens back to love-at-first-sight Broadway numbers like "Some Enchanted Evening," although not nearly as memorable.

Alan Menken was never a particularly unique songwriter. His music was always clearly geared toward contemporary pop no matter what the circumstances of the story; whether it was the Arabian Nights world of *Aladdin* or turn-of-the-century New York in *Newsies*, his music has always been interchangeable, formulaic, and inoffensive. The fact that the score won a Tony is more a reflection on Feldman's clever lyrics, written in "New Yawk" dialect and street slang, and Gattelli's scintillating choreography than its own musical singularity.

1600 Pennsylvania Avenue

Historical context: The White House and its occupants during the
    nineteenth century
Time period: 1800–1900
Broadway run: May 4, 1976–May 8, 1976 (7 p.)
Venue: Mark Hellinger Theatre
Book: Alan Jay Lerner
Score: Leonard Bernstein (music), Alan Jay Lerner (lyrics)
Cast album: None
Major characters: The President (Ken Howard), The President's Wife
    (Patricia Routledge), Seena (Emily Yancy), Lud (Gilbert Price)

HISTORICAL BACKGROUND

1600 Pennsylvania Avenue is one of two shows profiled in this book (the
other is *Assassins*) that is not devoted to either a specific event or epoch
in American history, but instead provides a sweeping summation of an
era or theme. The show tells the story of the first one hundred years of
the White House through the eyes of two pairs of residents: its presidents
and first ladies and four generations of a family of African American servants. Focusing on race relations, the show depicts a number of historical
events and circumstances from the nineteenth century, including Thomas
Jefferson's affair with his African American slave, Sally Hemings, the
burning of Washington during the War of 1812, James Monroe's refusal
to ban slavery in the capital city, the prelude and aftermath of the Civil
War (including the impeachment of Andrew Johnson), the disputed
1876 presidential election, and the presidencies of Chester Alan Arthur
and Theodore Roosevelt.

The incidents depicted in the musical, which begin with John and Abigail Adams moving into the newly completed "People's House," are based in fact, although Jefferson's affair with Hemings, a slave who bore six of Jefferson's children, had not been proven at the time the musical was written. It wasn't until 1998 when Jefferson and Hemings's forty-year affair was established through DNA tests.

On August 23, 1814, with British troops threatening to invade Washington, DC, President James Madison ordered the White House abandoned. Before leaving, Madison's wife, Dolley, remained behind to save important documents and works of art, including Gilbert Stuart's famous painting of George Washington. Just prior to setting the building on fire, British troops took advantage of a state dinner for forty that had been abandoned and calmly enjoyed the feast, using the White House's place settings and silverware.

Although James Monroe was an abolitionist, he owned an estimated 250 slaves during his lifetime. As president, he signed the Missouri Compromise of 1820, which banned slavery from territories north of the 36°30′ parallel, while at the same time admitting Missouri to the union as a slave state. Monroe was a nationalist who, like Abraham Lincoln, believed in preserving the union at all costs, and with the issue of slavery already threatening to tear the country apart, promoted the recolonization of freed slaves to Liberia through the American Colonization Society, formed in 1816.

Act I ends as the ineffective and hapless President James Buchanan proposes in song to ignore the problem of slavery by throwing a party for the combatants, followed by the election of Lincoln and the beginning of the Civil War. The audience is spared the harrowing four-year conflict, which apparently occurs during intermission; Act II opens with Andrew Johnson's disastrous presidency and subsequent impeachment, in which post–Civil War Blacks are famously promised "forty acres and a mule" as reparations.

Outgoing First Lady Julia Grant and her successor, Lucy Hayes, are given a schizophrenic showcase to represent the disputed 1876 presidential election, in which a compromise ended the Reconstruction Era, resulting in Rutherford B. Hayes, who had lost the popular vote to

Samuel J. Tilden, becoming the nineteenth president. A fifteen-member commission created to settle the election decided in Hayes's favor by one vote, in exchange for a list of demands from Southern Democrats: withdraw federal troops from the former Confederate states, appoint at least one Southern Democrat to Hayes's cabinet, construct a second transcontinental railroad to go through the South, help restore the South's battered economy, and permit Southern states to deal with Blacks without Northern interference.

Chester Alan Arthur, the incorruptible twenty-first president, came to power after the assassination of James Garfield, resulting in abrasive former New York Senator Roscoe Conkling referring to him as "His Accidency." In this scene, Arthur hosts one of his famously lavish White

Ken Howard and Patricia Routledge in *1600 Pennsylvania Avenue*.
PHOTOFEST

95

House dinner parties, with elite billionaire robber barons John D. Rockefeller and Cornelius Vanderbilt attending, complete with a minstrel show that pointedly highlights their corrupt business dealings. The musical ends with Theodore and Edith Roosevelt's plea for reconciliation for the nation's century of contentious tumult between the races.

PRODUCTION NOTES

In his memoir *The Street Where I Live*, Alan Jay Lerner made one brief reference to *1600 Pennsylvania Avenue* by writing simply, "Well, you remember the Titanic." Despite this, there is much to say about the troubled musical, known as being one of Broadway's most legendary and embarrassing flops. It had a long and interesting history, which culminated in its being universally slammed by critics, surviving for only seven performances in 1976, the year of America's bicentennial celebration.

Lerner got the idea to do a patriotic musical about the first hundred years of the White House in 1972, joined by Leonard Bernstein, whom Lerner had known since both attended Harvard in the late 1930s. It was viewed as a teaming of giants: Lerner, the writer of the book and lyrics for such legendary shows as *My Fair Lady* and *Camelot*, and the peripatetic Bernstein, who hadn't composed a Broadway musical since *West Side Story* fifteen years earlier.

Lerner initially titled the show "Opus One," after he had become depressed over the state of the nation in the wake of the Watergate break-in and subsequent landslide reelection of Richard Nixon. Bernstein and Lerner appeared to be perfectly suited for one another. In addition to their friendship at Harvard, both were Jews who spoke compassionately about social issues and were unified in their hatred of Nixon.

The show's title was soon changed to *1600 Pennsylvania Avenue*, the street address of the White House. The trouble began when Lerner told interviewers that he didn't believe in "message musicals," especially those dealing with teenage rumbles and switchblade knives, a clear slap at *West Side Story*, and a direct contradiction with what *1600* would turn out to be. The show was originally designed as a play-within-a-play, in which the four major actors would step out of character to comment on the plot from the present day. By the time the show went through its tryout stage in Philadelphia, the concept was abandoned, resulting in a disjointed and clunky book that lurched from one scene to the next. The ten presidents depicted are shown as ineffectual fops with no stomach for doing anything substantial, spending their presidencies contradicting good intentions with hypocritical behavior.

Theatrical impresario Saint-Subber, responsible for such hits as *Kiss Me, Kate, Barefoot in the Park,* and *The Odd Couple,* was brought on board as producer, but after two fruitless years, he backed out, saying that he loathed the show and tried in vain to get everyone else to abandon it as well. By that time, Lerner was going through a divorce from the fifth of his eight wives and deferred to Bernstein, rejecting much of his proven Lerner-and-Loewe formula.

Producers Roger L. Stevens and Robert Whitehead then hired Broadway director Frank Corsaro, but after reading through Lerner's book, Corsaro could not believe the fragmented mess that was the result of two years' work. But the esteemed presence of Lerner and Bernstein convinced Corsaro to reluctantly give the show the benefit of the doubt and preproduction continued.

In 1975, Lerner talked Coca-Cola into subsidizing the entire cost of the production (ultimately, $1.2 million), completely bypassing Stevens and Whitehead's authority and virtually ensuring that *1600 Pennsylvania Avenue* would come to fruition. By now, America was getting closer to the bicentennial, with celebrations planned in every community in the nation. A musical about the presidency was giving the show instant credibility, especially considering its glittering creative team.

Ken Howard, who had played Thomas Jefferson in *1776*, was hired to portray all the presidents while English actress Patricia Routledge was brought on to play the first ladies. Operatic baritone Gilbert Price played Lud Simmons, the show's patriarchal White House servant as well as his progeny, and Emily Yancy, an actress who up until that time had only played bit roles in television, was cast as Jefferson's illegitimate daughter Seena, and Lud's wife.

On February 23, 1976, the show finally opened in Philadelphia. By the time the first act ended, much of the audience had already fled. One patron was so upset after being refused a refund on his ticket that he ended up taking his frustration out on a pane of glass near the foyer. Corsaro knew that the show was failing because its basic premise was a preponderance of heavy-handed references to racial injustice. But despite Bernstein's objections, Lerner refused to close the show. When Corsaro and choreographer Donald McKayle asked to leave, their replacements, director Gilbert Moses and choreographer George Faison (both from *The Wiz*) banned Lerner and Bernstein from attending rehearsals.

Composer André Previn saw the show before it went to Broadway and was aghast at how awful it was, at one point grabbing hold of his seat with both hands and muttering to himself, "I'm going mad." At another, Previn turned around in his seat and noticed Bernstein in the last row of the theater, banging his head against a wall. When he finally cornered Lerner, the lyricist who had written some of the most enchanting songs in Broadway history made the understatement of the ages: "It needs a lot of work."

Like an impending tidal wave on a beleaguered coastal city, word began to get out about the coming disaster. Despite replacing directors, changing the dialog, and virtually overhauling the book, the show only got worse and Coca-Cola removed its name from the production. The presidents were made to look like fools, but it was worse in its representation of African Americans. *Time* magazine went as far as to call the show "racist." Other adjectives that were bandied about by critics included "embarrassing," "amateurish," and "a Bicentennial bore." In the end, it was a miracle the Broadway run lasted a mercifully brief seven performances.

SCORE

Bernstein and Lerner were so humiliated by the show's abject failure that they refused to permit a cast recording to be released. As badly as *1600 Pennsylvania Avenue* fared with critics and audiences, Bernstein's score has held up amazingly well in the years since the show's brief run. Lerner died in 1986 and Bernstein in 1990, but after their deaths, their estates authorized a choral version of the score titled *A White House Cantata*, which made its debut in 1997. Although live performances of the cantata are permitted, Bernstein's estate has refused all requests to allow exploitation of the original musical in any form, as a live performance, recording, or printed transcript.

Two songs from the detritus of the show rose from the wreckage to become stand-alone favorites, both sung in the show by Patricia Routledge. In "Take Care of This House," Routledge, playing Abigail Adams, is giving Lud, a runaway slave played by Gilbert Price, a laundry list of tasks required to maintain the White House. The song has since become a poignant allegory for the nation itself, a plea to preserve America's delicate and fragile democracy.

One other song survives as a bravura audition piece and cabaret number, "Duet for One (The First Lady of the Land)," Patricia Routledge's second-act tour de force, in which she plays both Julia Grant and Lucy Hayes in a schizophrenic musical dialog that takes place during President Hayes's inauguration. To perform both roles, Routledge was fitted with a specially designed double-sided wig. With a flip of her head and a change in voice, she flip-flopped between a wizened Julia Grant and an operatically challenged Lucy Hayes. On opening night, Routledge received a standing ovation for her showstopping performance. (A bootlegged audio recording of Routledge's opening night rendering of the song and the audience's rhapsodic response can be heard on YouTube.) On closing night, Routledge received another standing ovation, this time from the musicians in the orchestra pit.

All told, *A White House Cantata* preserved ninety minutes of music from the two-hour show. It has since been separated from the ponderous book, emerging as a neglected masterpiece, the most celebrated Broadway score that was never recorded. Its songs hop-scotched from genre to genre: charming waltzes, rousing marches, plus jazz, blues, minstrelsy, calypso, torch songs, and barbershop harmonies. Before his death, Bernstein recycled some of the songs into other productions, including his 1983 opera *A Quiet Place* and the song cycle *Songfest: A Cycle of American Poems for Six Singers and Orchestra* (1977), the latter work commissioned to honor the American bicentennial celebration.

Teddy & Alice

Historical context: President Theodore Roosevelt and his daughter Alice

Time period: 1901–1904

Broadway run: November 12, 1987–January 17, 1988 (77 p.)

Venue: Minskoff Theatre

Book: Jerome Alden, with Alan Jay Lerner as "artistic consultant"

Score: Richard Kapp (music), Hal Hackady (lyrics); some melodies based on works by John Philip Sousa

Cast album: ESS. A.Y Recordings (311168 H1), 1988

Major characters: Theodore Roosevelt (Len Cariou), Edith Roosevelt (Beth Fowler), Alice Roosevelt (Nancy Hume), Nick Longworth (Ron Raines), William Howard Taft (Michael McCarty), Henry Cabot Lodge (Raymond Thorne), Elihu Root (Gordon Stanley)

HISTORICAL BACKGROUND

When President William McKinley was assassinated in September 1901, forty-two-year-old vice president Theodore Roosevelt (1856–1919) became the twenty-sixth president of the United States, the youngest in history. Roosevelt brought a large family to the White House, including five children from his second marriage to Edith Kermit Carow and his seventeen-year-old daughter from his first marriage. Two days after the baby's birth in 1884, Roosevelt's first wife, Alice, had died of kidney failure, with Roosevelt naming the child after her.

The White House became a playground for the Roosevelt children, who roller-skated on the hardwood floors and threw spitballs at a portrait of Andrew Jackson. The family's menagerie of pets included a lizard, a badger, a one-legged rooster, and Alice's pet snake, Emily Spinach, which she would sometimes carry around in her pocket.

Known for her great beauty, Alice Roosevelt (1884–1980) became a celebrity and a fashion icon during her years in the White House. Her most famous frock was a grayish-blue dress that soon sparked a national craze, the color becoming known as "Alice blue." The dress was the inspiration for the song "Alice Blue Gown," which became a Broadway hit when Edith Day performed it in the 1919 musical *Irene*.

In addition to being admired for her beauty and fashion sense, Alice Roosevelt loved being the center of attention and attending nightly dinners, balls, and parties. She was constantly testing the president's patience with her controversial behavior: smoking cigarettes in public, betting at racetracks, jumping into swimming pools fully clothed, riding in automobiles with male companions without a chaperone, and pulling practical jokes on unsuspecting congressmen. She often interrupted meetings her father held in the Oval Office, prompting his famous comment to a friend, author Owen Wister, "I can either run the country or I can attend to Alice, but I cannot possibly do both."

Alice Roosevelt was more than just an incorrigible wild child. She was bright and well read; her father would often ask her advice on important issues of state. As sharp-minded and intelligent as she was, Alice was also stubborn and opinionated, and clashed often with her father, whose all-consuming ego led to her famous comment, "He always wanted to be the corpse at every funeral, the bride at every wedding, and the baby at every christening."

Alice and the president were not close personally. Roosevelt was still haunted by the death of his young wife, who was only twenty-two when she died. Alice's great beauty and startling resemblance to her mother no doubt affected Roosevelt. Alice would write in her diary of her relationship with Roosevelt, saying at one point, "We are not in the least congenial. . . . Why should he pay any attention to me or the things that I live for, except to look upon them with disapproval?"

In 1905, Alice accompanied a coterie of congressmen on a goodwill trip to the Orient, with stops planned for Hawaii, Japan, China, and the Philippines. Responsibility for Alice's behavior fell to Secretary of War

William Howard Taft. On the journey aboard the steamship *Manchuria*, she leaped fully clothed into the ship's swimming tank. That December, Alice became engaged to Nicholas Longworth III, a congressman from Ohio's first congressional district and a notorious playboy fourteen years her senior. The wedding, held at the White House on February 17, 1906, became the social event of the season, with more than a thousand guests attending and thousands more gathered outside, waiting for a glimpse of the bride in her blue dress. At the ceremony, Edith Roosevelt reportedly told her stepdaughter, "I want you to know that I'm glad to see you go. You've never been anything but trouble."

PRODUCTION NOTES

The musical *Teddy & Alice* was a fictionalized account of the stormy relationship between President Roosevelt and Alice. The show's origins began when Stone Widney, an associate of Alan Jay Lerner who had

Alice Roosevelt and her father, President Theodore Roosevelt, subjects of the 1987 musical *Teddy and Alice*. Photos taken c. 1902 during Roosevelt's first term.
LIBRARY OF CONGRESS PRINTS AND PHOTOGRAPHS DIVISION, COURTESY THEODORE ROOSEVELT DIGITAL LIBRARY, DICKINSON STATE UNIVERSITY

been researching Roosevelt's presidency for use in Lerner's disastrous musical *1600 Pennsylvania Avenue*, became intrigued by the caustic relationship between Roosevelt and his daughter and thought it might be worthy of a separate musical on its own.

It took seven years for the musical to come to fruition. Robert Preston was the first choice to play Roosevelt, but he was soon replaced by Len Cariou, star of Stephen Sondheim's *Sweeney Todd*. Cariou was intrigued by the show's premise, stating in an interview that Roosevelt was "the first modern-day President," a populist, and a man of the people.

In the musical, Roosevelt is seen not as a president as much as the commander of a battalion of children that has invaded the White House. The cast list was populated with real-life politicians, advisors, and cronies, including billionaire J. P. Morgan, foreign policy advisor Henry Cabot Lodge, Secretary of War Elihu Root, labor leader Samuel Gompers, and Roosevelt's distant cousins, Eleanor and Franklin Roosevelt, who would marry one another in 1905. (Eleanor and Franklin were fifth cousins once removed.)

The book was written by Jerome Alden, author of a one-man play about Roosevelt called *Bully*. The show's composer, Richard Kapp, decided on the novel approach of using the music of march king John Philip Sousa as the basis for many of the songs, in addition to writing original numbers as well. Lyricist Hal Hackady was brought on board to write his fourth Broadway flop, following *Minnie's Boys*, *Goodtime Charley*, and *Ambassador*. A televised version was aired on cable television in an attempt to attract financial backers and the musical finally staged its first tryout in Tampa, Florida, where John Driver replaced Widney as director.

The plot of *Teddy & Alice* begins with the Roosevelts and their brood entering the black-draped White House, remnants from the death of President McKinley, but the hallways are quickly enlivened with the antics of the Roosevelt children, along with their toys, animals, and belongings.

Much of the story involved Roosevelt's attempts to keep his daughter and Nick Longworth apart. Alice gets a ticket for driving her new gas-powered automobile at the outrageous speed of fifteen miles per hour in a ten-mile-per-hour zone, crashing it into a tree. In another scene,

Roosevelt is interrupted from discussions concerning the Panama Canal when Alice bursts in, offering her unsolicited opinion.

Roosevelt is so distracted by Alice's antics that he impulsively sends her on a goodwill tour to the Orient (which didn't occur until 1905, during his second administration) and prepares to run for reelection. At the end of Act I, Roosevelt's opponents are branding him at the 1904 Republican National Convention as a socialist and a tyrant, but he wins everyone over with a rousing, patriotic song and gets the nomination.

In Act II, Alice has just returned from the East with gifts from her journey as her relationship with Longworth is now becoming serious. She is intent, however, in not marrying him until she gains her father's approval, but T. R. stubbornly resists. He experiences an apparition from his late first wife, however, who convinces him to let Alice go. Fearing he will be defeated in the 1904 election, Roosevelt nevertheless prevails and gives his blessing. The show ends with Alice and Nick's wedding (which actually didn't take place until a year into T. R.'s second term).

Critics were not kind to *Teddy & Alice* when it made its Broadway debut in November 1987. The *New York Times* called the experience "an evening that combines the educational mission of 'My Weekly Reader' with the halftime show at a high-school football game," denouncing Kapp and Hackaday's "monotonous, march-laden score." Roosevelt's all-consuming malaise from the death of his first wife, along with jealousy over Alice's attention toward Longworth, monopolized the show's atmosphere. *Times* critic Frank Rich slammed Hackady's "inane" lyrics and accused the show's creators of having "no respect for the dead," since credited artistic consultant Alan Jay Lerner had died the previous year.

Teddy & Alice might have been more successful had greater attention been paid to Roosevelt's political accomplishments, rather than the distractions of Alice and his other children. There was certainly plenty of drama to be had in T. R.'s administration, but this kind of dramatic relevance would have been equally problematic. Cariou's performance was likened to that of Robert Preston as Harold Hill (not surprising, since the role was designed for Preston) while the sets were derisively described by one scribe as "Daddy Warbucks' mansion after a fire sale."

Teddy & Alice's failure was guaranteed when the musical didn't portray Roosevelt as anything beyond a frustrated father who wouldn't let his daughter have a life of her own. In the show, we are treated to a litany of Alice's madcap escapades that are entertaining, but Roosevelt's stubborn refusal to acknowledge his daughter's chosen suitor made the show seem like a bad episode of a situation comedy. Still, the relationship between father and daughter was portrayed as a touching one, so many historians believe that after more than thirty years since its disappointing Broadway run, *Teddy & Alice* certainly deserves another appraisal.

SCORE

In retrospect, Richard Kapp and Hal Hackady's uneven score was not as bad as its critics proclaimed. Four Sousa marches were used while six others were adapted by Kapp in addition to a handful of Kapp originals. The attempt to write new words to Sousa's most celebrated march, "The Stars and Stripes Forever," resulted in "Wave the Flag," a patriotic patter song at the end of Act I, modeled after Preston's work in *The Music Man*, with cumbersome words chanted by Cariou in the form of a speech Teddy Roosevelt gives at the nominating convention.

Cariou also sings "Make This a House," which uses the trio section from Sousa's "El Capitan" to inspire the new White House residents to rejuvenate the morbidly dark building, giving the effect of the tidying-up-of-the-nursery scene in *Mary Poppins*.

The best song of all might be "Can I Let Her Go," which takes its melody from Sousa's "The Thunderer," slowing it down from a rousing march to become a tender ballad in which Roosevelt distresses over Alice marrying Longworth and leaving him. The slower tempo revealed the sheer beauty of Sousa's melody, which bears a resemblance to "Drink to Me," the revolutionaries' song from *Les Misèrables*.

Although there was no official *Teddy & Alice* cast album, the closest to come to one was a collection of Sousa orchestral music that included six songs from the show. Three Len Cariou solos were sung by Gordon Stanley, who played Elihu Root, while Meg Bussert and Ron Raines, neither of whom were in the original cast, performed three others.

Ragtime

Historical context: Racism and immigration at the turn of the
   twentieth century
Time period: 1902–1906
Broadway run: January 18, 1998–January 16, 2000 (834 p.)
Venue: Ford Center for the Performing Arts
Book: Terrence McNally (based on the 1975 novel by E. L.
   Doctorow)
Score: Stephen Flaherty (music), Lynn Ahrens (lyrics)
Cast album: RCA Victor 63167-2 (1998)
Major characters: Mother (Marin Mazzie), Father (Mark Jacoby),
   Coalhouse Walker Jr. (Brian Stokes Mitchell), Sarah (Audra
   McDonald), Tateh (Peter Friedman), Harry Houdini (Jim Corti),
   Booker T. Washington (Tommy Hollis), Emma Goldman (Judy
   Kaye), Evelyn Nesbit (Lynnette Perry), Henry Ford (Larry Daggett),
   J. P. Morgan (Mike O'Carroll), Edgar, the Little Boy (Alex Strange)

HISTORICAL BACKGROUND

E. L. Doctorow's novel *Ragtime* is a work of historical fiction that placed
prominent Americans into a story about three families: one white, one
Black, and one immigrant, at the turn of the twentieth century. The plot
focused on racial intolerance, political anarchy, and its characters' desires
to be respected as individuals.

The white family, whose names are never identified except for Edgar,
the little boy with an uncanny clairvoyance, live in an elegant home in
New Rochelle, New York. Although Mother is the key member of the
family, it is Mother's Younger Brother who is actually the key to the novel's

story arc. A whiz at manufacturing explosives, he apparently has no direction in life, but after getting spurned by model/chorus girl Evelyn Nesbit, applies his talents to aid a violent takeover of the prestigious Manhattan library of billionaire tycoon J. P. Morgan.

Coalhouse Walker Jr. is a gifted Black ragtime piano player whose shiny new Model T Ford is vandalized by racists. When his frustration at getting justice results in his young wife's tragic death, he is turned into a vicious, unrepentant vigilante, with devastating consequences.

The immigrant Tateh is the third main character in the story, a Latvian Jew who descends into poverty after arriving in America because of anti-immigrant feelings and discrimination. A struggling silhouette artist, Tateh invents what became known as a "riffle book," a novelty item that simulates motion through successive drawings, which Tateh calls a

American revolutionary, anarchist, and agitator Emma Goldman, a key character in *Ragtime* (1998).
NEW YORK TIMES

"movie book." Through diligence and ingenuity, he eventually pioneers the motion picture industry.

The members of the three fictional families are influenced by a number of historical figures, including illusionist Harry Houdini (1874–1926), African American educator and orator Booker T. Washington (1856–1915), anarchist Emma Goldman (1869–1940), Gibson Girl model and actress Evelyn Nesbit (1884–1967), billionaire tycoon J. P. Morgan (1837–1913), explorer Admiral Robert Peary (1856–1920), and automotive industrialist Henry Ford (1863–1947).

Goldman, Washington, and Houdini became muses for three of the characters: respectively, Mother's Younger Brother, Coalhouse Walker Jr., and Tateh. Mother's Younger Brother is influenced by Goldman to join Walker's increasingly violent quest for justice, Walker appeals to Washington for advice, and Tateh looks to the immigrant Houdini as inspiration to believe in his abilities as an artist. The young boy, who idolizes Houdini, develops an admiration for him after the escape artist happens by his home in New Rochelle.

The historical figures' influence on the fictional characters' story arcs serve to reflect the emerging new century and its changing mores in American life. Henry Ford's invention of the assembly line, which enabled automobiles to become available to average Americans, resulted, although indirectly, in the humiliating desecration of Coalhouse Walker Jr.'s new Ford, triggering his descent into vigilantism. The sordid circumstances surrounding the Evelyn Nesbit love triangle, in which her jealous millionaire husband Harry K. Thaw murdered architect Stanford White, presaged Americans' fascination with the sensationalistic lives of celebrities. Booker T. Washington's majestic oratory predicted the civil rights movement of the 1950s and 1960s, while the standoff at the Morgan library became frighteningly familiar to a generation inundated by incidents of domestic terrorism.

The show's title served as a metaphor for America's rapidly changing society and continuing struggle for social justice. Just as ragtime was considered a radical and, to some, decadent development in music in its time, so were other taboo societal practices that were referenced in the musical, including illegitimate children, interracial marriage, equal rights for women, and respect for the dignity of Black Americans.

Production Notes

Ragtime was first developed into a motion picture in 1981, a film that was notable for being James Cagney's motion picture swan song. Cagney played another real-life figure, New York City fire commissioner Rhinelander Waldo, who is seen in the movie as the city's police commissioner.

When Terrence McNally was asked to transform the story into a musical, he immediately said yes. For McNally, *Ragtime* appeared ideally suited for the adaptation, noting, "It just sings, every page." McNally viewed the book as a demonstration of a key phrase from the Constitution: "life, liberty, and the pursuit of happiness," concepts to which each of the story's major characters aspire.

The show made its world premiere in December 1996 in Toronto, followed by its US opening seven months later at the Shubert Theatre in Los Angeles before finally making it to Broadway in January 1998 at the Ford Center for the Performing Arts on West Forty-Third Street.

The Broadway production was noted for its lavish attention to detail and large cast. Its ten-million-dollar budget included fireworks, explosive devices, and a working Model T automobile that was driven on stage at each performance. The novel's sweeping storyline had to be edited down to become manageable in a three-hour window and in the process, some key relationships from the book had to be distilled or eliminated altogether.

In the novel, Mother's Younger Brother's obsession with Evelyn Nesbit resulted in a brief affair, but in the musical, his love remains unrequited, leading to his frustration and desperate need for a purpose in life. Similarly, Coalhouse Walker's obsession for vengeance in the novel results in his abandoning the child he fathered by the murdered Sarah, with Mother eventually adopting the boy. In the musical, Mother merely cares for the child while waiting for Coalhouse's return. In the musical's bows, which serve as the postscript, the newly married Mother and Tateh are seen with the boy, whom it is assumed they have adopted.

The character of Evelyn Nesbit has a much larger role in the novel than in the musical. In the latter, she is used as comic relief, shown only as a ditsy, opportunistic chorus girl. In the novel, Evelyn has a much more interesting role, shown to have been brought up in a lower-class neighborhood and able to feel empathy for the plight of Tateh and his daughter. When she befriends them, she actually covets Tateh's little girl, having had no children of her own. When the girl becomes seriously ill, Evelyn nurses her back to health. Tateh eventually discovers her identity and takes his daughter out of the city. In the novel, Emma Goldman also interacts with Evelyn, applying her feminist principles into accusing the chorine of becoming a creature of capitalism.

Father's death in the sinking of the *Lusitania* occurs during the book's narrative but is mentioned only in the musical's postscript. The musical also entirely eliminates Tateh's wife, Mameh, who in the musical has already died before the family arrives in America. Harry Houdini has more of a direct relationship with characters in the book. When Houdini's car breaks down, Father invites him into his house and tells him his plans to travel to the North Pole with Admiral Peary.

Other historical figures referenced in Doctorow's novel were not represented in the musical adaptation, including journalist Jacob Riis, psychiatrist Sigmund Freud (who has a large role in the book), Mexican revolutionary Emiliano Zapata, and Austrian Archduke Franz Ferdinand. Manhattan District Attorney Charles S. Whitman turns up as a minor character in the musical, negotiating with Coalhouse at the standoff at the Morgan Library.

The historical characters play a much bigger part in the novel's narrative, interacting not only with the fictional characters but also with each other. McNally's adaptation simplified their roles by limiting their interactions to a few scenes, generally overseeing and commenting on the action as a celestial Greek chorus from elevated points on the stage.

Ragtime led the 1998 Tony Awards with thirteen nominations but lost to *The Lion King*, which garnered eleven, including Best Musical. Composers Lynn Ahrens and Stephen Flaherty's songs won *Ragtime* a Tony for Best Original Score, the finest of their career. The massive budget, however, proved to be the show's downfall, and the musical was not a financial success. When it was revived in 2009, its opulent scenic design was stripped down to its bare essentials, a skeletal hunk of metal representing the resplendent Model T in the original with a concoction of scaffolding and only minimal set pieces used. Despite the reduction in set pieces, the large cast and forty-two-piece orchestra kept costs high and the revival lasted only sixty-five performances, closing inside of two months.

SCORE

Lyricist Lynn Ahrens recalled that eight or nine songwriting teams auditioned to write the score for *Ragtime*, including John Kander and Fred Ebb. When Ahrens and her songwriting partner, composer Stephen Flaherty, got the job, they knew it was going to be an epic assignment.

In composing the music, Stephen Flaherty understood that, like the stories in the play, the music also had to represent a conflict between Black and white traditions. Ragtime was born in the brothels of St. Louis, with the Black composer Scott Joplin its foremost practitioner. The structure of ragtime is similar to marches, composed in strains in an AABA pattern as opposed to the familiar verse/chorus format that became popular in early Tin Pan Alley. Flaherty viewed Coalhouse Walker's piano ragtime as symbolic of the ongoing struggle between Blacks and whites; the left hand, with its unyielding rhythm, representing the rigid industrial revolution and the white establishment, while the right hand's syncopated melody representing Black Americans straining to be free of the bondage of the left hand's rhythm.

Each major historical figure is given a solo showcase: Evelyn Nesbit ("The Crime of the Century"), Henry Ford ("Henry Ford"), Harry Houdini ("Harry Houdini, Master Escapist"), Emma Goldman ("The Night That Goldman Spoke at Union Square"), and Booker T. Washington ("Look What You've Done"), but are also woven into the fabric of other songs, including "Atlantic City" and "Success."

Ahrens and Flaherty's score is one of the richest in Broadway history. Ahrens would often tell how the songs grew naturally from McNally's dialog, such as in Mother's first song, "Goodbye, My Love," in which she bids farewell to her husband as he sets off to explore the North Pole. Flaherty's melodies are imbued with the syncopated rhythms of ragtime in songs like "Gettin' Ready Rag" and "The Crime of the Century," and more subtly in the eloquent "New Music" and the strident "Success." Only in soaring ballads like "Make Them Hear You" and "Wheels of a Dream," which are more traditional Broadway fare, does Flaherty depart from the ragtime-flavored formula he created for the score. Even the music used to represent the Jewish immigrants (the klezmer-flavored "A Shtetl Iz Amereke") bears the rhythmic syncopation of ragtime, communicating its influence on other musical styles.

During her formative years as a lyricist, Lynn Ahrens wrote songs about American history for *Schoolhouse Rock*, a series of short, animated films for children's television. In "The Preamble" (which literally sets the words of the Preamble to the Constitution to music), Ahrens learned how to distill pertinent facts about a historical event into three minutes. In *Ragtime*, "The Crime of the Century" succinctly relates the facts concerning the sordid 1906 love triangle that saw railroad scion Harry K. Thaw murder Evelyn Nesbit's husband, architect Stanford White, in cold blood.

Ahrens felt a special affinity for the character of Tateh, who, like her own grandparents, emigrated from Eastern Europe in the early twentieth century. Ahrens's own father was a photographer, not dissimilar to Tateh the silhouette artist, and Ahrens felt a kinship in sharing her father's drive to live the American Dream through Tateh.

The double meaning of the word "ragtime" struck home in "Coalhouse's Soliloquy" when Coalhouse Walker destroys firehouses and murders firefighters in his vigilante rampage, bellowing, "Listen to that ragtime!"—the line followed by gunfire. Thus, Ahrens and Flaherty were able to equate ragtime's revolutionary music with Black vigilantism, a powerful argument threatening existing rules of society and music at the turn of the century.

Oklahoma!

Historical context: Territorial Oklahoma before statehood
Time period: 1906
Broadway run: March 31, 1943–May 29, 1948 (2,212 p.)
Venue: St. James Theatre
Book: Oscar Hammerstein II, based on the play *Green Grow the Lilacs* by Lynn Riggs (1931)
Score: Richard Rodgers (music), Oscar Hammerstein II (lyrics)
Cast album: Decca A-359 (78 rpm, 1943)
Major characters: Curly (Alfred Drake), Laurey (Joan Roberts), Ado Annie Carnes (Celeste Holm), Will Parker (Lee Dixon), Aunt Eller (Betty Garde), Jud Fry (Howard Da Silva)

HISTORICAL BACKGROUND

Lynn Riggs's play *Green Grow the Lilacs*, the fictional story on which *Oklahoma!* was based, takes place in territorial Oklahoma, prior to its achieving statehood. In 1906, three territories existed in the continental United States. Oklahoma would become the forty-sixth state on November 16, 1907, followed by New Mexico on January 6, 1912, and Arizona on February 14, 1912.

The history of Oklahoma's territorial status goes back to 1834, when Congress set aside land designated for Native Americans by passing the Indian Trade and Intercourse Act, which affected unorganized federal land "west of the Mississippi and not within the states of Missouri and Louisiana, or the territory of Arkansas." After the Civil War, ranchers moved into the area and established their own rules for setting land boundaries and resolving disputes. The Panhandle, which extended 169 miles long and thirty-four miles wide, was initially called Cimarron Territory. Attempts were made to establish a territorial government and persuade Congress to recognize the new territory, which would eventually lead to statehood, but efforts failed after the opening of Oklahoma's Unassigned Lands in 1889. (Had they been successful, *Oklahoma!* might have been called *Cimarron!*)

By the time Oklahoma became a territory on May 2, 1890, as a result of the Oklahoma Organic Act, its familiar borders had been established, incorporating the western half of what was called Indian Territory and the Panhandle, which became known as "No Man's Land." Three years later, the final region, a small patch designated the Cherokee Outlet, which had been held back from the 1890 territorial designation, was purchased and transferred to Oklahoma Territory.

Indian Territory, which constituted about half of the total area of Oklahoma, was the designated home for the Five Tribes (Cherokee, Chickasaw, Choctaw, Creek, and Seminole) who had been forced to relocate from their ancestral homelands in the Southeast after the Indian Removal Act of 1830, joining a number of other Indian nations that already lived in the region, including the Apache, Arapaho, Comanche, Kiowa, Osage, and Wichita. The Panhandle remained as a neutral strip of land.

The events in the fictitious story in *Oklahoma!* take place in Claremore, located in the Indian Territory in the northeastern part of the state. Claremore would become known as the birthplace of philosopher/entertainer Will Rogers (1879–1935), whose family was one of the area's first European American settlers, thus inspiring the designation of Rogers County after Oklahoma became a state.

Claremore's growth (its name was Clermont until 1882) was assured when railways were finally built during the 1870s. Census records reveal that between 1900 and 1910, when the events in *Oklahoma!* take place, the population of Claremore grew from 855 to 2,866 people, a rate of 235.2 percent, the largest gain for any ten-year span in its history.

PRODUCTION NOTES

Author and playwright Lynn Riggs was born on a farm near Claremore on August 31, 1899. In 1912, he entered the Eastern University Preparatory School in Claremore, and after graduating in 1917, worked in Chicago and New York before returning to Oklahoma in 1922. There he taught English and attended college at the University of Oklahoma until 1923, when he was forced to withdraw after contracting tuberculosis. He then moved to New Mexico and subsequently returned to New York, hoping to start a writing career on Broadway. His first major play, *Big Lake*, was produced in 1926. Others followed, all of which drew from Riggs's memories growing up on the Oklahoma plains.

While on a Guggenheim Fellowship in Europe, Riggs used memories of his upbringing in territorial Oklahoma to write a play about the lusty characters he came to know on the rolling countryside, colored by the melodious songs sung by cowboys that worked on its ranches. *Green Grow the Lilacs* was named for an American folk song whose roots go back to a traditional Scottish ballad titled "Green Grows the Laurel."

The original cast from *Oklahoma!*—Joan Roberts and Alfred Drake (in surrey), Celeste Holm and Lee Dixon (far right), Joan McCracken (left of the surrey).
PHOTOFEST

Folk songs and ballads played a big part in Riggs's play. His memories of these songs spurred the simple tale of Laurey Williams, a naive young girl who is brought up by her Aunt Eller after her parents' death. As the story begins, Laurey is playing hard-to-get with Aunt Eller's handsome cowpuncher, Curly McClain, while also fending off the advances of brutish ranch hand Jeeter Fry.

In the play's written introduction, Riggs writes that his intent was to "recapture, in a kind of nostalgic glow, the great range of mood which characterized the old folk songs and ballads I used to hear in my Oklahoma childhood; their quaintness, their sadness, their robustness, their simplicity, their melodrama, their touching sweetness." Indeed, at key moments in the play, the main characters break into song to illustrate their feelings. Although *Green Grow the Lilacs* was not a musical, music played a central role in its telling, but the songs that had been so integral in Riggs's memory would be the first elements to be jettisoned on its journey to becoming a Broadway musical.

Songs sung in the original 1931 play included a variety of traditional songs, including "Whoopee Ti-Yi-Ay, Git Along, You Little Dogies," "A Ridin' Ole Paint," "Sam Hall," "And Yet I Love Her Till I Die," and the title song, all of which were sung by Curly. Others included "The Miner Boy" (sung by Laurey), "Sing Down, Hidery Down" (Aunt Eller), "My Lover's Gone Off on a Train" (Ado Annie), "Custer's Last Charge" (Old Man Peck), and "The Little Brass Wagon" and "Skip to My Lou" (ensemble). In addition, other folk songs are mentioned as being sung, but were not incorporated into the script, including "Hello Girls," "I Wish I Was Single Again," "Home on the Range," "Goodbye, Old Paint," "Strawberry Roan," "Blood on the Saddle," "Chisholm Trail," and "Next Big River." Four songs were sung in the show by a twenty-five-year-old Texan named Maurice Woodward "Tex" Ritter, who played rancher Cord Elam. Ritter had been educated at the University of Texas at Austin and had been performing on Broadway since 1928. He would soon become a star in "B" Westerns and ultimately elected to the Country Music Hall of Fame.

Green Grow the Lilacs starred twenty-four-year-old Franchot Tone, who would later become a leading man in films, as Curly, singing in a play for the first time. Laurey was played by June Walker, who at twenty-six was already a theater veteran, having played her first role when she was just fourteen. (In 1957, Walker's son, John Kerr, would play Lieutenant Cable in the film version of *South Pacific*.) Theatre Guild board member Helen Westley played Aunt Eller and would later appear in 1945 in *Liliom*, the inspiration for *Carousel*, Rodgers and Hammerstein's follow-up to *Oklahoma!*

In *Green Grow the Lilacs*, Aunt Eller has a monolog that presaged a similar speech by Ma Joad in John Steinbeck's *The Grapes of Wrath* nearly a decade later. Aunt Eller is telling Laurey about the death of Laurey's father, Jack, after getting struck by a stray bullet, telling how she and her family survived through sheer determination, heartiness, and spirit.

The cast of *Green Grow the Lilacs* also included future acting mentor Lee Strasberg, who played the role of the Pedler (*sic*), and operatic baritone Richard Hale as Jeeter Fry, whose character's first name was changed to Jud in the musical.

Oklahoma! closely follows the story in *Green Grow the Lilacs*, although there are a number of differences. Ado Annie, who is described as "unattractive" and "stupid-looking," with taffy-colored hair pulled back from a freckled face, would become attractive and flirtatious in the musical. Her beau, Will Parker, is only mentioned once in the play, by Curly in the smokehouse scene, describing him merely as a Claremore boy "who can spin a rope and chew gum at the same time." For the musical version, Rodgers and Hammerstein decided to expand Will Parker's character in order to create a romance with Ado Annie, establishing a comical romantic subplot that was used in a number of musicals. Also added were supporting characters like Gertie Cummings (whose annoying laugh provided a comical running gag) and Andrew Carnes, Ado Annie's gun-toting father, based on the play's Old Man Peck.

The play failed to mention the overriding goal of the characters in the musical: Oklahoma's impending statehood, a device that would be added by Hammerstein. In the play, the story ends as Curly is arrested after accidentally stabbing and killing Jeeter Fry during the shivaree fight, but he escapes to spend his honeymoon night with Laurey. When the sheriff arrives to return him to jail, Curly pleads to allow him one evening with his new bride, as he sings "Green Grow the Lilacs" to her from their bedroom window.

Green Grow the Lilacs ran for only sixty-four performances, not a bad run during the Depression, earning praise from *New York Times* theater critic Brooks Atkinson, who called it "a sunny part of the American legend." In July 1940, Theatre Guild's Lawrence Langner invited his Connecticut neighbor Richard Rodgers to see a revival of *Green Grow the Lilacs* at the Westport Country Playhouse. Although noted film director John Ford was scheduled to direct the play, with John Wayne of *Stagecoach* fame playing Curly, neither showed up for the production. (Ford was ultimately listed as producer.) Replacing Wayne was Ward Bond, another actor regularly used by John Ford in Western films. The choreographer was a talented young actor/dancer named Gene Kelly. Other key roles were filled by Betty Field as Laurey and Mildred Natwick as Aunt Eller.

By 1942, Theatre Guild was teetering toward bankruptcy and the thought came to its governing board that a Rodgers and Hart musical might save it from going under. When he was approached to write a musical version of *Green Grow the Lilacs*, Rodgers thought it was a splendid idea, but his partner, Lorenz Hart, was suffering from severe depression and alcoholism and wanted no part of this "hillbilly show." So Rodgers turned to an old friend, Oscar Hammerstein II, who agreed to write not just the lyrics, but also the libretto.

At the time, Rodgers was in his prime after scoring the hit musicals *Pal Joey* (1940) and *By Jupiter* (1942) with Hart as lyricist. Hammerstein, however, hadn't had a hit in years and was viewed as representing an era that was passé in the 1940s, musicals heavily influenced by European operetta. Hammerstein surprised everyone but Rodgers by aptly expanding the play's spare story. He added the Will Parker/Ado Annie romance for comic effect and expanded the role of the Pedler, now called Ali Hakim, thus balancing one romantic triangle (Curly-Laurey-Jud) with another (Annie-Will-Ali).

When Hammerstein incorporated Oklahoma's impending statehood into the final scene, it gave the musical its raison d'être, resulting in the change of *Away We Go!*, the show's original title, to *Oklahoma!*, adding an exclamation point to accentuate the excitement felt by its characters and to ward off any impressions of barren barns and pallid prairies.

Oklahoma! revolutionized American musical theater through Rodgers and Hammerstein's ingenious integration of songs and dance into the story, transforming a marginally successful play into a major Broadway hit. Historically, *Oklahoma!* is a rich depiction of American life in Oklahoma's Indian Territory in 1906, on its way to statehood.

With the exception of the sullen Jud Fry, the musical's characters (all of whom are Caucasian, despite living in Indian territory) are imbued with enthusiasm, rambunctious joy, and the fortitude to accomplish anything as long as they possess good humor and frontier spirit. *Oklahoma!* represented the muscular, brawny arms of a still-expanding America at the turn of a new century. *Oklahoma!* reconciles the antipathies of its two opposing factions: farmers and ranchers, who ultimately find common ground and move inexorably toward the common goal of statehood.

SCORE

The major irony of *Oklahoma!* was the abandonment of Lynn Riggs's main purpose for writing the play *Green Grow the Lilacs*: memories of the plaintive traditional cowboy and folk songs from his childhood. None of the songs in the play were retained, with Rodgers and Hammerstein creating an entirely new score, written using vernacular accents, grammar, and speech patterns. This becomes apparent in the very first line of the musical's first song, "Oh, What a Beautiful Mornin'," as "meadow" becomes "medda" and "g's" are dropped from words like "morning" and "feeling."

Rodgers and Hammerstein's songs were written specifically for their characters, reflecting their interpersonal relationships and conflicts. One song, "Kansas City," gives details of the changing life on the increasingly urbanizing frontier, in which cowhand Will Parker returns to the ranch after winning a steer roping contest, marveling about innovations in the modernized city, describing gasoline-powered buggies, telephones, and indoor radiators.

In addition to its status as Broadway's most influential and revolutionary musical, *Oklahoma!* also resulted in the first complete "original cast" album, featuring performers from the original production performing studio versions of songs from the score. The practice of recording stage performers' renditions of songs from musicals was already a staple of British record companies, but *Oklahoma!* marked the first time the entire cast of a Broadway musical went into a recording studio to record all of its songs using the original orchestrations under the direction of the show's conductor, in effect creating an aural version of an actual stage performance.

The Music Man

Historical context: Life in small-town America in 1912
Time period: July 1912
Broadway run and venues: December 19, 1957–October 22, 1960
(Majestic Theatre); October 24, 1960–April 15, 1962 (Broadway
Theatre) (1,375 p.)
Book: Meredith Willson
Score: Meredith Willson
Cast album: Capitol Records WAO-990 (1957)
Major characters: Harold Hill (Robert Preston), Marian Paroo (Bar-
bara Cook), Marcellus Washburn (Iggie Wolfington), Mrs. Paroo
(Pert Kelton), Winthrop Paroo (Eddie Hodges), Mayor Shinn
(David Burns), Eulalie Mackecknie Shinn (Helen Raymond),
Charlie Cowell (Paul Reed), The School Board (The Buffalo Bills)

HISTORICAL BACKGROUND

The Music Man was composer Meredith Willson's love sonnet to his
hometown of Mason City, Iowa, where he was born in 1902. The story
and characters in the musical are entirely fictional, but what makes *The
Music Man* relevant to American history is its depiction of small-town
life in Middle America during a hot July in 1912.

Mason City, the county seat for Iowa's Cerro Gordo County, has
stayed remarkably small over the past century. Whereas the 1910 Census showed the city having 11,230 residents, today that has grown only
to 28,000. Cerro Gordo County's demographics have also been stable,
remaining predominantly white. In 1910, out of some 25,000 residents
only about 150 were African American. The townsfolk in Willson's

fictionalized River City are noted for their uniformly middle-class status as well as their overwhelming whiteness. The only hint of a lower social class comes when the town's dyspeptic Mayor Shinn scorns teenaged ringleader Tommy Djilas as a "hoodlum" and a "wild kid," sneering about Djilas's itinerant father, who is a day laborer who lives "south a'town." Djilas is a Serbian name, indicating Tommy's family were probably immigrants.

Willson illuminated his story using period language, including catchphrases, slang, and cultural references familiar to Americans of that era but foreign to 1957 audiences that saw the original production. It had only been forty-five years, but the script's references to such extinct commodities as hogsheads, demijohns, and pinchback suits; personages like composer Rudolf Friml and the band master known as The Great Creatore; and renowned harness race horse Dan Patch evoked the innocence of the times in which Americans lived, a charming and nostalgic journey to a world that had been gone for nearly a half century even at the time Willson's production was staged in mid-century.

Some of Willson's references were used anachronistically, such as the pulp magazine *Captain Billy's Whiz Bang*, which wasn't published until 1919, cracker-barrels (a term not coined until 1916), phrases like "I got the goods on him in spades" (which wasn't in general use until the 1920s), and a purported dream match between wrestling champions Frank Gotch and Ed "Strangular" Lewis, who never actually fought one another. Lewis, in fact, wouldn't become well known until 1920.

Today, *The Music Man* is used as a teaching tool to acquaint youngsters as well as Broadway theater veterans with meanings behind the quaint language and cultural references that populate the dialog and songs. Much can be learned about day-to-day life in America at the turn of the twentieth century just by studying the script for *The Music Man*, including how dry goods and liquids were measured, the personalities of the day, fashion, and societal mores, such as "how to keep the young ones moral after school," as traveling salesman Harold Hill sings in "Trouble," his fast-paced musical sales pitch. In that song, Hill predicts that pool halls would lead to "libertine men" and "scarlet women" dancing to ragtime at armory dance halls, implying that the musical form popularized by Scott Joplin was in some way corrupting. In truth, by 1912, Joplin's ragtime had been appropriated by New York music publishers and had become mainstream entertainment, no longer considered morally objectionable, as it had been when the music was confined to St. Louis bordellos and saloons.

Amid all the flag waving and civic harmony of the Fourth of July celebration in River City's Madison Park, there are also dark overtones to the story. The gossipy "Pick-a-Little, Talk-a-Little" ladies have turned reserved spinster librarian Marian Paroo into a social outcast due to her relationship with the unseen "Miser Madison." Lynch mobs meting out social justice through tarring and feathering appear to be prevalent while the stigmatizing of children with speech disorders and the racist portrayal of Native Americans through the Wa Tan Ye Girls' tableau at the high school gymnasium are also on display. (The latter has resulted in the Wa Tan Ye scene being removed altogether from regional productions of the show.) As a result, *The Music Man*'s reputation as the quintessential "all-American musical" has been somewhat tarnished as audiences have responded negatively to many of the social prejudices and practices that existed in America more than one hundred years ago.

Production Notes

The idea for *The Music Man* originated in 1951, when Broadway producers Ernie Martin and Cy Feuer suggested that Willson write a musical comedy about his formative years in Mason City. At the time, Willson was one of Hollywood's busiest composer/arrangers, writing the score for Charlie Chaplin's *The Great Dictator*, arranging music for William Wyler's *The Little Foxes*, leading an orchestra for the Armed Forces Radio Service, and acting on the *Burns and Allen* radio program. In the mid-1950s, Willson was appearing as a panelist on the Goodson-Todman television game show *The Name's the Same* when he was approached by Martin and Feuer, who noted Willson's uniquely common touch in writing compositions such as "May the Good Lord Bless and Keep You," written for radio actress Tallulah Bankhead, and penning his 1948 autobiography, *And There I Stood With My Piccolo*, a memoir about

Barbara Cook and Robert Preston in *The Music Man.*
PHOTOFEST

his growing up in Mason City in which he described playing flute under the baton of "March King" John Philip Sousa.

Initially called *The Silver Triangle*, Willson's story focused on traveling salesman Harold Hill, who passes himself off as an organizer of boys' bands, going from town to town selling musical instruments, and then skipping town just after the instruments arrive. Willson populated the town with colorful, realistic characters, including a janitor's spastic, wheelchair-bound son, who would eventually be refined to become Winthrop, the lisping younger brother of the town's spinster piano teacher, Marian Paroo.

Many of the supporting characters in the show were inspired by real people Willson had known, such as Tommy Djilas, a rebellious teenager based on a boy he knew named Kilroy, a young ruffian who displayed charismatic leadership qualities due to his having a job early in life and to whom the neighborhood children gravitated as a role model. Marian Paroo came from a medical records librarian from Provo, Utah, named Marian Seeley, whom Willson had met during World War II.

Willson spent several years developing *The Music Man* along with his wife Rini, the two pitching the show to potential investors by performing it live, with Willson playing piano and the two speaking all the dialog and singing the more than three dozen songs considered for the score. Eventually these were whittled down to nineteen. A string of leading men was considered to play Harold Hill, including Danny Kaye, Dan Dailey, and Phil Harris, before Willson finally settled on Robert Preston, who ended up defining the role, making it one of the most iconic characterizations in musical theater history. *The Music Man* made its debut in December 1957 and was an immediate hit, winning the Tony Award for Best Musical and running for more than three years. It has since thrived in revivals, national tours, and regional productions, becoming an institution in American musical theater.

SCORE

Willson used his own idea of integrating dialog with music by applying a "talking-rhymeless-rhythm" aspect to numbers like "Rock Island," the bravura opening number in which traveling salesmen complain to one another about the packaging of products they sell to the rhythm of a speeding locomotive. This idea was expanded into Harold Hill's two musical sales pitches, "Ya Got Trouble" and "Seventy-Six Trombones," in which he combines the patter of a fast-talking salesman with short bursts of melody. Willson's brilliance involved creating dialog that flowed rhythmically with a musical background, much as hip-hop would do forty years later.

Willson also used musical counterpoint to represent connections between pairs of characters. As an example, Harold Hill's flamboyance and reputation as a love-'em-and-leave-'em cad masked an innate loneliness, reflected by Marian Paroo, whose lovelorn, unrealistic visions of the perfect man had not resulted in a husband, leaving her at age twenty-six still unmarried and destined for spinsterhood. Willson's idea was to link these two people through different interpretations of the same melody:

for Hill a rousing march and for Marian a lilting waltz, resulting in the songs "Seventy-Six Trombones" and "Goodnight, My Someone," one of a series of such pairings in the score. In another, he juxtaposed Hill's "The Sadder-But-Wiser-Girl for Me" with Marian's "My White Knight," but the pairing was ultimately rejected, although both songs appeared as stand-alone numbers in the score.

An aficionado of barbershop quartets, Willson used the Buffalo Bills, winning entry of the 1950 International Quartet Champions of SPEBSQSA (the Society for the Preservation and Encouragement of Barber Shop Quartet Singing in America), more commonly known as the Barbershop Harmony Society, to provide countermelodies for two of his songs, pairing the traditional song "Goodnight Ladies" with the chattering "Pick-a-Little, Talk-a-Little," and "Lida Rose" with Marian's wistful ballad "Will I Ever Tell You."

Most people would be surprised to discover that barbershop singing stemmed from African American roots in the late 1800s. Groups would often improvise harmonies on popular songs, folk music, and spirituals, which were then mimicked by white minstrel show performers. By the early twentieth century, the nascent recording industry had utilized a number of white vocal quartets singing new compositions in four-part close harmony, which soon came to be associated with the style.

The accidental transformation of the bickering members of the school board into a harmonious barbershop quartet was one of many humorous devices used in *The Music Man*. The term "barbershop" had only been recently introduced in "Play That Barber-Shop Chord," the first popular song to reference the close-harmony, four-part male quartet sound, which was first recorded in 1910 by the celebrated African American minstrel performer Bert Williams and by the American Quartet, a vocal group that recorded prolifically in the early decades of the century.

Parade

Historical context: The trial of suspected child murderer Leo Frank
Time period: 1913–1915
Broadway run: December 17, 1998–February 28, 1999 (85 p.)
Venue: Vivian Beaumont Theatre (Lincoln Center)
Book: Alfred Uhry
Score: Jason Robert Brown
Cast album: RCA Victor 09026-63378-2 (1999)
Major characters: Leo Frank (Brent Carver), Lucille Frank (Carolee
   Carmello), Hugh Dorsey (Herndon Lackey), Governor Slaton
   (John Hickok), Jim Conley (Rufus Bonds Jr.), Mary Phagan
   (Christy Carlson Romano), Britt Craig (Evan Pappas), Newt Lee
   (Ray Aranha)

HISTORICAL BACKGROUND

On April 26, 1913, in Atlanta, Georgia, a thirteen-year-old girl named
Mary Phagan (1899–1913) was found raped and murdered in the base-
ment of the National Pencil Factory where she had worked before being
laid off the week before. The prime suspects were Newt Lee, the factory's night watchman; Jim Conley, the building's janitor; and Leo Frank
(1884–1915), the factory's twenty-nine-year-old superintendent. Frank
was a Jewish, Brooklyn-born, Cornell University graduate, a respected,
upstanding citizen who was also a philanthropist and president of the
local B'nai B'rith.

Arrested and railroaded through manufactured evidence and coerced
witnesses, Frank was found guilty in what was called "The Trial of the
Century," and sentenced to hang for Phagan's murder. In an attempt to

save her husband's life, Lucille Frank (1888–1957) convinced Georgia governor John M. Slaton (1866–1955) of her husband's innocence, resulting in the commutation in June 1915 of Frank's sentence to life in prison. This enraged local anti-Semites, who, on August 16, kidnapped Frank from Milledgeville State Penitentiary, drove 175 miles to Marietta, near where Mary Phagan had lived, and hanged him from the branch of a tree the next morning. Afterward, photographs of the lynching were published as postcards and sold to the public.

Although the Phagan case was never solved, testimony submitted in 1982 by Frank's former office boy, Alonzo Mann, pointed toward Jim Conley as being the likely murderer. Conley had reportedly threatened to kill Mann if he told what he knew and, subsequently, Mann never testified. In 1986, the Georgia State Board of Pardons and Paroles posthumously pardoned Leo Frank, although he has never been officially absolved of the Phagan murder.

The Leo Frank lynching resulted in the expansion of the Anti-Defamation League, which had been founded by the B'nai B'rith the same year the Frank trial took place. American preacher William J. Simmons founded the second Ku Klux Klan, inspired after viewing *The Birth of a Nation*, director D. W. Griffith's savage and controversial 1915 silent film that glorified the Klan's post–Civil War existence. Several individuals who had participated in Leo Frank's lynching became charter members of the new Klan. The movie was used to recruit new chapters, with thousands of white supremacists filling their ranks well into the 1920s.

PRODUCTION NOTES

Alfred Uhry, author of the stage play *Parade*, grew up in Atlanta, Georgia, and attended Brown University, where he wrote two musicals for the college's student-run theater group, the Brownbrokers. After moving to New York, he was supported in his work by Broadway composer Frank Loesser, who provided Uhry with a stipend as well as counseling and encouraging the young writer.

Uhry's career highlights include a trilogy of works set in Atlanta during the first half of the twentieth century, including *Driving Miss Daisy* (1987), which earned him the Pulitzer Prize for Drama and

Leo Frank, who was falsely convicted of the rape and murder of thirteen-year-old Mary Phagan, 1915. The scandal was the inspiration for the 1998 musical *Parade*.
LIBRARY OF CONGRESS PRINTS AND PHOTO-GRAPHS DIVISION / ATLANTA JOURNAL

Thirteen-year-old Mary Phagan.
LIBRARY OF CONGRESS PRINTS AND PHOTOGRAPHS DIVISION

became an Oscar-winning motion picture. Another was *The Last Night of Ballyhoo* (1996), a comedy/drama set in 1939 during the premiere of the film *Gone with the Wind*. This, too, was highly praised, and won Uhry a Tony Award for Best Play.

But it was Uhry's third work of the trilogy that had the greatest impact on his legacy. *Parade* was an emotionally rich but disturbing musical based on the Leo Frank trial, which won Tony Awards both for Uhry's libretto and Jason Robert Brown's score.

As a Jew growing up in the South, Uhry recalled stories his family told about the region. His grandmother was friends with Lucille Frank, while a great uncle once employed Leo Frank. But Uhry recalled that whenever the name of the doomed pencil factory manager came up, family members would leave the room. Uhry was fascinated by the case, which resulted in *Parade*, named for an annual event held on Confederate Memorial Day, a rallying point for defiantly proud veterans of the Confederacy after the South's defeat in the Civil War. It was on that particular holiday in 1913 that the Phagan murder took place. The Confederate Memorial Day parade frames the action of the story, represented at the start, middle, and end of the musical to show the passage of time.

Uhry's book juggles a quartet of antagonists, all intent on Frank's destruction: district attorney Hugh Dorsey, the frightened janitor Conley, opportunistic journalist Britt Craig, and right-wing zealot Tom Watson. Dorsey strikes a deal with Conley to testify against Frank in exchange for immunity after he was caught trying to escape from prison. As Act I ends, Frank and his wife, Lucille, emerge as martyrs with Frank's initial conviction and sentencing to death. Act II focuses on Governor Slaton's efforts to reopen the case and Lucille Frank's heroic quest to save her husband's life. After Slaton commutes Frank's sentence, a mob comes to the jail and kidnaps Frank, lynching him the next morning, in one of the most harrowing sequences in all of Broadway history.

In the *New York Times*, critic Ben Brantley noted director Hal Prince bringing similarly disquieting and often horrifying subject matter to the theater, in shows such as *Cabaret* and *Sweeney Todd*, but star Brent Carver's performance as Leo Frank was dismissed, described "as flat and iconic as a bleeding saint in a religious mural." The musical's focus is on the strength of the Franks' relationship, but Leo Frank is portrayed more as a symbol than as a fleshed-out human and isn't portrayed with empathy as was *Sweeney Todd*'s tortured central character. Other critics noted the frank and frequent use of racial slurs in the show (all justified and not gratuitous) as a reason for the show's underwhelming reception by the public. It was plain that the many unlikeable characters and themes of racism, anti-Semitism, and injustice were too depressing for audiences looking for a "feel-good" musical with a happy ending. The disturbing messages of racial intolerance and failures within the Southern justice system that are displayed in *Parade* are more relevant now than ever.

SCORE

Jason Robert Brown's majestic, emotionally charged score won a Tony Award, elevating the musical above the book's faults with some of the best work of Brown's career. The ghostly specter of the Confederacy permeates many of the songs in the score, beginning with the martial introduction, "The Old Red Hills of Home," which serves as the overture. Brown cleverly incorporates elements of patriotic songs like "The Stars and Stripes Forever" into the rousing number, which attempts to invite the audience to cynically identify with Georgian pride.

In contrast, Leo Frank is introduced as an uncomfortable alien in the South, complaining of its "endless sunshine" and uncouth, "foreign" (i.e., anti-Semitic) inhabitants. There are a few lighter elements in the score, such as the playful "The Picture Show," which showcases the innocent flirting of the doomed Mary Phagan with her young friend Frankie Epps, written in a jaunty, vaudeville flavor.

Brown's complex, richly layered score, with its Charles Ivesian references to Southern folk and sacred tunes, dissonant countermelodies, and the blending of sprightly musical styles with dark overtones and ominous ostinatos, is designed to heighten the tension that culminates in Frank's lynching, which looms over the story like the Sword of Damocles. Along the way are a number of bravura showstopping numbers: weaselly journalist Britt Craig's cacophonous, strutting "Real Big News," Jim Conley's relentless, falsified testimony ("That's What He Said"), and the Franks' regret-filled farewell, "All the Wasted Time."

Brown showed keen awareness of American musical styles of the period, utilizing elements from ragtime, marches, and spirituals, which he combined with nascent forms of country music and jazz, which were just beginning to develop in the mid-1920s. Brown had the help of veteran jazz musician/arranger Don Sebesky, who provided period-authentic orchestrations. To his credit, Brown remained faithful to the period without resorting to trite Broadway clichés.

Although *Parade* only survived for eighty-five performances during its Broadway run, Jason Robert Brown's powerhouse score ranks with Adam Guettel's *Floyd Collins*, based on another early-twentieth-century tale of tragedy in the South, as one of the most underappreciated modern scores in musical history.

Fiorello!

Historical context: The rise to fame of Fiorello La Guardia
Time period: 1915–1929
Broadway run and venues: November 23, 1959–May 6, 1961 (Broadhurst Theatre); May 9–October 28, 1961 (Broadway Theatre) (795 p.)
Book: Jerome Weidman and George Abbott, based in part on *Life with Fiorello* by Ernest Cuneo (1955)
Score: Jerry Bock (music), Sheldon Harnick (lyrics)
Cast album: Capitol Records SWAO-1321 (1959)
Major characters: Fiorello La Guardia (Tom Bosley), Ben Marino (Howard Da Silva), Marie (Patricia Wilson), Dora (Pat Stanley), Morris (Nathaniel Frey), Floyd (Mark Dawson), Thea (Ellen Hanley)

HISTORICAL BACKGROUND

Although Fiorello La Guardia (1882–1947) was best known for his eleven-year stint as the energetic and colorful three-term mayor of New York (1934–1945), it was his formative years, prior to his becoming mayor, that became the subject for this award-winning 1959 musical.

The son of an Italian immigrant father and a Jewish mother from the Austro-Hungarian Empire, La Guardia was born in New York but moved with his family to Arizona in 1890, where his father worked as a bandmaster for the US Army. With his mixed family ancestry and a quick mind, La Guardia would become fluent in both Yiddish and Italian. In 1898, the La Guardias moved to Trieste (now Italy) where young Fiorello worked at the US consulates at Budapest and Fiume, adding German, French, Croatian, and Hungarian to his linguistic toolbox, enabling him to secure a job as an interpreter for the US Immigration Service on Ellis Island after his return to America.

In 1910, La Guardia received his law degree from New York University and in 1916, he was elected to the House of Representatives as a progressive Republican. World War I interrupted his term, during which time Captain La Guardia served as a pilot in the air force. At war's end, he was discharged after being promoted to major and returned triumphantly to Congress, where he was reelected four times, supporting the women's suffrage movement but opposing the enactment of Prohibition.

The period of La Guardia's life covered in *Fiorello!* focused on the period spanning from 1915, when he was an eager young attorney, to his initial campaign for mayor in 1929, when he ran against but lost to the corrupt but popular Jimmy Walker, who was supported by the

Tom Bosley as Fiorello La Guardia.
PHOTOFEST

powerful Tammany Hall political machine. The musical ends in 1933 as La Guardia decides to run for mayor for a second time, a race he would ultimately win.

PRODUCTION NOTES

New York-born Jerome Weidman, who wrote the libretto for *Fiorello!* with producer George Abbott, shared much with La Guardia's background. Like La Guardia, Weidman was the product of immigrants. Both parents were Jewish; his father made his living in the garment industry. Like La Guardia, Weidman attended law school at NYU, where he began writing short stories for the *New Yorker* during the magazine's "golden age" of the late 1930s and early 1940s. His short stories and, later, his novels often dealt with the seamier underbelly of New York politics. *Fiorello!* marked his first work for Broadway, which resulted in his writing subsequent books for *Tenderloin* (1960), also with George Abbott, and *I Can Get It for You Wholesale* (1962), which launched the career of Barbra Streisand.

Fiorello! starred Broadway newcomer Tom Bosley, a dead ringer for the fireplug-sized La Guardia, in a performance that helped the show win the Tony Award for Best Musical and the Pulitzer Prize for Drama—one of only ten musicals to be so honored. Howard Da Silva (Jud Fry in *Oklahoma!*) played the fictional political boss Ben Marino, while Patricia Wilson played La Guardia's loyal secretary Marie, who is secretly in love with her boss.

Fiorello! accurately followed key developments in La Guardia's professional and personal life, including his courtship of and marriage to Thea Almerigotti (1894–1921), who he met in 1915 when she was working as a dress designer in New York's garment district. In the musical, Thea is not an immigrant, but Thea Wilson, the daughter of President Woodrow Wilson. Thea's activism was exaggerated in the musical by having her portrayed as the leader of the Nifty Shirt Waist Factory's female employees in a strike against management for better working conditions.

In 1918, La Guardia returned from the war and married Thea. In November 1920, they were blessed with a daughter, whom they named Fioretta, but, tragically, the baby contracted spinal meningitis and died on May 8, 1921, before she was six months old. Thea suffered a breakdown as a result of the strain of caring for the baby and became ill herself from tuberculosis, which led to her own death six months later, on November 29, 1921, at the age of twenty-six. The musical makes no mention of the La Guardias' daughter and delays Thea's death until La Guardia's first campaign for mayor in 1929, a plot device that worked better for the playwrights. La Guardia's second marriage, to his faithful congressional secretary Marie Fisher (1895–1984), was also based on fact.

Weidman and Abbott made a wise decision in limiting the story to a finite period in La Guardia's life instead of trying to jam too much history into too little time. This left them ample opportunity to develop La Guardia's character as well as those of Thea and the secondary fictional characters in the story, ignoring what many thought would be a profile of his years as mayor, when he was known as "The Little Flower" and famously read the Sunday funnies to children on his radio program during a newspaper strike.

To have Thea die early in the play would have robbed the story of two key emotional story arcs: Thea's relationship with La Guardia and her tragic death; and Marie ultimately becoming the second Mrs. La Guardia, after resolving near the end of the musical to give up hope, quit her job, and marry the first man who asked her.

Fiorello! made good use of demonstrating La Guardia's charismatic connection with his constituents by having him speak fluently in Yiddish and Italian during his campaign for Congress. He defies the political machine of fictionalized Republican district leader Ben Marino by challenging the corrupt practices of Tammany Hall and becoming an honest politician who is an activist for civic improvement and responsive to the needs of the underprivileged.

Although musicals based on famous Americans had been produced before (*Annie Get Your Gun* and *Gypsy* being the best-known examples), *Fiorello!* marked the first time a major Broadway musical was devoted to a famous American subject personally familiar to members of the audience, many of whom grew up listening to La Guardia's Sunday radio broadcast, "Talk to the People." *Fiorello!* was followed by a string of other biographical musicals during the 1960s, including *The Unsinkable Molly Brown* (1960), *Funny Girl* (1964), and *George M!* (1968).

SCORE

The tuneful, melodically rich score for *Fiorello!* was written by the team of composer Jerry Bock and lyricist Sheldon Harnick, who would follow *Fiorello!* with *Tenderloin*, *She Loves Me*, and their longest-lasting success, *Fiddler on the Roof.* Bock fashioned his melodies from simpler times; the sentimental waltz "Till Tomorrow" could easily have been written during the 1910s while "Home Again" evoked the many patriotic marches that were found on music racks on pianos in homes throughout America at the end of World War I.

From the beginning, La Guardia is compared with political activist and writer Upton Sinclair, described by his office manager, Morris, his law clerk, Neil, and his secretary, Marie, in admiring terms as an upstanding and honest politician, fighting "On the Side of the Angels." In the breezy, satirical waltz, "Politics and Poker," Ben Marino and his cronies are in the process of selecting a Republican patsy to run in the heavily Democratic district against the favored Tammany candidate.

Bosley's showpiece, "The Name's La Guardia," is the candidate's musical soapbox speech, in which La Guardia uses his charisma and multilingual abilities to dazzle and spellbind voters, much as Harold Hill did to the citizens of River City in "Ya Got Trouble." Another flashy campaign song takes place during Act II with "Gentleman Jimmy," a rousing tribute to Jimmy Walker, tinged with a Charleston beat and tap-dancing ensemble that would be paralleled in "Willamania" in *The Will Rogers Follies* three decades later.

Gypsy

Historical context: Gypsy Rose Lee and the demise of vaudeville
Time period: Early 1920s to the 1930s
Broadway run and venues: May 21, 1959–July 9, 1960 (Broadway Theatre); August 15, 1960–March 25, 1961 (Imperial Theatre) (702 p.)
Book: Arthur Laurents, based on the memoirs of Gypsy Rose Lee
Score: Jule Styne (music), Stephen Sondheim (lyrics)
Cast album: Columbia OL-5420/OS-2017 (1959)
Major characters: Rose Hovick (Ethel Merman), Louise Hovick (Sandra Church), June Hovick (Lane Bradbury), Herbie (Jack Klugman), Tulsa (Paul Wallace), Mazeppa (Faith Dane), Electra (Chotzi Foley), Tessie Tura (Maria Karnilova)

HISTORICAL BACKGROUND

The life and early career of Gypsy Rose Lee (1911–1970) is noteworthy for the purpose of this book because Lee presided over the demise of vaudeville and the brief ascension of burlesque during the dark days of the Depression. Burlesque has been described as "vaudeville's naughty twin," a bawdier combination of low humor, ribald skits, and suggestive songs presented in a revue-styled format. Although both forms got their start in the nineteenth century, vaudeville acts were deemed more suitable for family entertainment while burlesque, with its scantily clad, curvaceous females, broad parodies, and lowbrow comics, was aimed chiefly at male audiences.

The story arc of *Gypsy* serves as a microcosm for the transformation of many struggling vaudeville performers into burlesque attractions as an act of desperation to stay relevant in the live entertainment industry. When *Gypsy* opens, it's the early 1920s, and June Hovick (1912–2010) and her older sister, Louise, are juveniles performing in innocent vaudeville skits. As the girls grow older, June gets weary of the endless touring and the girls' domineering stage mother Rose (1890–1954) and in 1928 lies about her age and elopes with Bobby Reed, a boy in the vaudeville act. She eventually changes her name to June Havoc and has a brief career as a marathon dancer before becoming a star on Broadway and in movies.

Louise Hovick was not as talented a dancer or singer as June and eventually moved into burlesque, which was now being threatened with extinction by the Depression and the motion picture industry. In order to continue attracting its male clientele, many burlesque performers resorted to stripping, which was how Louise became famous. She eventually changed her name to Gypsy Rose Lee and redefined the striptease, creating a more elegant, even dignified act that was more tease than strip, to which she added brainy recitations and witty, sometimes risqué one-liners. Gypsy's act made her a headliner for Minsky's Burlesque, for which she worked for four years during the 1930s.

Although the musical ends with Gypsy on top of her profession, her reign would not last long. By this time, Minsky's had invaded Broadway itself, billing its shows as "The Poor Man's Follies," and offering productions featuring lavishly costumed chorus girls, racy humor, and sumptuous orchestras at a fraction of the price Florenz Ziegfeld was charging for his upscale extravaganzas.

As the Depression wore on, Minsky's got lewder and raunchier in order to stay in business. Upon being elected New York mayor in 1933, Fiorello La Guardia declared war on the burlesque houses, blaming them for the rise in lurid sex crimes. Under pressure from reformers and citizens opposed to the raunchy shows, La Guardia authorized raids on New York's fourteen burlesque houses, with Paul Moss, his handpicked commissioner of licenses, refusing to grant renewals of licenses. La Guardia declared "the end of incorporated filth" in New York and banned the use of the word "burlesque" in any theater advertising. By November 1938, Minsky's was out of business and so was burlesque.

Production Notes

The 1959–1960 Broadway season saw two biographically based musicals whose subjects were still living: *The Sound of Music* and *Gypsy*. Both shows dealt with strong women surviving challenging times: Maria Von Trapp, the Austrian matriarch of the Von Trapp Family Singers, who persisted despite the looming threat of Nazi Germany, and Rose Hovick, who shepherded her daughter Louise through the Great Depression. Despite having her name in the title of the musical, Louise was not the show's main character. As soon as Ethel Merman joined the cast, Mama Rose became the show's central and, ultimately, tragic figure, with Merman

Gypsy Rose Lee in the 1930s.
PHOTOFEST

making it her signature role, taking over the show with one of the most powerful performances in theater history.

After reading Gypsy Rose Lee's 1957 autobiography, *Gypsy: A Memoir*, producer David Merrick immediately thought of Ethel Merman as being perfect to play the feisty stage mother who literally pushed her two daughters onto vaudeville stages as soon as they could walk. Laurents's vision changed *Gypsy* from a lighthearted salute to the last days of vaudeville and burlesque to a musicalized *King Lear*, with Merman playing what has been called the most complex character in the history of Broadway.

Whereas the real Rose Hovick was, according to June Havoc, tiny, fragile, and beguiling, Arthur Laurents refashioned her into an ambitious monster, whose own show business failures drove her to stop at nothing to ensure her girls' success, even convincing elder daughter, Louise, to demean herself by resorting to stripping just to attain the fame and fortune that had eluded her.

The real Rose Hovick never had a chance to defend herself against how Merman portrayed her in her epochal performance; Rose died in 1954 at the age of sixty-three from colorectal cancer, complicated by a stroke suffered two weeks earlier. June Havoc had an opinion about *Gypsy*, but it was not complimentary. The actress claimed that the depiction of her mother was a grotesque caricature and nowhere close to what her mother was really like. As a result, June engaged famed attorney Louis Nizer to draw up an agreement requiring that the show would not depict Havoc past the age of seven. Although much of what was in the agreement was ignored, one demand came to fruition: that theater marquees and all printed advertisements, programs, and recordings would show the proper title of the show as *Gypsy: A Musical Fable*, implying that none of what was presented on stage should be taken as factual.

SCORE
Producer David Merrick's first inclination was to have Irving Berlin write the score for *Gypsy*. Berlin had written for Ethel Merman previously in *Annie Get Your Gun* and *Call Me Madam*, but the veteran songsmith didn't approve of the show's concept and turned it down. Merrick's next

choice was Cole Porter, but Porter was in poor health, having recently lost both of his legs to amputation, the lingering result of injuries suffered in a horseback-riding fall twenty-one years earlier. Next to be called was the team of Cy Coleman and Carolyn Leigh, but Merrick didn't like any of the four songs they presented to him at an audition.

Arthur Laurents had worked with twenty-eight-year-old wunder-kind Stephen Sondheim on *West Side Story* and proposed that Sondheim write the score, but Merman turned this idea down flat, demanding someone better known. Merrick then went to Jule Styne, who, at fifty-four, was a versatile, seasoned composer, and Styne's frequent partners, lyricists Betty Comden and Adolph Green. The trio got started on the songs in 1957 but Comden and Green didn't know what to do with the character of Rose. Eventually, they bowed out to work on the screenplay for a film version of the novel *Auntie Mame*.

With Styne on board, Laurents's next step was to again consider Sondheim to write the lyrics, but the talented young writer balked, pre-ferring to do the whole score himself. Before giving Laurents his answer, however, Sondheim asked his mentor, Oscar Hammerstein, for advice. Hammerstein urged Sondheim to take the job, reasoning that writing for a big star like Merman would be a boost to his career. Hammerstein also told Sondheim that he should write not just for the character, but for the character as portrayed by Merman. This idea of customizing songs to fit a particular actor's portrayal became a hallmark of Sondheim's future musicals and established his personal policy of never writing songs until a show was fully cast. Ultimately, Merman loved what Styne and Sond-heim wrote for her, especially the explosive showstoppers "Everything's Coming Up Roses" and "Rose's Turn."

Styne and Sondheim's score perfectly captured the brassy, upbeat atmosphere of 1920s vaudeville and the risqué world of burlesque that replaced it. It has since become one of the most admired scores in Broad-way history, its songs running the gamut of emotions, from Merman's rafters-raising solos to the comic duet "If Momma Was Married," the sprightly buddy song "Together, Wherever We Go," and the tender char-acter number for Louise, "Little Lamb." One of its many brilliant turns was the transformation of Baby June and Baby Louise's innocent "May

We Entertain You" into Gypsy Rose Lee's bump-and-grind theme song, "Let Me Entertain You." To do this, Sondheim designed an ingenious, flexible lyric to convey different meanings without changing the words for each stage in the girls' careers; playful when they sing it as children and suggestive when the grown-up Louise uses it in her striptease act. Within two years, Sondheim was writing ingenious, epoch-changing scores on his own, beginning with *A Funny Thing Happened on the Way to the Forum*.

Chicago

Historical context: Chicago murderesses Beulah May Annan and Belva
    Gaertner
Time period: Late 1920s
Broadway run: June 3, 1975–August 27, 1977 (936 p.)
Venue: Forty-Sixth Street Theatre
Book: Fred Ebb and Bob Fosse, based on the play *Chicago* by Maurine
    Dallas Watkins (1926)
Score: John Kander (music), Fred Ebb (lyrics)
Cast album: Arista AL-9005 (1975)
Major characters: Roxie Hart (Gwen Verdon), Velma Kelly (Chita
    Rivera), Billy Flynn (Jerry Orbach), Amos Hart (Barney Martin),
    Matron (Mary McCarty)

HISTORICAL BACKGROUND

On April 3, 1924, twenty-three-year-old Beulah May Annan (1899–
1928) from Owensboro, Kentucky, shot and killed Harry Kalstedt, a
man with whom she was having an affair, after meeting him at Tennant's
Model Laundry in Chicago, where she worked as a bookkeeper. Annan
and her husband, Albert, an auto mechanic, had moved to the Windy
City after marrying in 1920. Mrs. Annan confessed to the murder,
claiming she shot Kalstedt in self-defense to avoid being raped. During
her trial, she changed her story to say that she shot Kalstedt because he
was ending their affair. By the time the trial ended, Mrs. Annan said she
had told Kalstedt she was pregnant and had shot him during an argument when both reached for a gun in the room. According to newspaper
reports, instead of calling the police immediately after the shooting,

Annan lounged around the apartment, drinking cocktails, while playing a popular foxtrot record, "Hula Lou" (popularized by Sophie Tucker) over and over for four hours.

Annan's husband, Albert, not only backed up her story but also supported her throughout the trial, even withdrawing money from a bank account in order to pay for the services of high-powered lawyer William Scott Stewart. A day after Beulah was acquitted, she publicly dumped Albert, claiming he was "too slow." Four years after her acquittal, Beulah Annan was dead from tuberculosis at the age of twenty-eight.

On March 11, three weeks before the Annan murder, Belva Gaertner (1884–1965), a twice-divorced, twenty-nine-year-old cabaret singer who was separated from her second husband, William Gaertner, whom she had recently remarried, shot and killed Walter Law, a married man with whom she had been having an affair. Law was found in the Gaertners' car along with a bottle of gin and the gun, which was lying beside his body. A woozy Mrs. Gaertner was arrested at her apartment with her blood-soaked clothes strewn across the floor. She claimed she had been drinking and had no memory of the shooting. Like Annan, Gaertner was defended by Stewart and, in June, she was also acquitted, only days after Annan's trial had concluded with the same outcome. Gaertner survived longer than Annan did, living until 1965, when she died of natural causes at the age of eighty.

The two disconnected murders reflected Chicago's fascination with homicides committed by women during the Roaring Twenties, a time when tabloid stories about the suffragette movement and illicit Prohibition-era booze proliferated. No less than seven cases of jealous lover murders were currently in the news. The acquittals of Annan and Gaertner followed a pattern that saw Cook County juries refusing to convict female murderers of their deeds. The acquitted women became celebrities, exploited in sensationalistic stories by newspapers such as the *Chicago Tribune*, while rival Hearst papers sneered at the "sob sisters" who wept at trials, thus gaining the sympathies of the all-male juries.

One of the *Tribune's* journalists was Maurine Dallas Watkins (1896–1969), who had been working the courthouse beat for only a few months when the Annan and Gaertner murders took place. Watkins's

Beulah Annan, left, and Belva Gaertner, both on trial for
murder in 1924. The two were the prototypes for Roxie
Hart and Velma Kelly in *Chicago* (1975).
CHICAGO TRIBUNE

stories highlighted the attractiveness of the two women, playing up an
angle of "jazz babies" corrupted by leering men sloshed on illegal liquor,
with Annan characterized as the "beauty of the cell block" and Gaertner
"the most stylish of Murderess Row."

After working at the *Tribune* for eight months, Watkins returned to
school, studying journalism at Yale University's new School of Drama.
Remembering the cases she covered back in Chicago, Watkins wrote a
play that was initially titled *The Brave Little Woman* before publishing it as
Chicago in 1926. Watkins combined the stories of Annan and Gaertner,
renaming her characters Roxie Hart and Velma Kelly. Al Annan became
Beulah's mousy husband, Amos Hart, while William Scott Stewart was
combined with another famed Chicago defense attorney, W. W. O'Brien,
to become Billy Flynn, a flashy and opportunistic lawyer.

The play had a respectable run of 172 performances, which led to a national tour that reached Los Angeles, where it starred a young, unknown actor named Clark Gable as Amos Hart. In 1927, a silent feature film version was produced, directed by Cecil B. De Mille, which led to, in 1942, a big-budget Hollywood film, now retitled *Roxie Hart*, with Ginger Rogers starring in the title role and a mustachioed Adolphe Menjou playing Billy Flynn. The film rolled Velma Kelly and the other multiple murderesses in Watkins's play into one feisty, trigger-happy blonde named "Two-Gun Gertie" Baxter, played by bombshell Iris Adrian. Today, Watkins's play goes by its original subtitle, *Play Ball*, when it is staged, so as not to be confused with the musical.

PRODUCTION NOTES
Actress Gwen Verdon had wanted to do a musical version of Watkins's play ever since she saw *Roxie Hart*, the 1942 Ginger Rogers movie. However, Watkins, who was still living, had become a born-again Christian and refused to permit the adaptation, fearing it would glamourize the novel's unsavory themes. After Watkins died in 1969, her estate awarded the rights to Verdon, along with her husband, director/choreographer Bob Fosse, and producer Richard Fryer.

In 1973, Fosse was busy directing *Lenny*, a film based on the life of comedian Lenny Bruce, but the following year he set to work on the musical version of *Chicago*, asking John Kander and Fred Ebb, with whom he had worked on *Cabaret*, to write the score. Fosse cast Verdon in the role of Roxie Hart, with Verdon's good friend Chita Rivera playing Velma Kelly.

Shortly after rehearsals began on *Chicago*, Fosse suffered a massive heart attack. After three days in intensive care and a week of tests, he underwent bypass surgery, only to suffer another heart attack, which further debilitated him. Concerned that members of his cast would quit to take other jobs, Fosse gave personal loans to members of the dance ensemble and had his producers find temporary jobs for his cast until he could return. Jerry Orbach, who had been cast as Billy Flynn, was offered a production of *Macbeth* in Los Angeles but turned it down.

After a few months, Fosse was well enough to resume directing, with his loyal cast waiting for him. In late 1974, *Chicago* started rehearsals at the same time that *A Chorus Line*, a musical about struggling chorus dancers directed by Fosse's rival, choreographer Michael Bennett, was scheduled to open.

Transported from 1924 to the late 1920s, Fosse's *Chicago* was bleak and pessimistic, disguised by the glitz and pageantry of vaudeville at its most decadent. All of the show's characters (except for the guileless Amos Hart) were avaricious, duplicitous, and self-serving. *Chicago* had no love story and no protagonist, seen through a cynical lens that glorified crime and criminals, and celebrated yellow journalism and greedy lawyers.

Despite its decadent "razzle-dazzle," a star-studded cast, and Kander and Ebb's superlative score, *Chicago* was upstaged by the overwhelming success of *A Chorus Line*, which swamped it in the Tony Awards. To add insult to injury, some of the dialog from a 1978 production staged by the Los Angeles Civic Light Opera was censored by the opera's general managers, who red-circled language that might be deemed offensive by its regular subscribers. Indignant protests from Fosse, Verdon, and the entire cast resulted in only minimal changes, but *Chicago* continued to be plagued by controversy and bad luck during its initial Broadway run.

By the time it was revived in 1996, American society and, in turn, Broadway, had undergone a wholesale change. Amid the lurid O. J. Simpson murder trial, other shows were now incorporating even more sensitive and risqué material than was seen in *Chicago*, such as *Rent* and *Victor/Victoria*, both of which were hits. In this atmosphere, *Chicago*'s lurid story of merry murderesses, headline-chasing journalists, and unscrupulous lawyers was welcomed with open arms by the theater-going public. Fosse had died in 1987, but the new production, launched after a successful concert version in the *City Center Encores!* series, received ecstatic reviews and has since become the longest-running revival in Broadway history, winning six Tony Awards and running for more than nine thousand performances.

SCORE

John Kander and Fred Ebb viewed *Chicago* as an homage to vaudeville and burlesque, the two leading forms of live entertainment during the 1920s. Ebb, who co-wrote the book with Bob Fosse, staged the entire musical as a series of vaudeville acts, with Roxie Hart aspiring to be a Hollywood actress with Velma Kelly as her jealous rival.

Ebb saw the show's characters as performers, modeling each solo number on a specific vaudeville personality. Roxie was the embodiment of sultry torch singer Helen Morgan, who starred as Julie LaVerne in *Show Boat*. Velma was patterned after speakeasy owner Texas Guinan, known for the catchphrase, "Hello, sucker! Come on in and leave your wallet on the bar." Billy Flynn was Ted Lewis, the top-hatted showman and king of the corny clarinet, known for his effusive "Is everybody happy?" Mama Morton, the name given to the unnamed prison matron in Watkins's novel, was based on ribald Jewish nightclub entertainer Sophie Tucker, "The Last of the Red Hot Mamas." And when sad sack Amos sings "Mr. Cellophane," it was meant to summon forth the spirit of Black vaudevillian Bert Williams, intoning his doleful 1906 signature song, "Nobody."

The music evoked the 1920s "Jazz Age," although beyond the overture, the score reflected vaudeville and burlesque rather than Chicago jazz, which was then championed by the likes of Joseph "King" Oliver, Jelly-Roll Morton, and Jimmie Noone. Only in the syncopation-laced galop "We Both Reached for the Gun," introduced as "The Press Conference Rag," do the tempos approach those of frenetic razzmatazz hits from the period like "Charleston," "China Boy," and "Nobody's Sweetheart." Still, Kander and Ebb did a good job of replicating the sound of jazz of the era, with tuba and banjo highlighting the rhythm in many of the numbers.

Tangos were all the rage during the 1920s, which emerged from the brothels of Europe to become respectable, symbolized by records by French-Argentine superstar Carlos Gardel. Kander and Ebb used the style on the slinky "Cell Block Tango," in which six "merry murderesses" explain away their respective homicides, to the pervasive refrain, "he had it coming."

Picayune complaints aside, the score was a triumph, actually a more accurate musical representation of the period than *Gypsy*, another major musical that evoked the seamy side of vaudeville and burlesque houses of the 1920s.

Floyd Collins

Historical context: Floyd Collins in Kentucky's Sand Cave
Time period: January 30–February 16, 1925
Off Broadway run: February 9, 1996–March 24, 1996 (25 p.)
Venue: Playwrights Horizons
Book: Tina Landau
Score: Adam Guettel
Cast album: Nonesuch 79434-2 (1997)
Major characters: Floyd Collins (Christopher Innvar), Nellie Collins (Theresa McCarthy), Homer Collins (Jason Danieley), Jewell Estes (Jesse Lenat), Skeets Miller (Martin Moran), Miss Jane (Cass Morgan), Lee Collins (Don Chastain)

HISTORICAL BACKGROUND

On January 30, 1925, Floyd Collins (1887–1925) a thirty-seven-year-old cave explorer who had already discovered, explored, and commercially exploited Crystal Cave in central Kentucky, sought to do the same for another discovery, known as Sand Cave. Sand Cave served two purposes for Collins: a potential site for a commercial attraction; and to point the way to the more remote Crystal Cave, which was situated farther off the main highway.

Collins grew up with an innate curiosity about the underground caverns in Kentucky's Mammoth Cave complex, the world's longest cave system, consisting of hundreds of miles of interconnected underground passageways and cathedral-like rooms made from limestone, gypsum, and helictites. Collins was obsessed with exploring every possible entrance to a new passageway, using basic digging tools and an oil lamp for illumination. Eventually, he met Edmund Turner, a geologist who had come to Kentucky to study terrain and rock formations but became engrossed in Collins's cave explorations, hiring him at two dollars a day to accompany him in his research. Through Turner, Collins educated himself on cave environment and structure and became an expert on the best ways to navigate caves, crawling on his belly through narrow passageways and moving mud and rocks by hand to seek out new and wondrous formations.

On that January day, Collins ventured into Sand Cave, navigating his way through a narrow, descending crevice, where he found himself in an entirely new, undetected cavern. Retracing his steps, he was climbing through a V-shaped crevice in the ceiling when a large, fifty-pound rock pinned his left leg. Unable to extricate himself, Collins, with no communication devices, could only wait for someone to come to his rescue.

When Collins failed to emerge from Sand Cave, his brother Homer (1902–1969) went looking for him. Collins had asked Homer to accompany him, but Homer declined, saying he was going to Louisville to shop for a used car instead. By February 1, rescuers had located Collins, but

Floyd Collins, cave explorer trapped in Sand Cave, Kentucky, in 1925. His ordeal was the focus of the 1996 musical *Floyd Collins*. REPRODUCED BY PERMISSION FROM HOMER COLLINS AND JOHN LEHRBERGER, *THE LIFE AND DEATH OF FLOYD COLLINS* (DAYTON, OH: CAVE BOOKS, 2001), 92.

couldn't agree on a method for extricating him from the cave, resulting in chaotic confusion. Some local residents volunteered to bring food and drink to Collins but they panicked in the darkness and returned to the surface, leaving the provisions behind.

As word began to spread about Collins's dilemma, William "Skeets" Miller (1904–1983), a journalist from the Louisville *Courier-Journal*, arrived to check out the story. When told by Homer to "go get the story yourself from Floyd," Miller entered Sand Cave himself and began assisting in the rescue attempt.

Before long, tents were being constructed outside the cave, staffed by would-be entrepreneurs selling hot coffee and snacks. An attempt was made to organize and coordinate the rescue effort by drilling a shaft that had to go through sixty feet of solid limestone in order to dig Collins out. Rumors were spreading that Collins had already died, while others claimed that Collins had never entered the cave at all and that the whole incident was a publicity-seeking hoax.

By February 4, Collins's entrapment had become headline news in the *New York Times*. The National Guard was put in charge of the rescue effort. A force of seventy-five men worked around the clock digging the rescue shaft, but work was progressing at a snail's pace, offset by bad weather and encounters with large rocks, gravel, and thick, oozing muck.

Nearby Cave City became inundated with curious visitors and journalists from around the world, hungrily looking for a story. More than 4,500 automobiles with license plates from twenty states descended on the area, which was now taking on a carnival-like atmosphere. As temperatures dropped into the twenties, heavy rain left two feet of water at the bottom of the still-uncompleted rescue shaft.

On February 16, workers finally broke through to the Sand Cave passageway, only to find Collins three days dead from extended exposure, hypothermia, and starvation. Floyd Collins was thirty-seven years old. Unable to extricate him, workers left him there until they were finally able to remove his body two months later.

In April, a blind Atlanta, Georgia, preacher, the Reverend Andrew Jenkins, wrote a song called "The Death of Floyd Collins," which became a huge seller when rural recording artists Fiddlin' John Carson and Vernon Dalhart recorded it.

The attention to the attempt to rescue Floyd Collins resulted in increased interest in the Mammoth Cave region, leading to it becoming designated as a national park. A film documentary and several books were written about the incident, including a memoir by Collins's brother Homer, published in 1955, and *Trapped! The Story of Floyd Collins* by Robert K. Murray and Roger W. Brucker, published in 1982.

A 1951 motion picture, *Ace in the Hole*, directed by Billy Wilder, shifted the locale to Albuquerque, New Mexico, with a focus on Skeets Miller, the journalist who sympathized with Collins's plight and tried to rescue him. In the Wilder film, Miller was renamed Chuck Tatum, played by Kirk Douglas as a ruthless opportunist who sought to make money from the misfortune of the buried man, now called Leo Minosa. In the film, Minosa gets himself trapped while looking for ancient Indian artifacts buried in the cave. As in real life, Minosa also dies, although the fault was blamed on the journalist's deliberately delaying in getting the unfortunate man help in order to maximize the continuation of his sensationalistic stories about the incident.

PRODUCTION NOTES
Writer Tina Landau was looking for an idea for a musical when she discovered the tragedy of Floyd Collins in "Amazing American Stories," a collection published in *Reader's Digest*. The story ran for only a paragraph, but its title, "Deathwatch Carnival," sparked her interest and she took the idea to composer/lyricist Adam Guettel, grandson of Broadway legend Richard Rodgers. In writing the book for the musical, Landau decided not to use *Ace in the Hole*, the 1951 film version, with its fictionalized characters that focused more on an unscrupulous journalist than on the victim. What started out as a tragic tale of an Icarus-like man who flew too close to the sun ended up as a protest piece against yellow journalism, set in the atmospheric, haunting world of 1920s Appalachia. When it first appeared at the American Music Theater Festival in Philadelphia in 1994, what struck audiences was that the Collins tragedy represented the first American media circus, a cautionary tale that forecast how news-

papers, tabloid magazines, and local television news continue to exploit unfortunate tragedies on a daily basis.

Audiences that saw the show when it played off Broadway in 1996 were able to relate to the hallmarks of the Collins tragedy: the wildly distorted reports, false rumors, and opportunists who sought to make a buck off of others' misfortunes. Landau's book, however, didn't get all of its facts right. Its ironic implication was that Collins, in wanting to create a carnival atmosphere surrounding his cave, became the subject of a different kind of carnival, at his own expense. According to Homer Collins, greed was not the chief motivating factor in his brother's cave explorations. Instead, it was simply an obsession stemming from an innate curiosity about the unknown that consumed him. Monetary exploitation was just a means of turning his hobby into a lucrative business. In Homer's book, Floyd Collins is depicted as a serious cave explorer whose passion to find out what lay beyond the next underground passage is what led to his tragic destruction.

Landau's premise for *Floyd Collins* presented a unique dilemma: how to write a compelling story with its protagonist immobilized in one position for nearly the entire play. The story accomplishes this through immersive staging, innovative sound design, and claustrophobic lighting, sometimes with only Collins (played by Christopher Innvar) illuminated on stage.

Floyd Collins remained off Broadway, and rightly so. It would have been impossible to convey the constricting confinement of Collins's plight in a large theater. Even smaller theaters reduced the house size, seating audiences in onstage bleachers in a modified thrust stage setting.

In researching the story, Landau and Guettel traveled to Kentucky's cave country to get the full flavor of the region, seeking out and interviewing Collins's family descendants. To create the score, Guettel conducted meticulous research into the spare, Appalachian hill country music that was then flourishing in 1920s central Kentucky, deciding upon a small chamber group playing folk instruments such as guitar, banjo, and harmonica.

Landau was careful not to distort the facts of the tragedy. Real-life persons became characters in the play, including Homer Collins; Bee

Doyle, the owner of the farm where Collins found the cave; H. T. Carmichael, the engineer who devised the method of extricating Collins; and Jewell Estes, a local teenager who was the first to find Collins after he was buried.

Unfortunately, *Floyd Collins* was not a hit, playing for only twenty-five performances before closing on March 24, 1996. Regional productions began in 1999 and the show's reputation as a daring and innovative musical has grown in the years since its initial run.

SCORE

Tina Landau's original intent was not to create a musical documentary about Floyd Collins, but to tell the story from four different points of view. The first was to show Floyd Collins's innocent ambition; the second, his family's single-minded devotion in rescuing him. The third focused on a monolithic press that ignores or distorts facts, while a fourth shows the confrontational atmosphere between the locals and the outlanders who arrive with the machinery to get Floyd to safety. The musical was originally called "Deathwatch Carnival," but Landau eventually changed it to "Floyd Collins," to remind audiences of the true focus of the story, and to show that everything else in the play was merely a distraction.

Guettel reinforced this idea by devoting the first fifteen minutes of his remarkable score to Floyd, on stage alone, singing a soliloquy as he descends into his own private universe. Guettel's music was based on traditional Americana styles, tempered by the dissonant influences of modern composers like Bartok, Janacek, and Stravinsky, bringing an aura of uncertainty to Floyd's naively hopeful optimism. A pared-down orchestra featured a string quartet, acoustic folk instruments such as guitar, banjo, mandolin, and harmonica, plus piano and percussion. Songs meander like the twisting passages of Sand Cave itself, including a nonmelodic hoedown ("'Tween a Rock an' a Hard Place"); the beautifully contemplative "Daybreak"; the quirky, vaudeville-flavored "The Carnival"; the elegiac "Through the Mountain"; and the show's framing song, "The Ballad of Floyd Collins," the only song written with a discernible melody and traditional structure.

The Scottsboro Boys

Historical context: The 1931 trial of nine Black teenagers accused of rape
Time period: 1931
Broadway run: October 31–December 12, 2010 (49 p.)
Venue: Lyceum Theatre
Book: David Thompson
Score: John Kander (music), Fred Ebb (lyrics)
Cast album: Jay Records CDJAY-1421 (2010)
Major characters: Haywood Patterson (Joshua Henry), Clarence Norris (Rodney Hicks), Charles Weems (Christian Dante White), Andy White (Derrick Cobey), Roy Wright (Julius Thomas III), Olen Montgomery (Josh Breckenridge), Ozie Powell/Ruby Bates (James T. Lane), Willie Roberson (Kendrick Jones), Eugene Williams (Jeremy Gumbs), Interlocutor (John Cullum)

HISTORICAL BACKGROUND

During the Great Depression, unemployed Americans often hitched rides on freight trains hoping to find work in other towns. On March 25, 1931, nine Black youths, ranging in age from twelve to nineteen, boarded a Southern Railway train in Chattanooga heading west to Memphis, Tennessee. Somewhere around Jackson County, Alabama, a fight broke out when a group of whites spied one of the boys, eighteen-year-old Haywood Patterson (1912–1952), and attempted to throw him off the train, claiming it was a "white man's train." The dispute soon escalated, with all the Black passengers on board being threatened. A fight ensued, resulting in the aggressive white passengers being removed from the train. The whites proceeded to contact local authorities, who formed a posse that stopped the train at Paint Rock, Alabama, and arrested the African Americans, even though some had been scattered throughout the train's cars, with many not even knowing each other. Victoria Price and Ruby Bates, two young white women on the train who were facing potential vagrancy and prostitution charges, falsely accused the Blacks of rape, resulting in the boys being forcibly removed and arrested. A trial with an all-white jury was conducted in the town of Scottsboro, Alabama, resulting in eight of the nine being convicted, without hard evidence, and sentenced to death. Only twelve-year-old Roy Wright (1918–1959) was spared.

The American Communist Party and the NAACP came to the youths' defense and appealed the conviction, but the Alabama Supreme Court upheld it. Chief Justice John C. Anderson dissented on the grounds that the accused teenagers were permitted neither effective counsel nor a fair trial; the case was appealed to the US Supreme Court, resulting in new trials being ordered.

The retrial took place in Decatur, Alabama, where one of the purported rape victims recanted her story, testifying that none of the boys had touched her. Despite this, the second jury again found them guilty, but the judge set aside the verdict and granted a third trial, which resulted in yet another guilty verdict. Once again, the case was appealed to the US Supreme Court, which ruled that African Americans had to be included on juries. In 1937, charges were dropped for four of the nine defendants, although all ended up serving time in prison.

The case of "The Scottsboro Boys," as they came to be known, became famous as a blatant miscarriage of justice, resulting in landmark decisions relating to how jury trials are conducted in the United States and paving the way for the civil rights movement, which wouldn't begin for another two decades.

PRODUCTION NOTES
While conducting research for the shows *Flora the Red Menace* and *Steel Pier*, both of which took place during the 1930s, composer John Kander, lyricist Fred Ebb, director Susan Stroman, and book writer David

Thompson came across the case of the Scottsboro Boys. The group was looking for "something from a real moment in American history that mattered" and decided to develop the case as a musical to show that the youths were individuals and not a monolithic group, as their unified name came to describe them.

In adapting the story, Kander, Ebb, Stroman, and Thompson chose to write it in the style of a minstrel show, implying a subversive commentary on minstrelsy's negative stereotypes, which is still in evidence in many aspects of modern society and the entertainment world. It wasn't the first time that a Kander and Ebb show framed a show using traditional entertainment forms. *Cabaret* (1968) depicted the rise of Nazi Germany as seen through a tawdry jazz nightclub while *Chicago* (1975) utilized the decadence of 1920s vaudeville and burlesque shows as a framework in satirizing a city's corrupt justice system. In using these devices, Thompson said he was able to take audiences to dangerous places while making sure they enjoyed every minute of it. At the time the events in *The Scottsboro Boys* took place, minstrelsy was still a potent element in American entertainment. The show thus paralleled minstrelsy with the devastating, racist actions of the Southern criminal and jury systems in the story.

John Cullum starred as the Interlocutor, the standard master of ceremonies character in minstrelsy and the only white actor in the cast. As often occurred in minstrelsy, performers played a variety of characters and *The Scottsboro Boys* featured Black actors playing bigoted whites as well as females. Sharon Washington played civil rights figure Rosa Parks (1913–2005), who bookends the musical, appearing as she is about to board a city bus in Montgomery, Alabama.

Familiar elements from minstrel shows were used, including the stock characters Mr. Bones and Mr. Tambo, the traditional "Gentlemen, be seated" introduction, a semicircular seating arrangement, and popular dances from the period including tap, soft-shoe, and sand dancing. After directing big-budget shows for Mel Brooks's *The Producers* and *Young Frankenstein*, Stroman utilized spare production values for *The Scottsboro Boys*, just as in minstrel shows, which often used only chairs and tambourines as set pieces or props.

SCORE

In writing the score, John Kander studied early 1930s jazz recordings, which still showed the influence of ragtime, a musical style that had all but disappeared after the death of its most celebrated composer, Scott Joplin, in 1917, but reverberated in the pre-swing hot jazz and dance bands that permeated the early years of the Depression.

Fred Ebb's death in 2004 forced the production to be put in moth-balls until 2008, when Kander decided to resume production, completing the lyrics himself. Unlike other songwriting teams that preferred to work independent of one another, Kander and Ebb were a true team, writing songs around a kitchen table and bouncing ideas off one another. The last song Ebb worked on was "Nothin'," sung by Joshua Henry as Haywood Patterson, who is testifying to the boys' innocence at their initial trial. The song was written in the laconic style of Black minstrel performer Bert Williams, whose signature song was "Nobody" (1906).

All of the show's songs were performed in the lighthearted style typical of minstrel shows, even the grim "Electric Chair," whose grisly lyrics vividly describe the effects of electrocution on the human body. Musically, however, it's not far from uplifting songs like "A Spoonful of Sugar" from *Mary Poppins*, concluding with a sprightly tap dance. An exception is the wistful "Go Back Home," sung by Haywood and the boys after being convicted, as they resign themselves to await execution.

One week after the show opened, a group of about thirty members of a political group calling themselves The Freedom Party picketed the Lyceum Theatre, chanting, "*Scottsboro Boys* is no minstrel show! Shut 'em down! They got to go!" and handing out flyers that asked, "When is racist terrorism musical entertainment?" The picketers were oblivious to the fact that *The Scottsboro Boys*, with its nearly all-Black cast, was actually turning minstrelsy on its head by having Black actors make fun of whites.

The *New York Times* compared *The Scottsboro Boys* to *Bloody Bloody Andrew Jackson*, in its attempt to rewrite American history as musical comedy but admitted that the writers took the satire a little too far, turning the suffering of the nine unfortunate African Americans into a lighthearted sideshow. *The Scottsboro Boys* proved to be too uncomfortable for Broadway audiences, lasting only six weeks before closing.

Baby Case

Historical context: The Lindbergh baby kidnapping
Time period: 1932–1936
Off-Off Broadway run: New York Musical Theatre Festival (July 9–29, 2012)
Venue: The Griffin at the Pershing Square Signature Center
Book: Michael Ogborn
Score: Michael Ogborn
Cast album: None
Major characters: Charles Lindbergh/Bruno Richard Hauptmann (Will Reynolds), Anne Morrow Lindbergh/Anna Hauptmann (Anika Larsen), Walter Winchell (Michael Thomas Holmes)

HISTORICAL BACKGROUND

In 1932, Charles Augustus Lindbergh (1902–1974) was the most famous person in the world. His journey from obscure US Air Mail pilot to celebrated hero took place literally overnight, when on May 21, 1927, he became the first person to complete a nonstop transatlantic flight from New York City to Paris, flying alone in his single-engine monoplane, the *Spirit of St. Louis.*

The feat marked a turning point in aviation history, earning Lindbergh the Medal of Honor, presented to him at the White House by President Calvin Coolidge. A multitude of honors bestowed upon Lindbergh included a ten-cent Air Mail stamp issued by the US Post Office Department, depicting his plane and a map of the flight, a ticker tape parade up Broadway's "Canyon of Heroes," and Lindbergh being honored as *Time* magazine's first "Man of the Year."

WANTED

INFORMATION AS TO THE
WHEREABOUTS OF

CHAS. A. LINDBERGH, Jr.

OF HOPEWELL, N. J.

SON OF COL. CHAS. A. LINDBERGH

World-Famous Aviator

This child was kidnaped from his home
in Hopewell, N. J., between 8 and 10 p. m.
on Tuesday, March 1, 1932.

DESCRIPTION:

Age, 20 months   Hair, blond, curly
Weight, 27 to 30 lbs.   Eyes, dark blue
Height, 29 inches   Complexion, light
Deep dimple in center of chin
Dressed in one-piece coverall night suit

ADDRESS ALL COMMUNICATIONS TO
COL. H. N. SCHWARZKOPF, TRENTON, N. J., or
COL. CHAS. A. LINDBERGH, HOPEWELL, N. J.

ALL COMMUNICATIONS WILL BE TREATED IN CONFIDENCE

COL. H. NORMAN SCHWARZKOPF
Supt. New Jersey State Police, Trenton, N. J.

h 11, 1932

Reward poster of New Jersey state police.

1932 wanted poster for information about the kidnapping of
Charles A. Lindbergh Jr.
PHOTOFEST

The next five years saw Lindbergh barnstorm the world. In all, he visited all forty-eight states, delivered 147 speeches, and toured six-teen Latin American countries. In 1931, he helped design a navigator's wristwatch that was produced by the Longines watch company, a design that the company still produces today. A budding inventor, Lindbergh helped physicist Robert H. Goddard secure a Guggenheim endowment to continue research on rocket development. Lindbergh also invented the "Model T" perfusion pump, which helped make heart surgery possible. These activities helped keep Lindbergh in the news long after the ini-tial furor over his transatlantic flight had died down. By 1932 he was a household name and a bona fide hero to the American public.

On March 1, 1932, Lindbergh's twenty-month-old son, Charles Augustus Lindbergh Jr., was kidnapped from his crib at the Lindberghs' rural home in East Amwell, New Jersey. A ransom note was found on the nursery windowsill, demanding $50,000. Immediately following the announcement, reporters and souvenir hunters began swarming the Lindbergh estate. A distraught Lindbergh was inundated by theories about the identity of the perpetrators and false clues.

The day after the kidnapping, convicted felon Al Capone, who was serving time in Chicago's Cook County Jail for income tax evasion, offered a $10,000 reward for information that would lead to the capture of the kidnappers and the baby's safe return. Police ignored Capone's offer, but Capone insisted that he had the resources to help find the kid-nappers and offered to put up $200,000 bail and have his younger brother take his place in prison if he could be freed on bond, an offer that was flatly rejected by the Lindberghs.

On March 6, a letter from the kidnapper arrived, now demanding $70,000 in ransom money. Multiple notes followed, one accompanied by the baby's sleeping suit, to offer proof of the abduction. When the ransom demand was reduced back to $50,000, it was delivered through an intermediary, a retired school principal named John F. Condon. A final note from the kidnapper revealed that the baby could be found on a boat named *Nellie*, located near Martha's Vineyard, Massachusetts. A thorough search for the boat, however, proved unsuccessful.

On May 12, the story reached its sad conclusion, when the badly decomposed body of Charles Lindbergh Jr. was found, partly buried, four and a half miles from the Lindbergh home. An autopsy revealed that the child had probably been killed by a blow to the head shortly after the kidnapping.

An investigation was led by Colonel H. Norman Schwarzkopf, Superintendent of the New Jersey State Police, with the cooperation and assistance of the FBI. (Schwarzkopf's son and namesake became famous for commanding US forces in the 1991 Gulf War.) The lengthy search for the murderer ended on September 19, 1934, when Bruno Richard Hauptmann, a thirty-five-year-old German carpenter, was apprehended after a twenty-dollar gold certificate, part of the ransom money paid by the Lindberghs, was traced and found on him. It was discovered that Hauptmann had a criminal record for robbery, for which he had spent time in prison.

Hauptmann's trial began on January 3, 1935, which resulted in a guilty verdict, rendered on February 13. After multiple attempts for an appeal were denied, Hauptmann was sentenced to death; on April 3, 1936, he was electrocuted.

PRODUCTION NOTES

Philadelphia-born songwriter Michael Ogborn first got the idea to write about the Lindbergh kidnapping back in the 1980s, when Bruno Richard Hauptmann's widow, Anna, appeared on an episode of television's *Phil Donahue Show*. Also appearing on the broadcast was Scottish journalist Ludovic Kennedy, who considered the Hauptmann case a miscarriage of justice, leading to the publication of his book, *The Airman and the Carpenter*, in which he offered the possibility that Lindbergh himself may have been behind his own son's kidnapping. Kennedy's book was eventually turned into an HBO film, *Crime of the Century*, starring Stephen Rea and Isabella Rossellini.

It took ten years, but Ogborn finally completed his musical, which he managed to get staged in 2001 at his hometown's Arden Theater. Like *Parade* and *Floyd Collins*, *Baby Case* was more concerned with the media circus that engulfed the story than the kidnapping itself. As a result, Ogborn used real-life radio gossip columnist Walter Winchell (1897–1972) as a character to advance the action. Ogborn programmed the musical as if the audience were channel-surfing, the play exploring wildly bizarre details of the case, both factual and imagined, with a satirical eye pointed at the tabloid personalities who soon dominated the story.

Baby Case kept audiences' eyes glued to the stage, utilizing multiple moving platforms and black-and-white newsreel projections, while brightly colored costumes provided a visual contrast. Terry Nolen, who directed the initial workshop of the musical in 2000, likened it to a blending of Busby Berkeley and Bertolt Brecht.

In the show, Lindbergh is portrayed as both protagonist and antagonist, reflecting his heroism through a prologue documenting the aviator's famous trans-Atlantic flight, his marriage to Anne Morrow, and the birth of Charles Jr., but also indicating his arrogance and pro-Nazi tendencies. To acquaint the cast with the story, Ogborn had them visit scenes from the actual crime, including the courthouse in Flemington, New Jersey, where the trial took place, and even the jail cell where Hauptmann was being held.

All of this pointed to *Baby Case* becoming either an explosive flop or a cult classic. In 2012, eleven years after its Philadelphia tryout, it finally made its New York debut, at the prestigious New York Musical Theatre Festival. The *New York Times* heaped praise on the show's "rousing songs, big voices, stylish staging and choreography, first-rate lighting, and handsome period costumes." *Baby Case* received four Barrymore awards for Excellence in Theater, including Best Musical, but the road ended there. It continued to be produced sporadically in regional productions, most of them garnering positive notices, but the show has not gotten any closer to Broadway than the scene of the actual New Jersey trial. No cast album exists, but YouTube highlights from a 2013 production at the History Theatre in St. Paul, Minnesota, show it to have the same gaudy atmosphere and cynical lavishness that pervades its closest Broadway counterpart, *Chicago*.

SCORE
Michael Ogborn's score parallels the story's sensationalistic fervor with a plethora of sensational production numbers. Most musicals include

one or two 11:00 numbers that utilize the entire ensemble, but Ogborn did this throughout the show, producing one showbizzy spectacular after another. "The guy can write tunes," marveled musical director Jake Endres. Ogborn pulled no punches in his songs; nothing was off limits. One satirical number, "If I Could Take a Picture of You," takes place outside the courthouse where avaricious vendors are hawking autopsy photos of the dead baby; the song is performed in C major, the cheeriest key of all, to a galloping 6/8 time signature as if it were a sprightly Fred Astaire dance number.

In the History Theatre production, eleven actors played ninety characters, many switching hats on stage to change from one to the next. If you're going to satirize something as tragic as the murder of an infant, you may as well go all the way, and *Baby Case* certainly did that, but Ogborn's abilities carried it through. One is mystified as to why such a well-received show never got further than a New York festival, but maybe someday, some brave producer will take a second look at *Baby Case* and mount a revival for Broadway.

Of Thee I Sing / Let 'Em Eat Cake

Historical context: Politics in the 1930s

Time period: 1931–1933

Broadway runs and venues: *Of Thee I Sing:* December 26, 1931–October 1933 (Music Box Theatre); October 10, 1932–January 14, 1933 (Forty-Sixth Street Theatre) (441 p.)

Let 'Em Eat Cake: October 21, 1933–January 6, 1934 (Imperial Theatre) (90 p.)

Book: George S. Kaufman and Morrie Ryskind

Score: George Gershwin (music), Ira Gershwin (lyrics)

Cast album: CBS M2K-42522 (Brooklyn Academy of Music production, 1987)

Major characters: John P. Wintergreen (William Gaxton), Alexander Throttlebottom (Victor Moore), Mary Turner Wintergreen (Lois Moran), The Chief Justice (Ralph Riggs), Diana Devereaux (*Of Thee I Sing*) (Grace Brinkley)

HISTORICAL BACKGROUND

Current events were on the minds of book writers George S. Kaufman and Morrie Ryskind when they wrote these two Depression-era political satires, which were scored by George and Ira Gershwin. Although Kaufman was apolitical, Ryskind was an activist member of the Socialist Party who performed sketches at antiwar events during the 1930s. Ryskind's politics would eventually take a dramatic turn to the right when in 1940 he abandoned his leftist tendencies and actually opposed Franklin D. Roosevelt's bid for a third term as president.

Ryskind had written political satire with the Gershwins before, in a 1930 revision of Kaufman's 1927 musical *Strike Up the Band*, whose plot had to do with a war with Switzerland in a dispute over cheese. (In Ryskind's revival, chocolate replaced cheese as the motivating foodstuff.)

Kaufman and Ryskind's idea was to satirize the trivialities, smug hypocrisy, and phony patriotism of presidential elections. The first plot they devised involved two rival political parties fighting over which had the best national anthem. In 1916, President Woodrow Wilson signed an executive order designating "The Star-Spangled Banner" as the national anthem, but it wasn't officially codified until 1929 when House Resolution 14 was presented to Congress. After much consternation and argument, the measure was finally passed in March 1931.

America was also struggling with the overwhelming effects of the Depression and the ineffectiveness of President Herbert Hoover to manage it. Despite this, Kaufman and Ryskind refused to blame either the Democratic or Republican parties by not naming them in their libretto; they determined both were equally guilty of political malfeasance.

The main characters in *Of Thee I Sing* and its sequel, *Let 'Em Eat Cake*, were presidential candidate John P. Wintergreen and his foppish running mate Alexander Throttlebottom. Wintergreen was patterned after scandal-plagued but charismatic New York Mayor Jimmy Walker while Throttlebottom suggested the vacuous Calvin Coolidge. In *Of Thee I Sing*, both political parties absorbed direct hits in the sharp-edged satire. In fact, neither Kaufman nor Ryskind supported either party and both voted for Socialist Party candidate Norman Thomas in the 1932 election. In their scenario, Kaufman and Ryskind suggested that politicians chose to be Republicans on Mondays, Wednesdays, and Fridays, and Democrats the rest of the week.

In *Let 'Em Eat Cake*, produced two years later, Kaufman and Ryskind's satire got even more pointed, as Wintergreen, now the incumbent president, is faced by the challenger John P. Tweedledee, who wins the election in a landslide. Wintergreen asks the Supreme Court to overturn the election, and when that fails, he stages a coup d'état, with his supporters marching on Washington, clad in blue shirts manufactured by the Wintergreen Shirt Company. The coup results in Wintergreen becoming dictator and the White House renamed the Blue House, with the nine justices of the Supreme Court becoming the country's official baseball team.

The startling, dark storyline for *Let 'Em Eat Cake* takes on politicians, the military, fascism, the Supreme Court, the Union League, the Daughters of the American Revolution, the League of Nations, all forms of media, and even the fashion industry, in a farce about an America ruled by an authoritarian government. Critics deemed the nightmarish vision of a fascist America too preposterous to be believed, but the outlandish satire has since come closer than comfort to the truth when one considers the aftermath of the tumultuous Trump/Biden election of 2020.

PRODUCTION NOTES

When Kaufman and Ryskind first presented their idea to George Gershwin, the composer enthusiastically set to work writing a pair of national anthems to be pitted against one another at the end of Act I. But the writers soon decided to veer away from music as the motivating plot element and turn to love, which served to soften the harsh satire of government and campaign politics.

In the revised plot device, presidential candidate Wintergreen was to fall in love with a "typical American girl," the winner of an Atlantic City bathing beauty contest, who would become the new First Lady. The winner of the contest is Diana Devereaux, who is revealed by the French Ambassador to be "the illegitimate daughter of an illegitimate son of an illegitimate nephew of Napoleon," an important potential pedigree for an American First Lady. Wintergreen, however, falls in love with Mary Turner, his winsome young assistant, a more down-to-earth girl who bakes corn muffins, eventually serving them up to the unemployed. In the early months of the Depression, Herbert Hoover's infamous remark, "Prosperity is just around the corner," rang hollow with the American people as the nation's unemployment rate soared. The Gershwins satirize this with the song "Posterity Is Just Around the Corner," sung after President Wintergreen discovers he's about to become a father.

George Gershwin got so wrapped up in writing the score that he began performing some of his songs at parties, even before Kaufman and Ryskind had heard them. The notoriously acerbic Kaufman thought about establishing a "new device" involving eight men, whose job it would be to keep composers away from a piano until after a show is produced.

To play Wintergreen and Throttlebottom, Kaufman and Ryskind cast comic actors William Gaxton and Victor Moore, whose chemistry together worked so well that they remained a Broadway team for the next decade, Ryskind calling them Broadway's answer to Bob Hope and Bing Crosby. In 1933, the pair reprised their roles in *Let 'Em Eat Cake*.

Of Thee I Sing was a huge success, running at full or near capacity for more than a year. Democratic presidential candidate Franklin D. Roosevelt saw the show and was so delighted by it that he sent William Gaxton an autographed photo, inscribed to "President Wintergreen." When

Victor Moore and William Gaxton of *Of Thee I Sing* and *Let 'Em Eat Cake*.
PHOTOFEST

former president Calvin Coolidge died in January 1933, Ryskind deleted a line from the script that referenced Coolidge's name.

As early as late 1932, Kaufman and Ryskind started thinking about a sequel to *Of Thee I Sing*. Kaufman's wife Beatrice thought the story should continue with President Wintergreen's reelection campaign. The Gershwins, producer Sam Harris, and actors William Gaxton, Victor Moore, and Lois Moran agreed to reprise their respective parts, and the show, titled *Let 'Em Eat Cake*, was announced in April 1933. By summer, the Gershwins had completed most of the score. The Gershwins' songwriting routine involved Ira inventing a song title and then waiting until George came up with a melody before filling in the lyrics.

In the sequel, Wintergreen's challenger, John P. Tweedledee, defeats Wintergreen in a landslide election but Wintergreen is rebuffed by the Supreme Court when he tries to get Tweedledee's election reversed. Now out of work, Wintergreen starts his own company, after cabinet wives admire a blue shirt hand sewn by his wife, Mary. Wintergreen then declares a blue shirt revolution, an uncomfortable reference to the rise of Benito Mussolini's black shirts in Italy and Adolf Hitler's brown shirts in Germany.

Wintergreen's blue-shirted supporters march on Washington. The army arrests President Tweedledee and names Wintergreen dictator, as the White House becomes the Blue House. After a baseball game pitting the members of the Supreme Court against the League of Nations, the League wins and sentences Wintergreen and Throttlebottom to death for treason. Tweedledee becomes president of Cuba but when he can't remember the name of his vice president, Throttlebottom takes over, while Wintergreen adds blue dresses to his product line. In the end, democracy and capitalism triumph, although the fumbling bumbler Throttlebottom now rules as president.

By October, the show was completed; it made its debut in Boston with Kaufman himself directing. Reviews were positive and with high hopes, the production team, cast, and orchestra proceeded to New York's Imperial Theatre for its Broadway debut on October 21.

Unfortunately, the mood of the nation had changed, with America mired even further into the Great Depression. Some critics found nothing funny about a totalitarian American state, calling *Let 'Em Eat Cake* "bitter." A scene in which President Wintergreen is set to be executed by guillotine was viewed as too disturbing, even savage, for audiences to swallow. Others praised the production, including famed critic Brooks Atkinson, who called the sequel "a first-rate job of music show-making." Audiences, however, proved to be in no mood to laugh, especially with the prospect of Adolf Hitler's rise to power in January, making Kaufman and Ryskind's blue shirt satire a little too close for comfort. *Let 'Em Eat Cake* survived for only ninety performances, closing shortly after the new year.

SCORE

Of Thee I Sing won the Pulitzer Prize for Drama and became the longest-running book musical of the decade. Its satire of superficial political campaigns, meaningless debates, and hyped scandals was masked by the premise of "love" and the show's likable characters. Plainly aimed at the ineffectiveness of President Hoover, the show's running gag about Throttlebottom as an invisible, fumbling vice president was an impression that continued for decades, helped in part by the folksy assessment of John Nance Garner, FDR's vice president, of the office as being "not worth a bucket of warm spit."

Since the Pulitzer Prize was considered a literary award, only Ira Gershwin, Kaufman, and Ryskind were awarded the prize. This was ultimately rectified when George Gershwin, who died in 1937 of a brain tumor at the age of thirty-eight, was finally awarded a posthumous Pulitzer in 1998, the centenary of his birth.

After ten years of writing songs for lightweight Broadway musicals and revues, the Gershwins demonstrated an affinity for the light, satirical style of Gilbert and Sullivan, two of their chief inspirations. With the songs integrated into the story, few became hits that survived the duration of the show. Ira Gershwin would later explain that the brothers' songs were deliberately designed to complement the story and were not written in the traditional verse-chorus format as much of their previous works. The one song that did distinguish itself on its own was "Of Thee

I Sing, Baby," which inspired an aftershave and cologne that were manufactured and sold for the B. Altman & Company department store chain.

Songwriter Leroy Anderson ("Sleigh Ride," "Blue Tango") was a twenty-three-year-old Harvard graduate student and director of the Harvard University Band when he crafted an arrangement of the Gershwins' campaign song "Wintergreen for President," complementing George Gershwin's melody with quotations from Harvard fight songs. This ingratiated Anderson to Boston Pops Orchestra manager George Judd and launched his career as a composer and arranger for the Arthur Fiedler–led Boston Pops.

Despite the disappointing and brief run of *Let 'Em Eat Cake*, the Gershwins' score has since been reassessed by scholars. George Gershwin matched brother Ira's pointedly satirical lyrics with dissonant and complex harmonies, creating a more operatic-like continuity in the score, as opposed to a collection of individual songs. Only five songs were published from *Let 'Em Eat Cake*; four of them were recorded as a medley by Paul Whiteman and His Orchestra, released on a specially produced 78 rpm, twelve-inch "picture record" released by Victor Records. One song, "Mine," was recorded outside of the context of the show, a 1944 duet by Decca artists Bing Crosby and Judy Garland.

George Gershwin incorporated a dizzying array of musical styles into his score for *Of Thee I Sing*, beginning with the very first notes in the overture, as a lead trumpet quotes "The Girl I Left Behind Me" accompanied by distorted army bugle calls. He took on elements of Handel in "Union League," opera in "All Mothers of the Nation," and gave militant marches a satirical twist with the show's title song.

In *Let 'Em Eat Cake*, quotations from familiar tunes abound in the show's astonishing "Tweedledee For President" opening number, sung by Tweedledee's supporters, which shuffles from a card deck of American anthems, including quotations from "Dixie"; "The Battle Hymn of the Republic" (the two opposing Civil War anthems); Gilbert and Sullivan's "With Cat-Like Tread" (aka "Hail, Hail, the Gang's All Here") from *The Pirates of Penzance*; George M. Cohan's World War I classic "Over There"; Theodore Metz's "There'll Be a Hot Time in the Old Town Tonight"; and John Philip Sousa's "The Stars and Stripes Forever."

Everywhere in the score, familiar songs were perverted, twisted, and turned every which way, a cartoonish skewering of musical idioms, not leaving anything out, even assaulting the Gershwins' own Russian/Jewish/Yiddish musical heritage. In retrospect, *Let 'Em Eat Cake* remains a musical triumph and probably the Gershwins' most underappreciated score.

The Will Rogers Follies

Historical context: The life of Will Rogers, framed by American vaudeville
Time period: 1879–1935 (with flashbacks from Rogers's life)
Broadway run: May 1, 1991–September 5, 1993 (981 p.)
Venue: The Palace Theatre
Book: Peter Stone
Score: Cy Coleman (music), Betty Comden and Adolph Green (lyrics)
Cast album: Columbia Records, CK-48606 (1991)
Major characters: Will Rogers (Keith Carradine), Ziegfeld's Favorite (Cady Huffman), Wiley Post (Paul Ukena Jr.), Betty Blake (Dee Hoty), Voice of Mr. Ziegfeld (Gregory Peck)

HISTORICAL BACKGROUND

At the time of his death in Alaska in a plane crash, Will Rogers (1879–1935) was probably the best-known American outside of President Franklin Roosevelt. Born in the Indian Territory of Oklahoma to a Cherokee family, Rogers left home in 1901 at the age of twenty-two, traveling to Argentina to work as a horseman (known as a gaucho). He became skilled at riding horses and doing rope tricks and appeared at the 1904 St. Louis World's Fair, leading to a career in vaudeville. In 1908, Rogers married Betty Blake after a long and frustrating courtship, a marriage that would last until his death. In 1915, Rogers made his first appearance in Florenz Ziegfeld's *Midnight Frolic*, in which he added humorous topical monologs to his act, which started with him saying, "All I know is what I read in the papers."

Rogers's popularity grew and eventually he became a star with the *Ziegfeld Follies*, performing rope tricks punctuated by witty bon mots and stories. In 1918, his fame took him to Hollywood, where he began appearing in films for producers Samuel Goldwyn and Hal Roach. Rogers was one of the few silent stars who made a seamless transition to talkies, appearing in twenty-one talking and forty-eight silent movies.

Rogers became familiar to the average American by always playing himself. He never wore makeup in his movies and became known for his folksy commentary on anything that was current in the news. In 1922, he began his syndicated weekly newspaper column, "Will Rogers Says," walking a political tightrope by not taking sides for either Democrats or Republicans. In 1929 he added radio to his entertainment arsenal, and Americans now also became familiar with his voice and homespun delivery. Rogers became America's goodwill ambassador and was beloved by all. The feeling was mutual, as evidenced by the oft-repeated quote attributed to him, "I never met a man I didn't like."

The tragic plane crash that took Rogers's life at the age of fifty-six, and that of his longtime friend, black-eye-patched aviator Wiley Post, in Alaska on August 15, 1935, stunned the world, which went into immediate mourning. Today, many landmarks, buildings, highways, and schools have been named for him.

PRODUCTION NOTES

The entertainment world made Will Rogers the most popular and highly paid star of his lifetime and he excelled in every medium that existed: in vaudeville, on screen, in print, and on radio. Playwright Peter Stone's concept was to pay tribute to Rogers's life using the *Ziegfeld Follies* as a framework. Subtitled "A Life in Revue," the musical focused on Rogers's magical optimism and humor, taking into account some of the hardscrabble events that shaped his life.

Rogers's career spanned from the early 1900s until the Depression-era 1930s, summing up the development of show business in America during the first third of the twentieth century. The plainspoken, no-frills Rogers worked as a stark contradiction to Ziegfeld's ostentatious, gaudy revues, with the sight of the humble, gum-chewing Rogers, rope in hand, making wisecracks to statuesque, bodaciously dressed showgirls.

The show's plot was devised to act out scenes from Rogers's life, with Rogers played with aw-shucks humility by Keith Carradine. The voice of the unseen Ziegfeld was provided by a prerecorded Gregory Peck. For all of his talents, Carradine was never known for his singing ability, which contributed to his charm. There was nothing dramatic, tragic, or controversial about Rogers's private life (he was only married once, to the devoted Betty Blake, played by Dee Hoty), so the musical became a tool for director/choreographer Tommy Tune to load the production with as many gorgeous, high-kicking chorus girls and lavish costumes (designed by Willa Kim) as possible in one of the most visually dazzling productions ever seen on Broadway. Cady Huffman played the part of Ziegfeld's Favorite, an unnamed chorus girl, whose leggy presence serves as kind of a Greek chorus, leading us from one dazzling *Follies* number to another.

The show uses Rogers's courtship of Betty Blake as a device to demonstrate the one conflict in the musical: Betty's desire for Rogers to

Will Rogers (1879–1935).
PHOTOFEST

get off the road and spend more time with family. But Rogers felt obliged to be America's conscience and always puts her second to what he felt was his function in American society. When the Depression arrives (signaled by a giant sign lowered from the rafters that reads "1931"), stagehands repossess the showgirls' brightly colored costumes and Rogers goes on the radio (at the behest of President Hoover) to give an inspirational speech and preach support for those who had lost their fortunes and homes in the wake of the stock market crash.

Looming over the glitzy proceedings is an eye-patched Wiley Post (Paul Ukena Jr.), who periodically halts production numbers by cheerfully hollering from the balcony, "Let's go flyin', Will!" reminding the audience of the inevitability of Rogers's sudden and tragic death and casting a pall over the high-spirited dance numbers.

The Will Rogers Follies juxtaposed vaudeville, America's most ubiquitous form of entertainment before movies took over, with Rogers's rise, thus making the show an homage to vaudeville as opposed to a biographical musical. Vaudeville was depicted in other musical biographies, including *Annie Get Your Gun*, *Gypsy*, and *Funny Girl*, but none of those shows used trappings of vaudeville as the storytelling device itself, making *The Will Rogers Follies* an unusual and attractive musical. It would eventually win the Tony Award for Best Musical and Best Score.

SCORE

The razzle-dazzle score was composed by Cy Coleman with lyrics by the team of Betty Comden and Adolph Green, their last Broadway musical in a career that spanned nearly a half century, going back to *On the Town* in 1944. The songs ostentatiously celebrate (or satirize, depending on your point of view) the flamboyant, extravagant Ziegfeld Follies productions, beginning with the gaudy opening number, "Willamania."

The visual highlight of the show is "Our Favorite Son," representing Rogers's mock run for president in 1928. The song featured Keith Carradine as Rogers and Cady Huffman as Ziegfeld's Favorite, seated alongside a stage-length chorus line of showgirls clad in spangled red-white-and-blue outfits with tambourines for hats. Tommy Tune's intricate leg-and-arm-crossing choreography created a Busby Berkeley-like kaleidoscopic effect that had audiences cheering to the rafters.

Contrasting with the glitzy production numbers was Rogers singing the show's theme song, the earworm "Never Met a Man I Didn't Like," complete with an anachronistic electric steel guitar, a nod toward Broadway's idea of country music. In reality, the electric steel guitar didn't exist during Rogers's lifetime, the show employing the instrument in a style befitting of current-day Nashville. Another Rogers solo, "Give a Man Enough Rope," is about as country as Cole Porter's "Don't Fence Me In," but the score was not meant to accurately represent the period, only to suggest it, equating Rogers's Oklahoma roots with stereotypical Nashville country music hallmarks, including hoedown fiddle, jew's harp, banjo, and a 1960s-style harmonica resembling that of Nashville session man Charlie McCoy.

Between the contrived country songs, conventional Broadway ballads like Betty Blake's plaintive "My Unknown Someone," and the lavish vaudeville production numbers, the score was still competent enough to garner a Tony Award, although none of the songs became standards outside of the musical.

Pins and Needles

Historical context: The labor movement of the 1930s
Time period: 1937
Broadway run and venues: November 27, 1937–closing date unknown
(Labor Stage Theatre); January 1, 1939–June 22, 1940 (Windsor
Theatre) (1,108 p.)
Book: Arthur Arent, Marc Blitzstein, Emmanuel Eisenberg, Charles
Friedman, David Gregory, Joseph Schrank, Arnold B. Horwitt,
John Latouche, and Harold Rome
Score: Harold Rome
Cast album: None. (A twenty-fifth anniversary tribute LP was issued in
1962 on Columbia Masterworks OS-2210.)
Major characters: Various, played by Al Levy, Hy Gardner, Nettie
Harrary, Millie Weitz, Al Eben, Ruth Rubinstein, Lynne Jaffee,
Ruth Elbaum, Dorothy Harrison, Berni Gould, Harry Clark, Ella
Gerber, and Murray Modick

HISTORICAL BACKGROUND

In the years prior to America's involvement in World War II, the damage
brought on by the Depression resulted in a threat to the existence of labor
unions. With unemployment at 25 percent, unions lost many members
who were unable to pay their dues. While frustrated Americans on relief
participated in strikes and marches, others began supporting socialist and
communist political groups. To combat this, President Franklin D. Roosevelt implemented the National Industry Recovery Act (NIRA), by which
workers were given the right to organize into unions that subsequently
demanded a minimum wage and a ceiling on hours worked per week.

In 1935, the Supreme Court declared the NIRA unconstitutional, assigning lawmaking powers to the National Recovery Administration (NRA), which was instituted to implement the law, declaring that the federal government did not have the power to regulate non-interstate commerce. The NIRA was ultimately replaced by the Wagner Act, which helped strengthen labor unions.

When New York's Princess Theatre, located at 104–106 West Thirty-Ninth Street, opened in 1913, it was one of the smallest on Broadway. Despite its size, the venue had a profound effect on musical theater, hosting early productions that were some of the first to integrate music with plot, including collaborations between Jerome Kern, Guy Bolton, and P. G. Wodehouse. The Depression threatened to shut it down for good, but in 1933 it reopened as a movie house, renamed the Reo Theatre.

In 1937, it was renamed again as the Labor Stage, after being acquired by the International Ladies Garment Workers Union (ILGWU), which initially used it for a recreation center for workers who lived in the area. Shortly thereafter, the ILGWU's cultural department decided to stage a musical revue, which resulted in the unlikeliest smash hit in Broadway history, *Pins and Needles*.

PRODUCTION NOTES

The ILGWU had a cultural department whose members took classes on everything from mandolin instruction to tap dancing, elocution, and even embroidery. A musical revue was the idea of department head Louis Schaffer, who became head of the cultural department in 1934. In October of that year, Schaffer formed the ILGWU Players, using theater professionals to serve as instructors for its performers, assembled from various locals of the union.

The next year, Schaffer founded a theater company to help promote New York's labor movement, Labor Stage, Inc. In January 1936, the company leased the Princess Theatre and commissioned a young writer named Harold Rome to write songs for a new revue, also featuring sketches satirizing contemporary politics. The labor board thought the idea was "too frivolous," but Schaffer and Rome persisted, bringing a cast of fifty-five garment workers to the production.

Hy Gardner performing "I Wanna Be a G-Man" from
Pins and Needles.
PHOTOFEST

By June, the revue was complete and professional performers were
brought in to audition for the show at Labor Stage. The board approved
the production and gave Schaffer permission to begin rehearsals. In a surprising decision, Schaffer decided to use the untrained garment workers
in the show rather than hiring professional singers and actors.

Rehearsals lasted a year, with the cast rehearsing for three hours on
three evenings during the week, beginning after their regular work hours
concluded. Rome himself played one of the two pianos in the orchestra, and later credited the success of the show to the rapport developed
between the garment workers and the audience, likening it to the same
effect actors in *A Chorus Line* would have four decades later.

On July 4, 1937, *Pins and Needles* was ready and the cast completed its
final rehearsals at Unity House, the union's vacation resort in the Pocono

Mountains. On November 6, an invitation-only performance was held at Labor Stage, with the show's official debut taking place on November 27. It was an instant hit. Within a month, word of mouth resulted in sold-out houses and *Pins and Needles* becoming the talk of Broadway.

Many of the show's garment workers requested leaves of absence from their factory jobs to become full-time performers. Due to popular demand, a second company was established to perform specifically for union members on late afternoons before the regular evening perfor-mance. Nearly fifty skits and songs were prepared, which were rotated for each performance of nineteen to twenty-two selections. As time went on, some numbers were replaced in accordance with current events. Sketches about controversial figures such as Father Charles Coughlin and Nazi activist Fritz Kuhn and the Works Progress Administration (WPA), written by Mark Blitzstein, Arthur Arent, and Joseph Schrank, were removed because they were no longer timely. Pressure on Schaffer to promote racial equality resulted in two African Americans, Dorothy Tucker and Dorothy Harrison, being added to the cast.

With *Pins and Needles*'s success, Schaffer, who didn't pay any atten-tion to theater rules or conventions, took the original cast on the road. He later did the same thing with the second company, after replacing the first. In March 1938, a small contingent performed the show for President Roosevelt in the East Room of the White House. Another performed at the twenty-fifth anniversary celebration of the US Depart-ment of Labor.

On April 21, 1939, a revamped version was mounted and it also became a hit. On June 26, the show moved to the larger Windsor The-atre, where the third edition would make its debut in November. *Pins and Needles* finally closed on June 22, 1940, after nearly four years and an unprecedented (for a production featuring amateur performers) 1,108 performances.

SCORE

According to composer Harold Rome, *Pins and Needles* succeeded because "People wanted to hear what was going on." The show skewered controversial names in the news, such as FBI director J. Edgar Hoover in "I Want to Be a G-Man," in which Hoover was targeted for his attacks on personal civil liberties. Another target, gossip columnist Walter Winchell, didn't take the song's satirical jabs well, and subsequently banned Rome from his column for a year just for mentioning his name in the song's lyrics.

The most popular numbers in the show were "Sing Me a Song of Social Significance," "It's Better with a Union Man," and "Nobody Makes a Pass at Me." A faux love song, "One Big Union for Two," was inspired by the merging of the AFL with the CIO. As time went on, the gentle political satire got more pointed. The song "Four Little Angels of Peace" was sung by characters portraying Anthony Eden, Benito Mussolini, Adolph Hitler, and a generic Japanese character, all proclaiming their devotion to peace.

One song in the show, "Sunday in the Park," even made the Hit Parade, recorded by both the Hudson-DeLange Orchestra and Ted Weems's orchestra, the latter featuring its new young singer, Perry Como. In 1962, an LP commemorating the twenty-fifth anniversary of the show was recorded, the songs performed by Jack Carroll, Rose Marie Jun, its playwright Harold Rome, and a young ingénue named Barbra Streisand, currently a breakout star in Rome's book musical, *I Can Get It for You Wholesale*. The record, which came out on Columbia Masterworks, was released a month after the *Wholesale* cast album was issued. In keeping with the show's pro-union stance, the union affiliations of the arranger, musicians, and even the recording engineer were all listed in the album notes.

South Pacific

Historical context: Racial prejudice during World War II
Time period: 1941–1945
Broadway run and venues: April 7, 1949–May 16, 1953 (Majestic The-
atre); June 29, 1953–January 16, 1954 (Broadway Theatre) (1,925 p.)
Book: Oscar Hammerstein II and Joshua Logan, based on *Tales of the
South Pacific* by James A. Michener
Score: Richard Rodgers (music), Oscar Hammerstein II (lyrics)
Cast album: Columbia MM-850 (78 rpm) (1949)
Major characters: Ensign Nellie Forbush (Mary Martin), Emile De
Becque (Ezio Pinza), Bloody Mary (Juanita Hall), Luther Billis
(Myron McCormick), Lieutenant Joseph Cable, USMC (William
Tabbert)

HISTORICAL BACKGROUND

The setting for *South Pacific* was a different kind of theater: the Pacific
theater in World War II. James Michener's 1947 Pulitzer Prize–winning
novel set the exotic beauty of two remote islands against an overlooked
dilemma faced by servicemen and women during the war: the tedium
of waiting for something to happen. The setting and the tropical atmosphere were what attracted Rodgers and Hammerstein to Michener's
novel, but they soon decided that the war was the story's MacGuffin. The
real issues were the latent racist attitudes of two people, Ensign Nellie
Forbush, a US Navy nurse, and Lieutenant Joseph Cable, a US Marine
officer transferred from Guadalcanal, and how that affected their respective destinies in the story.

Michener's novel was a compilation of nineteen short stories, each inspired by real people and incidents that occurred while Michener was a lieutenant commander in the US Navy stationed at a naval base on the island of Espiritu Santo in the New Hebrides, a group of volcanic islands in the South Coral Sea that is now known as Vanuatu. In explaining his premise for the book, Michener said that his intention was "to report the South Pacific as it actually was." Observing, firsthand, the sailors, nurses, and natives on the islands, Michener drew from a rich collection of personal experiences as he went on inspection tours and supply runs as part of his official duties. The emotionally rich stories showed a dichotomy between America's patriotic devotion to democracy and the deeply ingrained racial prejudices instilled in many of its citizens.

Three of the stories in Michener's novel were the sources for the plot of *South Pacific*. The first was "Fo' Dolla'," which focused on Lieutenant Joseph Cable, an officer newly stationed on the island, and his relationship with Liat, a beautiful Tonkinese girl and the daughter of Bloody Mary, a street-smart merchant who sold tribal souvenirs to American sailors. Mary was intent on finding a husband for Liat who could give her a better life than what she had on the island. Like most sailors, Cable was ready for action, whether it was sexual or military, and instantly fell in love with Liat after being introduced to her by her mother. Cable, however, resisted marrying her because of his fears of being ostracized back home because of Liat's race.

The second story, "Our Heroine," concerned a romantic relationship between Ensign Nellie Forbush, a spirited young nurse from Otolousa, Arkansas, and Emile De Becque, an aristocratic French plantation owner much older than she. Although Forbush is attracted to De Becque, she has doubts about their future together after she discovers that he has fathered eight children out of wedlock with various native women. Nellie is repulsed when she learns that De Becque actually lived with nonwhites. *South Pacific* is free of racial slurs, but Nellie's prejudice is plainly communicated nonetheless; in the musical, she is able to overcome it.

The third story, "A Boar's Tooth," described a sacred pig-killing ceremony, a sacrificial ritual that was a central superstition of Vanuatu tribal life. The prize of the ceremony is a pig's circular tusk, which became a focus of desire for Luther Billis, the show's enterprising comic figure. In the novel, Billis is a Seabee (a name derived from the initials for "Construction Battalion," a branch of the US Navy) who is introduced in the story "Dry Rot." In "A Boar's Tooth," Billis is described as a "big dealer" liberally tattooed enlisted man who in civilian life worked as a car salesman. Billis is described as never wearing a shirt, revealing a large, sagging belly, deep tan, long hair, and a thin golden earring, making him resemble a pirate right out of *Treasure Island*. He befriends an officer named Tony Fry for the purpose of gaining access to the Japanese-held island of Vanicoro (the inspiration for the musical's mysterious Bali Ha'i), where they lead a surreptitious expedition to retrieve boars' tusks from the natives, hoping to sell them as exotic bracelets for fifteen dollars apiece.

In the musical, Billis runs the laundry for the other sailors but is still depicted as somewhat of a schemer, albeit a lovable one, a precursor to television's peacetime military con man and swindler, Sergeant Ernie Bilko (Phil Silvers) on *The Phil Silvers Show*, which ran from 1955 to 1959. Like Bilko, the crafty Billis talks Cable, who has been sent on a dangerous reconnaissance mission to Bali Ha'i, to take him along, hoping to acquire a stash of the prized boars' tusks.

Michener's novel documented how Americans thought and behaved during World War II, with courage, bravery, and collective sacrifice tempered by resentment and prejudice.

PRODUCTION NOTES

After reading *Tales of the South Pacific*, director-writer Joshua Logan recommended that Richard Rodgers look at the short story "Fo' Dolla'," the chapter concerning Lieutenant Cable and Liat. At the time, Rodgers was confined to his bed with a back ailment and decided instead to read the entire novel. After finishing, he had his partner, Oscar Hammerstein, read it as well before coming to the decision to secure the dramatic rights for the entire book, so as to gain flexibility in combining characters or situations from other parts of the work.

Rodgers thought that the story in "Fo' Dolla'," was too close to Puccini's opera *Madama Butterfly*, so he and Hammerstein turned their attention to "Our Heroine," the Nellie Forbush story that became the main focus of the musical's plot. The Cable-Liat romance would be retained as its subplot. Rodgers and Hammerstein's shows often used a secondary romance as comic relief, but in *South Pacific* it was added to reinforce the show's central theme of racism in American culture. A third story, focusing on Luther Billis's schemes, would become the source of comic relief.

To play the aristocratic De Becque, Rodgers repaid a favor to Edwin Lester, a West Coast–based producer, by hiring Italian opera star Ezio Pinza, who had recently left the Metropolitan Opera with a desire to go into musical theater.

For the part of Nellie Forbush, Rodgers wanted a young, attractive actress with a lively disposition who could also project "believable innocence." He and Hammerstein had recently seen actress Mary Martin in a West Coast performance of *Annie Get Your Gun*, in which Martin played the title role. When Martin found out that she would be paired with an opera basso, she was frightened by the prospect of singing with him and made Rodgers and Hammerstein agree that she would not have to sing a duet with Pinza. As a result, they sang together on only one song, "Twin Soliloquies (Wonder How It Feels)," in which they alternated their respective lines.

South Pacific was the most successful show of Rodgers and Hammerstein's partnership, playing for 1,925 performances, second only to *Oklahoma!* Like Michener's novel, the musical won the Pulitzer Prize for Drama, in addition to winning ten Tony Awards, including Best Musical, Best Score, and Best Libretto. It remains the only musical to win Tonys in all four acting categories (for Martin, Pinza, Juanita Hall as Bloody Mary, and Myron McCormick as Luther Billis).

SCORE

Rodgers and Hammerstein's score is one of only a handful in Broadway history in which all of its songs live outside of the musical in the popular repertoire. (*My Fair Lady* is another.) Although De Becque's sweeping "Some Enchanted Evening" is the show's romantic and musical high point, there were others to rival it, including Cable's "Younger Than Springtime" (the only song not written specifically for the show), "A Wonderful Guy" (Nellie's unbridled declaration of love), and "This

Nearly Was Mine" (De Becque's elegant torch song). The latter two songs were waltzes, Rodgers's melodic strong suit.

Stories have been told about how quickly and easily Rodgers wrote the hypnotic melody to "Bali Ha'i," the exotic song that told of the mystical powers of the mysterious, fictional South Seas island. Hammerstein had sweated for a week writing the lyrics, but after handing Rodgers a sheet of paper with the lyrics written on it, Rodgers disappeared into the next room where a piano was handy and returned in five minutes with the melody. "If you know your trade," Rodgers said, not-so-modestly, "the actual writing should never take long."

Mary Martin and Ezio Pinza in *South Pacific.*
PHOTOFEST

The song that summed up the thematic essence of *South Pacific* (and also inspired the title of this book) is a minute-long song by a frustrated Cable, who can't bring himself to marry Liat despite an overwhelming, almost religious obsession for her. "Carefully Taught" (alternately known as "You've Got to Be Carefully Taught") explained Cable's concept of learned racism. Nellie Forbush may have been an innocent, naive girl from a Southern state, where bigotry is not an alien concept, but Cable was a Princeton-educated, intelligent officer from the North, and expressed anger at himself for not being able to commit to a relationship with someone of another race. Rodgers asserted that "Carefully Taught" wasn't written specifically to be a message song, but it is clear that Hammerstein was making a statement that racism is not innate, but the result of indoctrination from the moment of birth. Rodgers and Hammerstein included the song because it fit perfectly with Cable's character and situation, as he expressed his feelings about the superficiality of racial barriers.

In the novel, the Cable-Liat liaison ends ambiguously, with Cable ending their relationship. Hammerstein, pressured to satisfy censors who objected to the characters' onstage miscegenation, had Cable killed in the reconnaissance mission, implicitly punishing those who would have an affair with someone from a different race. Hammerstein's daring decision to keep "Carefully Taught" in the score, despite pressure to remove it, was tempered by his reluctance to have Cable pay with his life for his romantic folly. Despite this, many Southern theatrical venues refused to perform the song when *South Pacific* was staged. In 1953, the show was staged in Atlanta, resulting in a bill introduced in the Georgia legislature that outlawed entertainment containing "an underlying philosophy inspired by Moscow." In a sober pronouncement, Georgia legislator David C. Jones suggested that somehow the song was an implicit threat to the "American way of life." He may have been right.

Allegiance

Historical context: The incarceration of Japanese Americans during World War II
Time period: 1941–1945
Broadway run: November 8, 2015–February 14, 2016 (111 p.)
Venue: Longacre Theatre
Book: Marc Acito, Jay Kuo, and Lorenzo Thione, based on the personal experiences of George Takei
Score: Jay Kuo
Cast album: Broadway Records 888295386746 (2016)
Major characters: Sam Kimura (George Takei), Kei Kimura (Lea Salonga), Tatsuo Kimura (Christòpheren Nomura), Sammy Kimura (Telly Leung), Frankie Suzuki (Michael K. Lee), Hannah Campbell (Katie Rose Clarke), Johnny Goto (Marcus Choi)

HISTORICAL BACKGROUND

After the Japanese invasion of Pearl Harbor on December 7, 1941, approximately 120,000 Americans of Japanese heritage were forced to leave their homes and enter ten concentration camps, most of them in the western United States. The camps were surrounded by barbed-wire fences and patrolled by armed guards with orders to shoot to kill anyone who tried to escape. Very few escapes were ever attempted and most camp life was orderly, although many were overcrowded with less than comfortable conditions.

Japanese inmates were permitted to live as normal lives as they could while they were incarcerated. Schools were established, including high schools, which even had football teams that competed against those of local schools outside of the camps. Work was available for "residents" in schools, hospitals, garment factories, cabinet shops, and silk screen shops, all run by camp officials. Workers were paid paltry salaries ranging from twelve to nineteen dollars a month.

Actor George Takei, best known for his role as Lieutenant Hikaru Sulu, senior helmsman on the starship *Enterprise* on the original *Star Trek* television series (1966–1969), was five years old in the spring of 1942 when his family was taken from their Los Angeles home and forced to live in a horse stable at Santa Anita Park before being sent to the Rohwer War Relocation Center in Arkansas. Before boarding the train, Takei's father was forced to sell all of the family's belongings for very little money; the family was permitted to keep only what they could carry with them. The five-year-old Takei viewed the train trip to Arkansas as an adventure and was puzzled as to why so many people on the train were crying. At the time, Takei had an aunt and infant cousin living in Hiroshima, Japan; both would be killed in the atomic bomb attack of August 6, 1945.

Rohwer was built on swampland in an unincorporated area in Desha County, Arkansas, located in the southeastern part of the state. The Takeis were later transferred to another camp at Tule Lake, on the northern border of California. After the war ended, the Takeis were freed but were given no reparations and had to live on Los Angeles's Skid Row for five years before they were able to find a permanent place to live.

Takei's memoir, *They Called Us Enemy*, was published in 2019 as a graphic novel, telling of Takei's experiences from the viewpoint of a five-year-old. The book, which was illustrated by Harmony Becker, became a *New York Times* bestseller.

PRODUCTION NOTES

The idea for a musical based on Takei's experiences took shape after a chance meeting between Takei, his husband Brad, Broadway composer Jay Kuo, and producer Lorenzo Thione, who were sitting together at an off Broadway show. The next day, the four happened to be seated next to each other again at a performance of *In the Heights*. During the show, Takei broke into tears after the character of Kevin Rosario, who owns a taxi service, sings the song "Inútil," about his father's inability to support his family. Kuo and Thione asked Takei why the song had that effect on him and Takei told them the story of his family's incarceration during World War II. This prompted the germination of the production that would become *Allegiance*.

Allegiance was the first Broadway musical created and directed by Asian Americans, utilizing a predominantly Asian American cast. Takei played Sam Kimura, a World War II veteran at a Pearl Harbor anniversary ceremony reminiscing about his life. The younger version of Sam, played by Telly Leung, was changed from a five-year-old boy to a college graduate looking forward to a career in politics. After volunteering for military service, he is turned down because of his Japanese heritage.

The Kimuras are a farming family from Salinas, California, whose lives are uprooted when they are sent to the Heart Mountain Relocation Center in Wyoming. Heart Mountain was a real internment camp that opened on August 11, 1942, its first trainloads of prisoners arriving from Los Angeles, Santa Clara, and San Francisco counties in California and Yakima County in Washington. At its peak, Heart Mountain housed more than ten thousand inmates, making it the third largest town in the state. It closed on November 10, 1945.

The musical had little to do with Takei's actual experiences but did a good job displaying the Japanese inmates' defiant refusal to passively submit to the oppression experienced at the camp. As with *South Pacific* and *Show Boat*, miscegenation plays a part in the story. At the camp, Sammy falls in love with Hannah (Katie Rose Clarke), a white Quaker volunteer nurse, which creates tension in Sammy's community. As with Lieutenant Cable in *South Pacific*, Hannah suffers Broadway punishment by being killed off for her sins during a camp uprising. Respected Filipino actress Lea Salonga (*Miss Saigon*) played Sammy's older sister Kei, who serves as a substitute mother figure for Sammy and leader of the camp's resistance effort, along with her lover, Frankie (Michael K. Lee).

Reviews of *Allegiance* were mixed but chiefly negative. Staged toward the beginning of the tumultuous 2016 presidential campaign, anti-immigrant feelings heightened interest in *Allegiance*, but despite encouraging comments from critics about Salonga and others in the cast, the show closed after barely three months and 111 performances.

Score

Much of the fault for the abbreviated run of *Allegiance* was blamed on Jay Kuo's undistinguished score. Despite including ostentatiously inserted Japanese-sounding musical tropes and token use of traditional instruments like the shakuhachi and koto, Kuo's songs were lushly orchestrated generic Broadway fare, with clunky, contrived, and preachy lyrics. At the beginning of the musical, after hearing President Roosevelt's famous "day of infamy" speech, Sammy's father, Tatsuo, says, "This will not be good for us," speaking in clipped speech like an American Indian in a 1940s B-movie.

The clichéd dialog and mediocre songs helped bring down the musical's worthy and timely message of tolerance and racial equality. The most embarrassing number was "Get in the Game," in which baseball is used as a motivating factor in getting the camp inmates to "have fun" while being incarcerated, set to a big band arrangement, sounding more like Mickey and Judy getting ready to put on a show in *Babes in Arms*. The *Wall Street Journal* went so far as to call *Allegiance* "of no artistic value whatsoever, save as an object lesson in how to write a really bad Broadway musical."

Bandstand

Historical context: GIs returning home after World War II
Time period: August–December 1945
Broadway run: April 26–September 17, 2017 (166 p.)
Venue: Bernard B. Jacobs Theatre
Book: Rob Taylor and Richard Oberacker
Score: Richard Oberacker (music), Richard Oberacker and Rob Taylor (lyrics)
Cast album: Broadway Records (BRYSL-CD-04) (2017)
Major characters: Donny Novitski (Corey Coft), Julia Trojan (Laura Osnes), Nick Radel (Alex Bender), Wayne Wright (Geoff Packard), Jimmy Campbell (James Nathan Hopkins)

HISTORICAL BACKGROUND

Problems faced by servicemen and servicewomen returning home from World War II were addressed in motion pictures such as the Oscar-winning *The Best Years of Our Lives* and the musical revue *Call Me Mister*. Two of the most honored shows in history, *The Sound of Music* and *South Pacific*, dealt with the tragic and the lighter aspects of the war. The underappreciated *Bandstand* goes one step further in its addressing post-traumatic stress disorder (PTSD) and survivor's guilt issues, which presented an opposing viewpoint of the "greatest war" propaganda that has been promulgated in the media through motion pictures and other media.

More than a half century after the end of the war, Rob Taylor, whose father was a pilot in the Army Air Corps during World War II, decided to write a high-octane musical that would combine the excitement of the swing era with real situations faced by those who served in the armed forces. Through his father, Taylor understood that in the days before psychoanalysis, PTSD, previously called "shell shock" in World War I and "combat fatigue" in World War II, was a real condition that affected many servicemen and women. In addition, ex-GIs often had difficulties picking up where their lives had left off before the war. Relationships changed, jobs were hard to come by, and many were unable to cope with the return to normal day-to-day living.

Taylor's writing partner, Richard Oberacker, had known Broadway choreographer Andy Blankenbuehler since high school, so after drafting a script, the pair recruited Blankenbuehler to design the energetic dances the show would require.

PRODUCTION NOTES

The story tells of Cleveland native Donny Novitski, whose career as a nightclub piano player was interrupted by the draft. During the war, Donny witnessed the death of his best friend, and after being discharged, he returns home to find all the music jobs taken by younger musicians. He decides to start his own six-man swing combo, utilizing other returning vets, all of whom have also been emotionally and/or physically damaged by their respective experiences. Calling themselves the Donny Nova Band, the group enters a national radio contest in New York, in which bands vied for a spot in an upcoming MGM film musical. Joining the group as its singer is Julia, the Gold Star widow of Donny's best friend. Julia wants to know details of her husband's death, but Donny can't bring himself to discuss it.

The band's other members include Jimmy, a silky-smooth saxophonist; Wayne, a devoted family man who plays trombone; Nick, a supercilious and snippy trumpet player; alcoholic bassist Davy; and PTSD-afflicted drummer Johnny.

At the time *Bandstand* was produced in 2017, Broadway's use of musicians had expanded, with actors often doubling as onstage musicians in shows like *Once* and *The Band's Visit*. In *Bandstand*, this practice is integrated into the story, which jockeys back and forth between the band members' attempts to deal with their wartime experiences and a conventional Hollywood success story as they rehearse and make their way, one dance hall at a time, to New York for the contest. "Not one of us feels like a hero," Donny says at one point, haunted by the tragic death of his friend, while Johnny, whose memory was shattered by his own traumatic experiences, can only say, "I'm lucky I don't remember." The show might have been more effective had the band members' memories been more fully explored, but what remained was still enormously entertaining, due in part to the exuberant production values and a believable, heartfelt book.

The musical made its first appearance in 2015 at the Paper Mill Playhouse with most of the main cast going on to perform in the Broadway version two years later. One of the cast members, Joe Pero, who played the role of Nick, suffered an injury and was unable to make an appearance in the Broadway production until the middle of its run, which ended after 166 performances.

The *New York Times* noted the dichotomy between the "peppy celebration of can-do spirit" and "the more somber exploration of what American servicemen experienced when they marched home from World War II." *Bandstand*'s lack of success was blamed on its uneven storyline, which veered away from the band members' physical and emotional issues to concentrate on the more mundane aspects of the story, like personal relationships and the band members' musical ambitions.

SCORE

Oberacker and Taylor's score evoked the "band-within-a-band" trend that started with the Benny Goodman Trio and Quartet in the mid-1930s, when hot jazz musicians in swing orchestras split off to play small-unit jam sessions during dances. The popularity of the Goodman groups, which included Teddy Wilson, Lionel Hampton, and Gene Krupa, inspired other bandleaders, such as Bob Crosby (younger brother of Bing) and his Bobcats, Artie Shaw and His Gramercy Five, and Jimmy Dorsey's Dorseyland Jazz Band to do the same.

Actors were hired based on their ability to play instruments, rather than mime to pit musicians. The music was more jitterbug jump than swing, which was more suitable to Blankenbuehler's energetic and complex choreography. The song "Breathe" was one of the show's standout numbers, cleverly constructed around the bugle call melody for "Reveille," to which service personnel awoke each morning.

In one scene, bassist Davy and drummer Johnny summon up the memory of big band musicians Ray Bauduc and Bob Haggart (who had a hit with "Big Noise from Winnetka"), in which drummer Bauduc would use his drumsticks to beat on the strings of Haggart's string bass. With a compelling story, sympathetic characters, and a slam-bang score, *Bandstand* deserved more examination than it got and is a valuable addition to the catalog of shows that dealt with war and its aftereffects.

Finian's Rainbow

Historical context: Racism in Postwar America
Time period: 1947
Broadway run: January 10, 1947–October 2, 1948 (725 p.)
Venue: Forty-Sixth Street Theatre
Book: E. Y. Harburg and Fred Saidy
Score: Burton Lane (music), E. Y. Harburg (lyrics)
Cast album: Columbia MM-686 (78 rpm album) (1947)
Major characters: Sharon McLonergan (Ella Logan), Finian
  McLonergan (Albert Sharpe), Og (David Wayne), Woody
  Mahoney (Donald Richards), Senator Billboard Rawkins
  (Robert Pitkin), Susan Mahoney (Anita Alvarez)

Historical Background

Before the civil rights movement, before *Brown v. Board of Education*, and before Martin Luther King Jr., E. Y. Harburg, known to all as "Yip," was as much of a human rights activist as he was a lyricist. Harburg would describe *Finian's Rainbow*, his thinly veiled attack on racism in the United States, as being "twenty-five years ahead of its time." He recalled that ever since he was seven or eight years old, he identified with oppressed people. After seeing a production of *Peter Pan*, he fell in love with fantasy and with characters who were larger than life.

Growing up in a family of poor Russian-Jewish immigrants on New York's Lower East Side, Harburg, born Isidore Hochberg, became enthralled with the Yiddish theater, introduced to its rich language, stories, and melodies by his father, who had no problem skipping synagogue services to take his son to what became Harburg's "substitute temple."

In addition, Harburg knew the Gershwin brothers, and shared their love for the light operettas of W. S. Gilbert and Arthur Sullivan, all of which contained the blend of political satire and light comedy that Harburg grew to adopt.

Embracing a talent for lyric writing, Harburg wrote some fifty musicals during the Depression, in addition to penning words to such classics as "Brother, Can You Spare a Dime" (with composer Jay Gorney), the anthem of the downtrodden whose lives had been wiped out by the stock market crash and the surging unemployment of the 1930s. Harburg's lyrics embraced not the forgotten man as much as the inequities of the capitalist system. At the end of the 1930s, he would collaborate with composer Harold Arlen to write the score to the film fantasy *The Wizard of Oz*, using his innate sense of optimism to write the words to what many view as the century's greatest song, "Over the Rainbow."

Although not a member of the Communist Party, Harburg nevertheless was fed up with capitalism's economic system and also developed a strong disdain for the politics of certain Southern politicians, most notably two Mississippi segregationists: Senator Theodore Bilbo and US Representative John Rankin. Both men were outspoken proponents of segregation, with Bilbo extolling white supremacy in inflammatory speeches that regularly made the national news and Rankin proposing a bill in Congress to prohibit interracial marriage. In addition, both men regularly expressed racist views against African Americans, Japanese, and Jews.

When Harburg and playwright Fred Saidy decided to write *Finian's Rainbow*, Jim Crow attitudes were still alive and well in America, especially in the South. The armed forces remained segregated, anti-lynching legislation was prevented from passage by Southern senators, and poll taxes were still in force in the South. The only step forward to achieving racial equality was Jackie Robinson's recent breakthrough with the Brooklyn Dodgers as major league baseball's first Black ballplayer, his efforts rewarded with epithets and racist behavior from fans, opposing players, and even some of his teammates.

Drawing inspiration from Irish stories in James Stephen's *The Crock of Gold*, Harburg and Saidy fashioned a tale about immigrant Irishman Finian McLonergan and his daughter, Sharon, who arrive in a village in the mythical state of Missitucky after having stolen a pot of gold from a leprechaun named Og. Finian hopes to bury the gold in Fort Knox under the belief that it would grow.

Meanwhile, local union leader Woody Mahoney is fighting on behalf of Black and white sharecroppers who are being threatened with eviction at the command of racist Missitucky Senator Billboard Rawkins (an obvious amalgam of the names of Bilbo and Rankin). When Sharon, who is unknowingly standing on her father's pot of gold, makes a wish for Rawkins to turn Black so he could see how Black people live, her wish comes true.

Harburg's biting social commentary about the state of racism in America and the hostile feelings many felt toward immigrants after World War II was balanced, even disguised, by the endearing charm of the score, the show's whimsical humor, and the magical fantasy of the story.

PRODUCTION NOTES

Finian's Rainbow wasn't the first time Yip Harburg and Fred Saidy collaborated on a musical dealing with real-life American social problems. *Bloomer Girl* (1944), which we looked at in a previous chapter, examined women's rights and the emancipation of slaves during the days of the Underground Railroad. In that show, Saidy collaborated with S. M. Herzig on the book, while Harburg wrote lyrics to Harold Arlen's music.

In addition to the bold concepts inherent in Harburg and Saidy's book, *Finian's Rainbow* also featured Broadway's first ensemble with both Blacks and whites singing and dancing together, giving new meaning to the term "integrated musical." After the overture, the opening scene begins with Black folk musician Sonny Terry, a member of the leftist Almanac Singers contingent from New York, playing blues harmonica.

Harburg slyly combined one story—the capitalist principle of investing money in a financial entity—with another involving a fight against segregation, a deliberate amalgamation because it was Harburg's belief that the two institutions were related.

Missitucky's Rainbow Valley represented a kind of utopian world to Harburg, one where people of different races lived together in a land "where every American has everything" but is threatened by raging capitalism

David Wayne and Ella Logan in *Finian's Rainbow*.
PHOTOFEST

and raving racists. Despite the fantasy element, reality can be found under every rock. Even the sainted Glocca Morra, which serves as an Irish equivalent to the Garden of Eden in the show, was the name of an actual hamlet located in a small section of Fermoy in Ireland's County Cork.

SCORE

Finian's Rainbow contains what is arguably the best work Yip Harburg ever did. The score is filled with memorable songs that survive outside of the musical, in the repertoire not only of pop singers but also in jazz, due to the fact that Burton Lane's singable melodies were easy to improvise from. At the time, big band vocalists were going out on their own and looked to Broadway for new material and shows like *Finian's Rainbow* helped provide a good source for vocal repertoires.

"Old Devil Moon" and "How Are Things in Glocca Morra?" proved to be the show's two major hits, but others, like the enchanting "Look to the Rainbow," the pseudo-gospel singalong "That Great Come-and-Get-It Day," and the breezy "If This Isn't Love" also became standards. "Look to the Rainbow" is probably the best example of Harburg's innate optimism, a concept that does not occur often in satire, which is usually written by dyed-in-the-wool cynics. But Harburg was adept at communicating his political commentary in a jovial, whimsical way, revealing a refreshingly non-acerbic approach to satire that marked his unique songwriting style.

In writing the witty lyrics, Harburg forced rhymes in ingenious ways, either by adding suffixes, as in "Something Sort of Grandish," or leaving syllables out, as in Og's delightful solo "When I'm Not Near the Girl I Love," in which Harburg rhymes "fickle" with the partial word "par-TI-cul'." The song makes use of a palindrome-like structure that turns phrases backward to create new meanings as well as utilizing playful alliteration. Ask Yip Harburg how a leprechaun might write a song and that's exactly what you got.

"The Begat" is one of the most brilliantly written songs in the annals of musical theater, of which its most inventive lyricist, Cole Porter, was no doubt envious. The song, a lampoon of African American spirituals, features a laundry list of biblical begetting, targeting motion picture censors, congressional filibusters, the DAR, the GOP, income tax adjusters, and in an especially brilliant turn of a phrase, "sons of habitués," which, when sung properly, most likely raised the hackles of puritan-minded theatergoers.

Harburg was clever enough to bury his socialist ideology into the lyrics rather than have them fully exposed in the show's dialog. This was done deliberately; Harburg was a big believer in the power of songs to affect people's beliefs in a way that dialog could never do. Satire has always been used to communicate a point of view by entertaining the listener and when he was at his best, as he was in *Finian's Rainbow*, Yip Harburg delivered as sharp a satire as any show in Broadway history.

Million Dollar Quartet

Historical context: Four rock 'n' roll legends meet in Memphis
Time period: December 4, 1956
Broadway run: April 11, 2010–June 12, 2011 (489 p.)
Venue: Nederlander Theatre
Book: Colin Escott and Floyd Mutrux
Score: Jukebox musical featuring rock 'n' roll, R&B, and gospel
Cast album: Caroline Records 17558033 (2011)
Major characters: Elvis Presley (Eddie Clendening), Johnny Cash
(Lance Guest), Jerry Lee Lewis (Levi Kreis), Carl Perkins (Rob
Lyons), Sam Phillips (Hunter Foster)

HISTORICAL BACKGROUND

On December 4, 1956, Elvis Presley and his friend Cliff Gleaves were
driving through Elvis's old stomping grounds in Memphis, Tennessee,
when they passed the Sun Recording Studios at 706 Union Ave. There
they spied a parking lot full of Cadillacs. Elvis had left Sun Records the
year before, after owner Sam Phillips cultivated Presley's musical talent
and turned him into the hottest star in popular music. Since January, he
had been recording for his new label, RCA Victor, beginning a string of
million-selling records including "Heartbreak Hotel" and "Hound Dog,"
making him an instantaneous superstar.

Upon seeing the Cadillacs, Presley spun his car around, parked, and
walked into the studio, where he found Carl Perkins rehearsing for a
recording session. Perkins was the composer of "Blue Suede Shoes,"
which became Sun Records' biggest-selling single. When Presley covered it for RCA, his recording eclipsed Perkins's Sun single in popularity.

Perkins was at work rehearsing with his brothers Jay and Clayton, drummer W. S. Holland, and Sun's new session pianist, a raw-boned, blond-headed piano player from Ferriday, Louisiana, named Jerry Lee Lewis, who had just recorded his first single for Sun, "Crazy Arms," the record released only days before.

Before long, an impromptu jam session was taking place, with Phillips astutely rolling tape in the control booth, realizing not only the historical importance of the moment, but the potential publicity he could get for having Elvis return to where it all had started for him. Phillips immediately got on the phone, called his biggest current star, Johnny Cash, and told him to hightail it down to the studio. Then he put in a call to entertainment reporter Bob Johnson of the *Memphis Press-Scimitar*, inviting him to come down with a photographer. Elvis sat down at the piano and started fooling around with a few Christmas melodies and

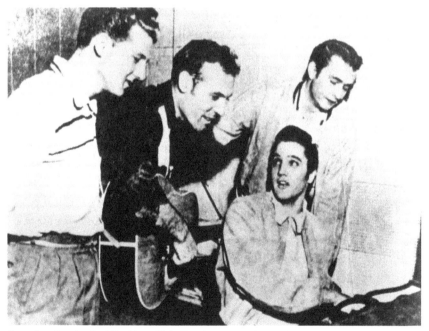

Jerry Lee Lewis, Carl Perkins, Elvis Presley (seated), and Johnny Cash, December 4, 1956, at the Sun Studio in Memphis.
RCA/PHOTOFEST

then launched into Lowell Fulson's blues hit "Reconsider Baby," followed by his most recent hit, "Don't Be Cruel." Elvis marveled to the others about having seen a skinny singer with Billy Ward and His Dominoes doing the song better than he had ever done it. (The singer was a young Jackie Wilson.)

Next, Elvis launched into a rockabilly version of the Civil War favorite "Home Sweet Home," joined by Perkins playing lead guitar, which segued into the New Orleans spiritual "When the Saints Go Marching In." Now in a sacred mood, the group started reeling off one hand-clapping gospel number after another: "Just a Little Talk with Jesus," "I Shall Not Be Moved," "Down by the Riverside," "On the Jericho Road," and others, with Lewis singing harmony and providing responsive answers to Elvis's lead.

Johnny Cash arrived in time to pose for a single photograph of the four of them grouped around the piano, with Elvis at the keyboard. Although it was believed that Cash left the session before the singing started, Cash himself insisted that he was there for the recording but was positioned far enough away from the others that he could not be easily heard. He said that he was already there when Elvis, who was returning to Tennessee after shooting a movie in Hollywood, arrived with showgirl Marilyn Evans on his arm.

According to Cash, Elvis, who had recorded Bill Monroe's "Blue Moon of Kentucky" on his first Sun record, wanted to learn other Monroe songs, which Cash knew well. The group then sang a string of Bill Monroe tunes, tried out the new Chuck Berry single, "Brown Eyed Handsome Man," and finished with covers of a number of country songs, with Presley doing a reasonable impression of Hank Snow on "I'm Gonna Bid My Blues Goodbye." After crooning Gene Autry's "You're the Only Star in My Blue Heaven," Elvis said his goodbyes, hopped into his Cadillac, and left.

In his *Press-Scimitar* story the next day, Bob Johnson noted, "That quartet could sell a million." The headline for the story gave the session its name, "Million Dollar Quartet." The tapes languished in Sam Phillips's studio until 1969, when producer Shelby Singleton purchased the Sun Records catalog. After reissuing much of the better-known material by Presley, Cash, Lewis, Perkins, and others, Singleton leased the cat-alogue to the Charly label in England. It was then that the legendary Million Dollar Quartet tapes were discovered.

In 1981, Charly Records issued seventeen tracks from the session on an LP, using mainly public domain gospel numbers, to reduce the neces-sity of paying mechanical royalties. In 1987, they released the entire ses-sion, which was released in the United States by RCA Victor, with album notes written by an English music historian named Colin Escott. Escott had been a fan of Sun recordings since the early 1960s, when he would note the phrase "Recorded by Sun, Memphis" printed at the bottom of London Records labels released for the British market. This developed into an all-consuming passion for Escott, who collaborated with another English Sun fan Martin Hawkins, to write the 1975 book *Catalyst*, the first book to focus on the history of the legendary label. In 1992, Escott and Hawkins expanded on the material when they wrote *Good Rockin' Tonight: Sun Records and the Birth of Rock 'n' Roll*.

Production Notes
In writing the musical with producer/screenwriter Floyd Mutrux, Colin Escott wanted to make a point about how unusual the impromptu session at Sun was. Today, such meetings are contrived by promoters, managers, or record companies, but in addition to capturing the four stars, for the only time in their lives, in one room, it also marked one of the few times Elvis Presley was recorded in an unguarded moment, just enjoying the company of friends, and playing and singing songs they all knew and enjoyed. It was this feeling that Escott wanted to communicate as the musical took shape in 2006, beginning with regional performances in Florida and Washington, then moving on to Chicago, and finally, in 2010, to Broadway. The show became a hit and was nominated for three Tony Awards.

With no real story to tell, Mutrux and Escott decided to begin the show with Sam Phillips reminiscing about the session. He then steps into the scene, reliving it along with the audience. Mutrux and Escott understood that to make the show more than just about a jam session, there had to be some dramatic elements added, so they had Presley and the volatile Lewis almost getting into a fight, added two vocals by Elvis's girlfriend, and had Cash and Perkins announcing to Phillips that they were going to leave Sun and record for Columbia. (The latter was an occurrence that indeed happened, but not at the same time. Cash wouldn't opt out until the fall of 1957; Perkins left in 1958.)

There is also a dramatization of a rant by Lewis that came during a later session that became legendary after Phillips captured it on tape, with Lewis telling Phillips he was playing "the devil's music." But there were enough true, factual events fitted into the story to make the between-songs chatter by the quartet realistic, a mark of Escott's devotion to historical accuracy.

The believability of the performances depended heavily on musical ability, so the actors portraying Presley, Cash, Perkins, and Lewis not only had to look and sing like the real thing but also play like them. Eddie Clendening was praised for not making his Elvis appear as the camped-up, "thank-you-very-much" stereotype of the 1970s, but as a young twenty-one-year-old who loved listening to country, gospel, and rhythm and blues, but was already being manipulated by his manager, "Colonel" Tom Parker and just wanted a chance to hang out with his Sun buddies before moving on to his next publicity-controlled event.

Levi Kreis was a revelation as Jerry Lee Lewis, perfectly portraying the uncontrollable, cocky "wild child," as Lewis would describe himself. Kreis raked and pounded at his piano, shaking his blond mane of hair just as Lewis was known to do, unintimidated by the other already established stars. Kreis would win the show's only Tony for his performance. When Kreis and the real "Killer" met for the first time, Lewis, the last survivor of the quartet, gave his blessing on Kreis's performance.

Million Dollar Quartet was a surprise hit, and has continued in national tours for the past decade. Regional productions are attentive to casting and ensure that only actors who can sing and play their own instruments are hired.

SCORE

The score for *Million Dollar Quartet* uses only three songs out of the twenty-two in the score that were actually performed by Presley, Cash,

Perkins, and Lewis on that December day in 1956: Berry's "Brown Eyed Handsome Man" and the spirituals "Down by the Riverside" and "Peace in the Valley." The rest of the songs were compiled from a carefully cultivated playlist of 1950s hits, making sure to showcase each of the performer's own catalog of hits, including Cash's "I Walk the Line" and "Folsom Prison Blues," Perkins's "Matchbox," and Lewis's "Whole Lotta Shakin' Goin' On" and "Great Balls of Fire." Elvis contributed "Hound Dog," Dean Martin's "Memories Are Made of This," and his first single, a cover of Arthur "Big Boy" Crudup's "That's All Right." In this instance, poetic license actually made the show better, since the original tapes were unstructured, with songs repeated or ending abruptly midway through. Despite problems with creaky dialog and forced introductions, the exuberant, effective performances by the actors made *Million Dollar Quartet* an enjoyable, if somewhat fictionalized version of one of the most historic events in popular music history.

Li'l Abner

Historical context: Cold War politics during the 1950s
Time period: 1956
Broadway run: November 15, 1956–July 12, 1958 (693 p.)
Venue: St. James Theatre
Book: Norman Panama and Melvin Frank (based on comic strip characters by Al Capp)
Score: Gene de Paul (music), Johnny Mercer (lyrics)
Cast album: Columbia OL-5150 (1956)
Major characters: Li'l Abner (Peter Palmer), Daisy Mae (Edith Adams), Mammy Yokum (Charlotte Rae), Marryin' Sam (Stubby Kaye), General Bullmoose (Howard St. John), Pappy Yokum (Joe E. Marks)

HISTORICAL BACKGROUND

When Al Capp started his comic strip *Li'l Abner* in 1934, it was just one of hundreds competing for the attention of newspaper readers across America. In those days, reading a daily comic strip was as necessary to Americans' lives as that first cup of coffee. Over the next forty-three years, *Li'l Abner* became an American institution, reflecting the political and social events in the news of the day and introducing such institutions as Sadie Hawkins Day and the Shmoo into American life.

For many Americans, *Li'l Abner* represented how the world viewed the American South: backwoods yokels who were either stupid (Abner Yokum), lazy (Pappy Yokum), or unkempt (Moonbeam McSwine). Unscrupulous politicians and greedy capitalists were personified by such characters as tycoon J. Roaringham Fatback, marketing consultant

J. Colossal McGenius, and blowhard Senator Jack S. Phogbound. Pulchritudinous, barefooted females like Daisy Mae Scragg, Appassionata Von Climax, and Stupefyin' Jones exhibited the power of feminine wiles over helpless, ineffectual males. The characters' heavily accented Southern dialect produced words that entered the American lexicon, including "natcherly," "druthers," and "nogoodnik." At a time when comic strips were little more than humorous diversions, *Li'l Abner* attacked daily issues head on, the main precedent for politically oriented comic strips to come such as *Pogo*, *Doonesbury*, and *MAD* magazine.

At its peak, *Li'l Abner* was seen by some seventy million readers in more than nine hundred newspapers. Capp's devastating humor targeted sanctimonious politicians and capitalism before his political direction moved toward the right in the 1960s when he started taking on antiwar activists and the hippie movement. Simply put, there was no comic family that had a greater influence on American life for a longer time than the citizens of Dogpatch, and, in turn, the strip became a mirror for how some Americans responded to current events.

PRODUCTION NOTES

By the time 1956 rolled around, *Li'l Abner* had been entrenched in American society for two decades. There was no one who wasn't aware of the antics of dimwitted bachelor Abner and the fetching Daisy Mae, whose endless pursuit of Abner as her husband finally resulted in her catching him in 1952. In 1959, Capp credited this landmark event to McCarthyism, which had threatened Americans' ability to laugh at any facet of American life for fear of being called anti-American and subsequently couldn't make fun of government, business, or any other aspect of American life except for marriage. So Daisy Mae and Abner got married.

In 1954, Alan Jay Lerner struck on the idea of turning the comic strip into a Broadway musical. He approached Burton Lane to the write the music but soon Lerner abandoned the idea to work on a musical version of George Bernard Shaw's *Pygmalion*, which would become *My Fair Lady*.

The next to pick up the gauntlet were Norman Panama and Melvin Frank, a Hollywood-based writing team that had written such successful films as *White Christmas* and *The Court Jester*. Together, they put together a libretto based on Capp's characters and asked esteemed choreographer Michael Kidd to direct and choreograph. For the songs, Kidd brought in composer Gene de Paul and lyricist Johnny Mercer, with whom he had worked on the acclaimed film musical *Seven Brides for Seven Brothers* (1954).

Although much of Capp's sharp-edged satire from the strip was sanitized, he was still able to make fun of post-McCarthy capitalism during the Eisenhower years, which included commentary on nuclear testing, big business, and right-wing Southern politics. With Mercer's sharp pen and keen ear for Southern dialect, the songs for the Broadway version of the musical were some of the best of the entire decade.

Tina Louise, Edith Adams, and Julie Newmar in *Li'l Abner*.
PHOTOFEST

Much of the show's political commentary was geared toward a relatively new character of Capp's, General Bullmoose, a cold-blooded capitalist tycoon who made his first appearance in the strip in 1953. Capp created the character after hearing Charles W. Wilson, the former head of General Motors, tell a Senate subcommittee, "What is good for the country is good for General Motors, and vice versa." In the strip, this became "What's good for General Bullmoose is good for everybody!" Wilson would later serve as President Eisenhower's secretary of defense.

In the show, General Bullmoose, played by Howard St. John, wants to control all the businesses in Dogpatch, but especially the formula for Yokumberry Tonic, a liquid that makes men strong and muscular, but has a side effect of impotence that baffles the women of Dogpatch, especially Daisy Mae.

Playing the title role was twenty-four-year-old Peter Palmer, who had a football player's physique and a voice big enough for the part. Edith (later known as Edie) Adams was a Juilliard graduate who studied at the Actors Studio in New York. Newly married to comedian and television pioneer Ernie Kovacs, Adams had starred opposite Rosalind Russell in *Wonderful Town* in 1953 before being cast as the voluptuous but virtuous Daisy Mae.

Showstopping belter Stubby Kaye signed on as Marryin' Sam, the preacher who specializes in two-dollar weddings, while corncob-pipe-chomping Mammy Yokum was played by comedienne Charlotte Rae. The show's statuesque female characters, including Adams as Daisy Mae, Tina Louise as Appassionata Von Climax, and Julie Newmar as Stupefyin' Jones, were clad in the skimpiest, form-fittingest outfits imaginable, leading Walter Winchell to call *Li'l Abner* "the best girlesque show in town." In fact, the women's outfits in the show, fashioned by costume designer Alvin Colt, perfectly matched those drawn in the strip by Capp, who laid claim to having invented the miniskirt in 1934, three decades before it came into fashion.

One element of the story involved the government's intention to use Dogpatch as a testing site for the atomic bomb. Nuclear tests were controversial during the 1950s, a decade during which the proliferation of nuclear weapons was of great concern to many Americans. The belief that building up its arsenal of nuclear bombs would deter Soviet aggression in the world, resulting in the development of nuclear test sites in the United States, also prompted fear of cancer from radioactive fallout. Schoolchildren were taught "duck and cover" techniques in regularly scheduled drills, hiding under their desks, as if that would save them from nuclear annihilation.

In November 1943, a nuclear reactor was developed at the Oak Ridge National Laboratory in Oak Ridge, Tennessee. The X-10 Graphite Reactor was designed by scientists from the top-secret Manhattan Project to produce plutonium to be used in the manufacture of nuclear bombs. The site was located near the small town of Clinton, Tennessee, the location designated for all fissionable materials production, an area so remote that scientists began calling it "Dogpatch," showing the pervasiveness of *Li'l Abner* and Al Capp's fictional backwoods hamlet in American popular culture.

This example of fiction inspiring reality took another U-turn in a key plot element in the musical when Congressman Senator Jack S. Phogbound (played by Ted Thurston) announces that since Congress had declared Dogpatch the most unnecessary town in the country, it was going to have to be evacuated for use as a nuclear test site, which would be overseen by government scientist Dr. Rasmussen T. Finsdale (Stanley Simmonds). Such an event was not unknown to Americans. In 1950, the town of Ellenton, South Carolina, and four other nearby communities were acquired by the US Atomic Energy Commission for the purpose of using the land for construction of a nuclear power plant. As a result, seven thousand residents (as well as all the graves from the town graveyard) along a 250,000-acre tract of land near the Savannah River had to be relocated.

Li'l Abner was deemed a success, surviving for two full seasons and nearly seven hundred performances, but much of this was due to the excellent score and the novelty of a comic strip coming to life on stage (a Broadway first). Although the story took some Cappian potshots at government bureaucracy, nuclear proliferation, corporate greed, and Southern politics, the musical's watered-down plot focused on what *Li'l Abner* had become known for: Daisy Mae's frustrating pursuit of Abner.

A successful film version was made in 1959, with nearly all of the original Broadway cast reprising their roles (excepting Adams, who was replaced by Leslie Parrish as Daisy Mae, and Rae, replaced by Billie Hayes as Mammy Yokum).

SCORE

For many, Michael Kidd's choreography and the de Paul/Mercer songs were the high points of *Li'l Abner*. The score proved to be the source for much of the show's political commentary. Its humor, however, took the form of sly sideswipes rather than head-on collisions at such controversial topics as welfare, which is only suggested in the show's opening song, "It's a Typical Day." "Jubilation T. Cornpone," sung with expansive gusto by Stubby Kaye as Marryin' Sam, celebrates the founder of Dogpatch, a cowardly Civil War general who never saw a battle he couldn't run away from.

The song that best captured the spirit of Al Capp's political commentary was "The Country's in the Very Best of Hands," in which Marryin' Sam sarcastically sings of the skyrocketing national debt, thickly worded Senate bills that no one can understand, rising taxes, unproductive farm bills, and the ongoing animus between Democrats and Republicans.

General Bullmoose has his say in "Progress Is the Root of All Evil," in which he bemoans the fact that money doesn't buy political favor as much as celebrity, referencing presidential losers like Thomas E. Dewey and Averill Harriman, who lost their respective elections because of a lack of "mass appeal."

The score also featured two charming duets, "I'm Past My Prime," in which Daisy Mae bemoans her advanced age (seventeen!) as the reason for Abner's disinterest, and "Namely You," a romantic duet for marriage-minded Daisy Mae and the romantically indifferent Abner.

Bye Bye Birdie

Historical context: Elvis Presley is drafted
Time period: 1958
Broadway run and venues: April 14, 1960–October 22, 1960 (Martin
  Beck Theatre); October 24, 1960–January 14, 1961 (Fifty-Fourth
  Street Theatre); January 16, 1961–October 7, 1961 (Shubert
  Theatre) (607 p.)
Book: Michael Stewart
Score: Charles Strouse (music), Lee Adams (lyrics)
Cast album: Columbia Masterworks (KOL-5510/KOS-2025) (1960)
Major characters: Albert Peterson (Dick Van Dyke), Rose Grant
  (Chita Rivera), Conrad Birdie (Dick Gautier), Kim MacAfee
  (Susan Watson), Mr. MacAfee (Paul Lynde), Hugo Peabody
  (Michael J. Pollard)

HISTORICAL BACKGROUND

Born in Tupelo, Mississippi, in 1935, Elvis Presley was driving a truck
for a living when he walked into the studios of Sam Phillips's Memphis
Recording Service in 1953 to make a demo record as a gift for his mother.
Two years later, he was the star performer on Phillips's Sun Records label
and was soon signed to record for RCA Victor, one of the top record
labels in the music industry. With his hip-shaking onstage actions that
thrilled female teens and horrified parents, Presley became a worldwide
phenomenon, derisively called "Elvis the Pelvis" by his detractors but
idolized by teenagers throughout the country. Magazines followed his
every move and each live performance inspired hysterical shrieking from
his young fans.

A major upheaval in the lives of American teenagers occurred when on March 24, 1958, the twenty-three-year-old Presley was inducted into the US Army, interrupting his soaring career. He had received his draft notice the previous December 20 but resolved to do his duty to his country by being sworn in and serving his time. After the announcement, the army received tens of thousands of letters from distraught fans, requesting that Elvis be spared, but Presley was intent on being a good citizen, although he requested and was granted a sixty-day deferment so he could complete shooting his latest movie, *King Creole*, not for selfish reasons but because he didn't want the filmmakers to lose money by not being able to finish production.

Induction day was a major news story; Elvis registered at Kennedy Veterans Hospital in Memphis, with his manager, "Colonel" Tom Parker handing out *King Creole* balloons to the throng of weeping fans mourning his departure from the popular music scene. In his first week of basic training at Fort Hood, in Killeen, Texas, Presley received some two thousand fan letters. When he returned to his Graceland mansion on a June furlough, swarms of teenagers were there waiting for him.

On September 22, 1958, Elvis arrived at the Brooklyn Army Terminal, where he was to set sail aboard the Navy troopship *General Randal* for the voyage across the Atlantic to his army base in Friedberg, Germany. At the Women's Army Corps in nearby Fort Hamilton, a WAC named Mary Davies was asked by a public relations representative if she would like to represent Elvis's female fans and attend a press conference being held for the singer before his departure. A phalanx of reporters with flashbulb cameras was there along with television crews and newsreel reporters documenting the event. Although his gear had already been stowed aboard the ship, a prop duffle bag was supplied for a photogenic farewell staged for the cameras. Elvis knew Davies had been selected for the photo op and motioned for her to come up to the front of the room to give him an official farewell embrace. A photograph was taken of the pair, with Elvis's arm wrapped around Davies as he signed a memorandum commemorating the occasion. Over the next week, the photo would be published in hundreds of newspapers across the country.

Elvis Presley's induction into the army marked the end of the initial stage of the development of rock 'n' roll, which began with the crossover success of Bill Haley's recording of "Rock Around the Clock" and the ascendancy of Presley in 1956. Rock 'n' roll had been deemed music for degenerates by many conservative media watchers as well as on Broadway, which saw rock 'n' roll as a threat to its domination of musical entertainment during the 1950s. The decade is now deemed "The Golden Era" of Broadway musicals, dominated by traditional adult-oriented musicals like *The King and I*, *West Side Story*, and *Gypsy*. But rock 'n' roll had become the elephant in the room that Broadway producers tried to ignore, until its popularity made it too large of a demographic to dismiss. In time, something needed to be done to address the pervasiveness of rock 'n' roll in American society, even it meant ridiculing it. *Bye Bye Birdie* proved to be that vehicle.

PRODUCTION NOTES

A musical satirizing the rock 'n' roll craze of the 1950s had been in the works since at least 1957, when a Broadway stage manager named Edward Padula approached songwriters Lee Adams and Charles Strouse, both newcomers with no Broadway credits, to come up with an idea for a story. In the summer of 1958, Strouse had collaborated with Fred Tobias in writing the song "Born Too Late" by the Poni-Tails, a female teenaged singing trio from Ohio, so he was already acquainted with catering to the teenage market.

Padula's initial idea was a musical he called "Let's Go Steady," concerning a teenaged girl who decides to lose her virginity. Gower Champion was slated to direct and choreograph. This soon morphed into a vehicle for madcap comedian Dick Shawn, one of the first entertainers to do a comic impression of Elvis Presley. When the "Let's Go Steady" idea fizzled, Michael Stewart was brought on board and came up with a different plot concerning a couple whose marriage was on the rocks, but whose children conspire to talk them out of it, a story that later became the Disney feature film *The Parent Trap*.

While Stewart was mulling over other ideas, Elvis Presley received his draft notice and the ensuing media circus was more than enough to

Elvis Presley signs a memorandum commemorating his departure to serve in the US Army, taken September 22, 1958. Elvis has his arm around WAC Mary Davies. The event inspired the "one last kiss" moment in *Bye, Bye Birdie* (1960).

prompt Stewart to write a treatment about a hip-swinging rock idol who gets drafted and his manager's efforts to milk it for all he could. When the story about Mary Davies and the Elvis send-off hit US newsstands, Stewart had the subplot that he needed. His rock star draftee would be called "Conrad Birdie," a thinly veiled take on Conway Twitty, the stage name for Harold Jenkins, one of many Elvis-inspired singers of the day.

In Stewart's story, Albert Peterson, Conrad Birdie's manager, who also wrote and published his songs, sees his silver-lamé-clad meal ticket about to leave the country and decides to write a farewell song for Birdie to sing to a randomly selected teenager; he would then dramatically kiss her before departing for the army, all before hordes of screaming teenagers and flashing cameras.

A young, rubber-limbed, twenty-four-year-old comedian named Dick Van Dyke was hired to play Albert, while actress Chita Rivera, fresh from her acclaimed performance as Anita in *West Side Story*, played Albert's secretary and love interest, Rosie.

Actors who could play rock 'n' roll idols were not exactly a stock-in-trade character type for New York's theatrical pool, but eventually a struggling actor named Dick Gautier was brought on board to play the show's title character. Gautier had been working as a cabaret singer, stand-up comic, character actor, and even a caricaturist when he was hired. He was initially reluctant to play a rock 'n' roll star until it was explained to him that the part required him to represent what many in the theater industry thought of rock 'n' roll stars: overly preening, talentless, beer-guzzling, motorcycle-obsessed numbskulls. Gautier played Birdie to a T in a performance that earned him a Tony nomination. Van Dyke won the Tony for Best Featured Actor in a Musical.

Bye Bye Birdie perfectly summed up the hysteria of the early rock 'n' roll movement, focusing on exaggerated impressions of the lives of gossip-obsessed teenagers, first viewed glued to their telephones, the "social media" mechanism of the era, in the show's opening number. Titled "The Telephone Hour," the song featured a bevy of teens spreading rumors while attached like umbilical cords to their phones. Sixty years have passed since *Birdie*'s debut, but teenagers remain basically unchanged in today's world of smartphones, proving the axiom "The more things change, the more they stay the same."

Another pop culture reality was inserted into *Birdie* when Stewart decided to have Conrad Birdie's farewell kiss to Sweet Apple, Ohio, teenager Kim McAfee (played by Susan Watson) take place live on *The Ed Sullivan Show*. Throughout the 1950s and 1960s, the Sullivan show, which was basically an outgrowth of vaudeville, with its array of singers, dancers, acrobats, and comedy acts, marked a performer's concept of the pinnacle of success. Although Sullivan himself didn't appear in the musical, he was cast to play himself in the 1963 motion picture version of *Birdie*.

Today, *Bye Bye Birdie* is viewed as a nostalgia piece, a way of fondly looking back at a more innocent era in American history, when teenagers would fawn over celebrities and display oversize photos of their heroes on their bedroom walls, screaming and fainting in ecstasy if they should ever encounter one.

When *Birdie* came out in 1960, its subject was not only still contemporary but still relevant. By the time it reached Broadway, Elvis had been back from his Army hitch for a month and had returned to making movies, resuming his mantle as the King of Rock 'n' Roll.

The show also satirized the music publishing business, a major factor in the dissemination of rock 'n' roll. In 1960, the Brill Building in Midtown Manhattan was the center of the publishing world, housing myriad publishing companies and small studios equipped with rickety upright pianos on which songwriters labored and demonstrated their tunes. The Brill was where any hack songwriter could become instantly rich if a star like an Elvis Presley would only record their songs. The lengths Albert Peterson went to ensure that his song, "One Last Kiss" would be performed on live television provided *Bye Bye Birdie* with its central plot motivation.

SCORE

Although *Bye Bye Birdie* was the first musical to target younger audiences, much of its score consisted of standard Broadway fare. Charles Strouse and Lee Adams's songs were filled with cheery melodies like "Put On a Happy Face" and "Got a Lot of Livin' to Do" but could hardly be considered rock 'n' roll. Of the other songs in the score, only "One Last Kiss," the tango-flavored song Birdie sings to Kim on the Sullivan show, and "Honestly Sincere," an Elvis-style number sung by Birdie to his teenage minions to demonstrate his self-conscious humility, showed any kind of homage to currently popular musical styles.

Paul Lynde, who played Kim McAfee's frustrated father in the Broadway version and the movie, made a name for himself with his performance of the comic song "Kids," which older theater patrons not only loved but identified with. The nation's almost religious piety to Ed Sullivan was satirized in "Hymn for a Sunday Evening," in which the four members of the McAfee family don choral robes to intone their devotion to the venerable variety show host.

Fly Blackbird

Historical context: The civil rights movement
Time period: 1961
Off Broadway run: February 5, 1962–c. June 1962 (127 p.)
Venue: Mayfair Theatre
Book: Clarence Bernard Jackson, James V. Hatch, adapted by Jerome Eskow
Score: Clarence Bernard Jackson (music), James V. Hatch (lyrics)
Cast album: Mercury OCS-6206 (1962)
Major characters: William Piper (Avon Long), Carl (Robert Guillaume), Josie (Mary Louise), Mr. Crocker (John Anania), Police Matron Jonsen (Helon Blount), Police Officer Jonsen (Leonard Parker)

Historical Background

In 1960, four African American college freshmen from the North Carolina Agricultural and Technical State University sat down at a "whites-only" Woolworth's lunch counter in Greensboro, North Carolina, and politely requested service. When the white waiter refused and suggested they order a take-out meal instead, the students steadfastly remained in their seats. Neither the store manager nor a police officer was able to budge the students, until the manager finally had to close the store early. This incident initiated the sit-in movement, in which African Americans staged similar protests in other Southern cities, which eventually spread to thirteen Southern states.

Inspired by the movement, two UCLA instructors: theater arts professor James V. Hatch, who was white, and pianist/composer Clarence

Bernard Jackson, who was Black, collaborated to write the civil rights musical *Fly Blackbird*. The civil rights movement was just beginning, and Hatch and Jackson were inspired by Blacks' increasing demands for social justice and equality.

PRODUCTION NOTES

Hatch and Jackson actually started work on the play in 1959, an entire year before the sit-ins began, but accelerated the process when they realized that the time was right to make a bold statement in musical theater about equal rights and the true nature of African Americans, who, if they were cast at all in Broadway productions, inevitably played degrading stereotypical roles, either as clownish characters, servants, Pullman porters, or shoe shine boys.

Fly Blackbird premiered in 1961 as a one-act show at the Metropolitan Theatre in Los Angeles. A year later, the fully realized musical made its debut off Broadway, which received a positive notice from *New York Times* critic Milton Esterow, who called the show "provocative and exhilarating," noting hypocrisies in both Blacks and whites in American society. Although the story in *Fly Blackbird* was thin, its strong libretto conveyed a meaningful message.

Fly Blackbird starred Avon Long, a veteran character actor who had played the part of Sportin' Life in the 1942 revival of *Porgy and Bess* and the 1952 revival of *Shuffle Along*. In the story, Long plays William Piper, a song-and-dance man known to the public as "Sweet William," who is now head of the Caribou Lodge, a Harlem fraternal order. Piper, a civil rights activist, is encouraged when his daughter becomes the first Black to be elected head of her class at Sarah Lawrence College. Students at the college demonstrate but are arrested and sent to jail. The plot continues as the students disrupt the station house with high-spirited antics, songs, and humor, refusing to be complacent during their incarceration and using their voices to call other students to arms to affect change and equal rights for African Americans.

On March 25, 1962, a letter to the editor was published in the *New York Times* concerning *Fly Blackbird*, which had been open for seven weeks. The letter's author was Robert Guillaume, a young actor who was appearing in the show playing the part of Carl. At thirty-four, Guillaume was already a seasoned performer, having toured the world in 1959 with the musical *Free and Easy* and who had recently made his Broadway debut in the unsuccessful *Kwamina*, with a score by Richard Adler and featuring a nearly all-Black cast. (One of its stars was Adler's wife, Sally Ann Howes.)

In his letter, Guillaume bemoaned the fact that roles for Blacks on and off Broadway had been mainly restricted to condescending stereotypes, commenting wryly, "If there was a Negro performer, his part only succeeded in reminding us of our service past." In addition to *Fly Blackbird*, Guillaume cited the play *Purlie Victorious* as the only other show featuring predominantly Black casts or written either in part or fully by Blacks, closing with the statement, "Where in tarnation are the Negro patrons?"

On April 29, 1962, an editorial by *New York Times* theater critic Howard Taubman praised *Fly Blackbird*, noting that the show, which was playing across the street from *How to Succeed in Business Without Really Trying*, served notice that the Negro "is through being patronized by the theatre." Taubman said the musical "uses the indirect power of song and dance rather than the blunt weapon of words to create its fresh, outspoken atmosphere," making its points through humor and delight rather than grim anger. In 1962, the trend toward Black-dominated musicals was only just beginning; it was not yet a movement but was making inroads in that direction. Just as the Freedom Riders were proudly asserting Blacks' rights as citizens, so were Blacks in the theater in the early 1960s. Taubman optimistically closed his piece by predicting that "the Negro not only will assume the place in the arts that his fullest gifts entitle him to but also will enrich them for all of us." On May 26, 1962, *Fly Blackbird* won Best Musical in the annual Obie Awards, which honored off Broadway shows.

SCORE

The first song in *Fly Blackbird* sets the show's tone with Avon Long's optimistic gospel-like "Everything Comes to Those Who Wait." In the strident "Now," Carl says that he doesn't want to wait fifty years for the next opportunity. "If there's a job, I want to work; if there's a school, I want to learn; if there's a house, I want to live in it; if there's a seat, I want to sit in it; if there's a bus I want to ride UP FRONT . . . NOW!" Real estate operator Mr. Crocker, who serves as the show's antagonist, represents white America by mocking the Blacks, saying that he has problems, too, and telling them not to complain ("I'm Sick of the Whole Damn Problem").

In the exuberant "The Housing Cha Cha," a white student looks enviously at the dark skin of a Black student and inquires, "Sea and Ski?" to which the Black student responds, "Heredity!" In another scene, a white character is conversing with a Black character and tells him, patronizingly, "Some of my best friends are colored people," to which the Black responds, "ALL of my best friends are colored people."

Not just Black stereotypes were decried. In "The Gong Song," Piper wonders, with an exaggerated accent, why Oriental detectives in Hollywood movies are always introduced with bashing gongs or temple blocks, say "Ah, so!" and are accompanied by melodies written in a pentatonic scale.

The two most pointedly satirical songs were "Mister Boy" and "Old White Tom," part of a dream sequence in which the prison matron dreams of a time when the Negro will be restored to his proper place in society, one step behind the white man, and grinning. The musical concludes with a joyous, pseudo-gospel anthem that proclaims, "Wake up, there's a new day waiting at your door." The score's incisive, frequently exciting songs were ahead of their time, with sharply satirical lyrics and a jazzy, brash score, orchestrated by Gershon Kingsley.

Freedom Riders: The Civil Rights Musical

Historical context: The civil rights movement
Time period: May–December 1961
Off Broadway run: August 1, 2017–August 5, 2017 (as part of the New York Musical Theatre Festival)
Venue: Theatre Row's Acorn Theatre
Book: Richard Allen and Taran Gray
Score: Richard Allen and Taran Gray (music and lyrics)
Cast album: None
Major characters: John Lewis (Anthony Chatmon II), Diane Nash (Brynn Williams), John Seigenthaler (Ciarán McCarthy)

HISTORICAL BACKGROUND

On December 5, 1960, the US Supreme Court, in a ruling on *Boynton v. Virginia*, overturned a judgment convicting an African American law student for trespassing at a bus terminal restaurant designated as "whites only." Furthermore, the ruling held that segregation in public transportation was a violation of the Interstate Commerce Act. The outlawing of racial segregation on public transportation led to the Freedom Rides, in which Black and white activists rode on interstate buses across the South to test states' segregation laws, even though the Supreme Court had already ruled that such laws were unconstitutional and illegal.

The first Freedom Riders left Washington, DC, bound for New Orleans, on May 4, 1961. Between then and December, sixteen Freedom Rides took place, on Greyhound and Trailways buses as well as on railroads. On the first Freedom Ride was John Lewis (1940–2020), a twenty-one-year-old student activist and future chair of the Student Nonviolent

Coordinating Committee (SNCC). Many of the riders, both Black and white, were brutally attacked during the trips, but the rides continued throughout the year. While attempting to enter a whites-only waiting room in Rock Hill, South Carolina, Lewis was assaulted by two white men, but continued on another ride two weeks later. Lewis would later lead the 1965 march across the Edmund Pettus Bridge in Selma, Alabama, on what came to be known as "Bloody Sunday." Later, he became a highly respected congressman from Georgia's fifth congressional district and a renowned American statesman and advocate for civil rights.

College student Diane Nash (born 1938) was, at the time, the leader of the SNCC student movement in Nashville, Tennessee. Nash not only organized campaigns to integrate Nashville lunch counters but also helped organize further Freedom Rides throughout the South.

John Seigenthaler (1927–2014) was a twenty-four-year-old administrative assistant to US Attorney General Robert F. Kennedy. In his capacity as assistant to John Doar, the assistant attorney general for civil rights, Seigenthaler was sent to Alabama to secure protection for the Freedom Riders, working with Alabama Governor John Malcolm Patterson. Knocked unconscious with a lead pipe while trying to protect Freedom Rider Susan Wilbur, who was being chased by an angry mob, Seigenthaler became editor of the *Tennessean* newspaper and later worked on Kennedy's 1968 presidential campaign. Fifty years later, Lewis, Nash, and Seigenthaler would become the main characters in a musical that would bring the stories of the Freedom Riders to life.

PRODUCTION NOTES

Freedom Riders: The Civil Rights Musical attempted to musicalize the historic trips of the courageous participants of the Freedom Rides. Richard Allen, a writer and producer for film and television, wrote the show as well as its songs, working with Taran Gray, a San Diego–based songwriter and music producer. The musical was produced as part of the 2017 New York Musical Theatre Festival (NYMTF), an annual three-week event during which more than thirty new musicals were staged at various theaters in Midtown Manhattan's theater district. The first such festival took place in 2004 and they continued until 2019. It shut down

Freedom Riders John Lewis and Jim Zwerg, after being beaten by a mob in Montgomery, Alabama, 1961 (from *Eyes on the Prize*, a 1987 documentary directed by Henry Hampton).
BLACKSIDE INC./PHOTOFEST

in January 2020, before the COVID-19 crisis forced productions to cease on all live theater. *Freedom Riders* was staged over five days at Theatre Row's Acorn Theatre.

Although the Freedom Rides had been thoroughly documented in articles, books, and documentaries, a musical had never been attempted. The dramatic heroism and courage of many of the riders inspired Allen, after he saw a 2011 PBS documentary and a special that aired on the network's *American Experience* series. In 2015, Allen, who is Black, started work with Taran Gray, who is white.

In watching the PBS production, Allen learned how the activists on the rides bonded while singing together. The songs they sang included popular numbers, ancient spirituals, modern gospel, and whatever kind of music they all knew, which helped inspire courage and release tension, leading Allen to reflect on the importance of music in the Black community. John Lewis himself testified to the value of music, saying later, "Without singing, we would have lost our sense of solidarity. It gave us hope in a time of hopelessness."

The riders would alter the lyrics to such well-known songs as "We Shall Not Be Moved," "Hallelujah, I'm a Bum," and "Walking Up the King's Highway" to fit whatever situation or locale they were in at that particular time, much as folk singers did during the turbulent times of the 1930s and 1940s labor movement. Even after they were arrested and thrown in jail, riders sang in four-part harmony to maintain solidarity and to communicate to riders in adjacent cells that they were OK.

In the show, the scene where John Lewis, played by Anthony Chatmon II, is brutally attacked in a whites-only waiting area, is dramatized with Chatmon singing a song in which he dreams of a world where true equality exists.

Seigenthaler was included as a character to show that there were whites involved in the Freedom Riders movement as well as Blacks. Diane Nash herself phoned in feedback to the cast during rehearsals and Lewis posed for photographs with Allen and Gray at the US Capitol and attended a rehearsal, where he got to meet Chatmon.

In addition to the three main characters, other historical figures were featured in the musical, including Robert Kennedy, Dr. Martin Luther King Jr., and civil rights activist James Farmer. Gray later said that it was his intent to not only humanize the larger-than-life participants of the rides but to show that ordinary people could do extraordinary things. In 2016, *Freedom Riders* won the BETA Award from the New York Musical Theatre Festival, followed by being awarded Outstanding Musical and the Social Relevance and Impact Award at the 2017 festival.

SCORE

Allen and Gray's score was dismissed by one critic who said that the songs were too derivative, with little diversity and repetitious lyrics. In an interview with *Playbill*, Taran Gray noted, "We broke a bit of a rule with a few of the musical theater songs that don't progress the storyline, where the music suspends the moment, and there's a pause in the story." Like many musicals depicting African Americans during the 1960s, the score relied heavily on popular music styles like Motown and pseudo-gospel numbers, although the cast delivered the score with enthusiasm and passion, notably the first act's rousing finale, "Freedom Song," and the stirring "The Call," sung by Meagan Flint. Another highlight was the powerful "Der Lawd," written to resemble a chain gang chant, the singers accompanied only by a pounding drum. Other songs, such as "We'll Get There," sung by Ciarán McCarthy as John Seigenthaler, were inspirational but interchangeable with a multitude of "I want" songs from other musicals.

Samples of the score found on YouTube bear out the score's impression as containing some truly inspirational songs as well as conventional Broadway fare. The lyrics highlight the empowerment and passion of the riders, sung with the fervor of Southern gospel revivals. The message delivered by *Freedom Riders* helped the show win the NYMF Award for Outstanding Musical, garnering special citations for Allen and Gray for the show's social relevance.

Hair

Historical context: San Francisco's "Human Be-In" and the hippie
   lifestyle in New York's East Village
Time period: 1967
Broadway run: April 29, 1968–July 1, 1972 (1,742 p.)
Venue: Biltmore Theatre
Book: Gerome Ragni and James Rado
Score: Galt MacDermot (music), Gerome Ragni and James Rado
   (lyrics)
Cast album: RCA Victor LSO-1143 (Off Broadway, 1967); RCA
   Victor LSO-1150 (Broadway, 1968)
Major characters: Claude (James Rado), Berger (Gerome Ragni),
   Sheila (Lynn Kellogg), Ron (Ronald Dyson), Woof (Steve Curry),
   Crissy (Shelley Plimpton), Hud (Lamont Washington), Jeanie
   (Sally Eaton)

HISTORICAL BACKGROUND

On January 14, 1967, America's growing counterculture movement was
symbolized by the "Human Be-In," a gathering of more than twenty
thousand people at Golden Gate Park in San Francisco. The event was
prompted by two recent occurrences: a new California law banning use
of the psychedelic drug LSD, which went into effect on October 6, 1966,
and the November election of Republican Ronald Reagan as California
governor.

The Be-In was the idea of Michael Bowen, a visual artist who helped
instigate what was called the Love Pageant Rally, also staged at Golden
Gate Park, on the day the LSD ban went into effect. Bowen's partner

in the venture was Allen Cohen, poet and editor of the underground newspaper the *San Francisco Oracle*. Posters displayed through the city promised the Be-In to be "A Gathering of the Tribes," featuring speeches by psychologist and psychedelic drug advocate Timothy Leary; Richard Alpert, Leary's colleague in the Harvard Psilocybin Project; comedian Dick Gregory; poet Allen Ginsburg; social activist Jerry Rubin; and performances by many San Francisco rock stars and groups, including the Grateful Dead, Janis Joplin, Santana, and the Steve Miller Band.

The Be-In was designed to attract young people who had in common a variety of goals, all of which furthered the youth movement's theme of questioning authority. Golden Gate Park, located adjacent to San Francisco's Haight-Ashbury neighborhood, was a magnet for those who celebrated free love, communal living, and opposition to the Vietnam War, and supported ecological awareness, promoted use of marijuana and psychedelic drugs, and rejected middle-class morality by aspiring to a spiritual life devoid of material enrichment. It was there that Leary first uttered the memorable phrase, "Tune in, turn on, drop out," which would become a slogan for the hippie generation.

The Be-In marked the official beginning of the youth counterculture movement, establishing San Francisco as its center. Before long, communities similar to Haight-Ashbury were popping up around the country. The East Village, a neighborhood on the East Side of Lower Manhattan, became New York's focus for artists, musicians, students, and disaffected hippies.

PRODUCTION NOTES

Hair was the idea of two men: James Rado, who created the role of Richard the Lionheart in the 1966 play *The Lion in Winter*, and Gerome Ragni, a struggling actor who had been performing since 1954. Rado and Ragni met in 1964 when both were cast in the short-lived *Hang Down Your Head and Die*, a revue centered on opposition to capital punishment.

After appearing in the 1966 play *Viet Rock*, which vehemently denounced America's involvement in Vietnam, Rado and Ragni teamed up to write a musical that would focus on the hippie movement and its attitudes toward American society. While visiting the Whitney Museum of Art on Madison Avenue, they became fascinated by a pastel drawing by Cincinnati-born artist Jim Dine simply titled "Hair," which would become the name of their new musical. The drawing reminded them of the long hair worn by those in hippie culture, which came to represent a cultural flag, a symbol of youthful rebellion as well as the equalizing of perceived gender roles.

Rado and Ragni decided to do the show after reading stories about New York's flourishing hippie culture. In developing the musical, they spent time in the East Village, getting to know teenagers who were dropping out and dodging the draft as well as those who had been expelled from school for refusing to cut their hair. They hung out with them, let their own hair grow long, and attended their own versions of San Francisco's Be-In. Eventually, many cast members of the show were recruited from the people with whom Rado and Ragni spent time in the East Village.

The cast of *Hair*.
PHOTOFEST

After writing a script and lyrics for the songs, Rado and Ragni approached Joe Papp, founder of the New York Shakespeare Festival's Public Theater, which was still under construction in the East Village, who asked them who was writing the music for the songs. Through jazz songwriter Nat Shapiro, Rado and Ragni were introduced to Canadian composer Galt MacDermot, who fit their lyrics to melodies in a matter of a few weeks. MacDermot wasn't a Broadway composer; he earned his living as a session pianist on demonstration records and at recording sessions. MacDermot was enamored with jazz and rock 'n' roll at the time and was delighted when Rado and Ragni told him they wanted the music to have a rock feel to it. In addition, MacDermot had spent three years in Cape Town, South Africa, absorbing the intricate rhythms of African drumming. Jazz drummer Bernard Purdie would help MacDermot fashion the rhythms for many of the numbers in the score and played in the original off Broadway band.

There was no linear story in *Hair*, which consisted of a revue-like series of songs that defined the lifestyle of the group, which Rado and Ragni called the Tribe, taking its cue from the original Human Be-In, which was promoted as "A Gathering of Tribes." To further the identification of the ensemble with Native Americans, the show's original off Broadway poster showed Rado and Ragni posing alongside nineteenth-century images of Native Americans wearing beads and feathered headdresses. The show, described as "An American Tribal Love-Rock Musical," made its off Broadway debut on October 16, 1967, featuring a five-piece rock band including MacDermot on piano.

After the show's six-week run ended, Rado and Ragni moved to get the show transferred to Broadway. Producer Michael Butler, thinking *Hair* was about American Indians, came to see it at the Public Theater and was delighted, even though he quickly realized it had nothing to do with Indians. Butler then had Rado and Ragni rewrite the script, adding thirteen new songs to the score, and the retooled production made its Broadway debut at the Biltmore Theatre on April 29, 1968. The show was a sensation, with publicity hyped by a controversial but discreet nude scene at the end of Act I.

Score

Although rock music culture was satirized in 1960's *Bye Bye Birdie*, *Hair* was the first bona fide rock musical, its writers keenly attuned to the contemporary rock scene of the 1960s and the multi-genre musical palette of Top 40 radio. *Hair* forced Broadway to acknowledge the existence of rock music and the new, younger market, triggering other rock musicals over the next five years, including *Joseph and the Amazing Technicolor Dreamcoat*, *Jesus Christ Superstar*, *Pippin*, and *Grease*.

In keeping with the culturally diverse cast (fully one-third were actors of color), the score was equally wide-ranging, including early funk, acid rock, R&B, country-and-western, soul jazz, Black gospel, British Invasion, and even Gregorian chant. The Broadway production added four additional musicians, including two trumpets. Bernard Purdie, who played drums in the off Broadway production, was unavailable for the Broadway run, so MacDermot hired noted jazz drummer Idris Muhammad and added bassist Jimmy Lewis, both well versed in the 1960s soul jazz idiom. As a result, the new score was saturated with soul, jazz groove, and rhythmic drive.

The songs cut a wide swath of issues relevant to 1960s culture, all of which were being extolled by America's youth: attacking racism, destruction of the environment, restrictive drug laws, air pollution, political corruption, sexual repression, nuclear proliferation, religion, the war in Vietnam, language, conventions of the American education system, and middle-class society. It proved to be a lot to load into any one musical, but *Hair* managed to do it with a score that revolutionized Broadway as no musical had done since *Oklahoma!* a quarter century before. Four of the songs became major pop hits: "Aquarius/Let the Sunshine In" by the Fifth Dimension, "Easy to Be Hard" by Three Dog Night, "Good Morning Starshine" by Oliver, and the title song by the Cowsills. In addition, Nina Simone's medley of "Ain't Got No" and "I Got Life" became a top five hit in the United Kingdom.

More than two dozen songs were included, more than double the number in a conventional musical, with very little spoken dialog. Many songs ended abruptly and had no discernible structure, as if they were improvised. In addition to the score's high spirits and enthusiasm, actors broke the fourth wall by invading the audience, handing out flyers inviting patrons to attend their Be-In, dancing in the aisles, balancing on the arms of theater seats, and hanging from scaffolding in the fly area. By the time the final sing-along anthem "Let the Sunshine In" was sung, youthful audiences were won over and often sang along. One could argue that *Hair* was Broadway's first immersive musical. There was nothing about *Hair* that wasn't different.

Assassins

Historical context: Presidential assassins, successful and foiled,
   throughout history
Time period: 1865–1981
Off Broadway run: December 18, 1990–February 16, 1991 (73 p.)
Off Broadway venue: Playwrights Horizons
Broadway run: April 22, 2004–July 18, 2004 (101 p.)
Broadway venue: Studio 54
Book: John Weidman
Score: Stephen Sondheim
Cast album: RCA Victor 60737-2-RC (1991)
Major characters: Balladeer (Patrick Cassidy), John Wilkes Booth
   (Victor Garber), Leon Czolgosz (Terence Mann), John Hinckley
   (Greg Germann), Charles Guiteau (Jonathan Hadary), Giuseppe
   Zangara (Eddie Korbich), Samuel Byck (Lee Wilkof), Lynette
   "Squeaky" Fromme (Annie Golden), Sara Jane Moore (Debra
   Monk), Lee Harvey Oswald (Jace Alexander)

HISTORICAL BACKGROUND

The assassination of Abraham Lincoln on April 14, 1865, was only the
first in a series of attempts on the lives of US presidents, a lineage of
notoriety that became a blot on American history. After Lincoln's death,
attacks on presidents occurred with frightening regularity. Whereas in the
nineteenth century only Andrew Jackson, Lincoln, and James A. Garfield
were targeted, the twentieth and twenty-first centuries have seen plots
foiled or carried out upon fifteen presidents, including every one since
Richard Nixon. In all, four assassinations were successful: Lincoln (1865),

Garfield (1881), William McKinley (1901), and John F. Kennedy (1963). *Assassins* dealt with nine assassination attempts on American presidents.

1. On April 14, 1865, Abraham Lincoln was ambushed while watching the play *Our American Cousin* at Ford's Theatre in Washington, DC. The plot was masterminded by a frustrated, megalomaniacal actor named John Wilkes Booth (1838–1865). Lincoln's killing was part of a conspiracy meant to avenge the South's defeat in the Civil War. The night Lincoln was shot, unsuccessful attempts were also made by Booth's conspirators, targeting Vice President Andrew Johnson and Secretary of State William H. Seward. Lincoln died of a bullet wound to the head early the next morning, at the age of fifty-six. Booth escaped the scene but suffered a broken leg after leaping from the balcony where Lincoln and his wife were sitting and landing on the theater stage. A posse pursued Booth for eleven days as he and fellow conspirator David Herold made their way south, where they thought they would be treated as heroes. The hunt ended when Booth was cornered in a Virginia barn and died of a gunshot wound. A Union cavalryman named Boston Corbett claimed to have fired the shot that killed Booth, but it has since been determined that Booth most likely committed suicide rather than be captured. On July 7, 1865, Herold and three other conspirators were hanged for their parts in the conspiracy.

2. On July 2, 1881, less than four months into his term as president, James A. Garfield was shot by a disappointed office seeker named Charles Guiteau (1841–1882), as the president arrived at a railroad station in Washington, DC. Garfield spent an agonizing summer in severe pain as incompetent doctors actually hastened his death by probing for the bullet with bare fingers and unsterilized instruments. As a result, Garfield developed an infection and died on September 19 at the age of fifty. After a highly publicized trial, Guiteau was found guilty and hanged on June 30, 1882.

3. President William McKinley, who was in the first year of his second term as president, was shot on September 6, 1901, while attending

the Pan-American Exposition in Buffalo, New York. The assassin was twenty-eight-year-old anarchist Leon Czolgosz (1873–1901), a Polish American who was employed as a steelworker. Inspired by a speech by activist Emma Goldman, Czolgosz had developed a virulent resentment against the US government, blaming it for encouraging laws that favored the rich over the poor. While in a reception line, Czolgosz shot McKinley in the stomach with a pistol he had hidden in a bandaged hand. The fifty-eight year old McKinley died eight days later on September 14 of an infection from the wound. Czolgosz was arrested immediately and although the jury believed that he was insane, nevertheless convicted him of first-degree murder. He was electrocuted on October 29, 1901.

4. On February 15, 1933, President-elect Franklin D. Roosevelt was giving a speech from an open car in Miami, Florida, which also contained Chicago mayor Anton Cermak when shots rang out from a sniper standing on a rickety metal folding chair. The would-be assassin was Guiseppe Zangara (1900–1933), an Italian immigrant and naturalized citizen who had been suffering from abdominal pain for some years, later attributed to adhesions on his gallbladder. Five people were hit in the attack, including Mayor Cermak, who died nineteen days later, but Roosevelt escaped unharmed. In jail, Zangara confessed, stating in broken English, "I kill kings and presidents first and next all capitalists." He was electrocuted on March 20, 1933. His last words were, "Push the button! Go ahead, push the button!"

5. The fourth president to die at the hands of an assassin was John F. Kennedy, who was shot while riding in a motorcade in Dallas, Texas, on November 22, 1963. Lee Harvey Oswald (1939–1963), a twenty-three-year-old former Marine and communist sympathizer, fired his shots at Kennedy's motorcade from the sixth floor of the Texas School Book Depository, hitting both the president and Texas governor John B. Connally. Kennedy was mortally wounded by a rifle shot to the head; efforts to save his life failed and he was pronounced dead a half hour later at Parkland Memorial Hospital. He was forty-six years old. After escaping the scene and shooting a police officer on

the streets of Dallas, Oswald was finally cornered in a movie theater and arrested. Two days later, he was shot by Dallas nightclub owner Jack Ruby while being transported from the Dallas city jail to the county jail. Despite numerous unproven conspiracy theories claiming Oswald was a patsy and framed for the killing, investigations still point to him as being Kennedy's sole assassin.

6. On February 22, 1974, forty-four-year-old Samuel Byck (1930–1974), who was suffering from severe bouts of depression after a divorce and a succession of financial failures, hijacked an airliner with plans to crash it into the White House, where he hoped President Richard Nixon would be present. After killing a Maryland police officer, Byck stormed a DC-9 Delta Air Lines flight, shot both pilots, and threatened to blow up the plane. Cornered by police, Byck committed suicide to avoid being arrested.

7. President Gerald Ford survived two assassination attempts only seventeen days apart. On September 5, 1975, Ford was receiving a crowd on the grounds of the California State Capitol in Sacramento when Lynette "Squeaky" Fromme (born 1948), a member of the Charles Manson cult, drew a forty-five-caliber pistol and aimed it at Ford. Four cartridges were in the pistol's magazine, but none were in the firing chamber, and Fromme was quickly restrained by a Secret Service agent. She spent thirty-four years in prison before being paroled in 2009.

8. In the second attempt on Gerald Ford's life, five-time divorcée Sara Jane Moore (born 1930), who had a fascination with revolutionaries like kidnapped heiress Patricia Hearst, took a shot at the president while he was standing on the street across from the St. Francis Hotel in downtown San Francisco. Her first shot missed due to a faulty sight on her gun, and before she could fire again, she was grabbed by a former Marine. Sentenced to life in prison, Moore, like Fromme, was released in 2007, at the age of seventy-seven.

9. On March 30, 1981, President Ronald Reagan had just delivered a speech at the Washington Hilton in Washington, DC, and was on his

way to his limousine when John Hinckley Jr. (born 1955), a twenty-five-year-old would-be singer-songwriter, fired shots at Reagan in an attempt to impress actress Jodie Foster. Reagan was seriously wounded but survived the attack, along with three others: a police officer, a Secret Service agent, and Reagan's press secretary James Brady. Brady was permanently disabled because of the shooting and became a symbol for anti-gun laws until his death in 2014. Hinckley was apprehended but found not guilty by reason of insanity, remaining under psychiatric care until his release in 2016.

Production Notes

The idea to write a musical about presidential assassins came to Stephen Sondheim after he read a script called *Assassins* by playwright Charles Gilbert. Sondheim, who was judging entries for the Musical Theatre Lab, made a mental note about the idea but soon forgot about it. The idea reappeared in his mind when theatrical producer John Weidman suggested Sondheim do a musical about Woodrow Wilson and the Paris Peace Conference, which reminded Sondheim of *Assassins*. He contacted Gilbert and worked out a deal to develop the idea.

Sondheim knew at the outset that he couldn't do a conventional musical about presidential assassins using an ordinary chronological timeline. Having challenged storytelling conventions before in *Company* (1970), whose disjointed vignettes were framed in a revue-type setting, and *Merrily We Roll Along* (1981), which was played in reverse time sequence, Sondheim knew how to bend time and space, and came up with the tantalizing idea of having America's presidential assassins interact with one another.

The result was a sneeringly cynical musical that grouped the nine assassins in a *Twilight Zone*–like revue of comic malevolence through which the bizarre confluence of its deluded characters plays out, their perverted rationales tied together in the setting of a carnival shooting gallery.

Sondheim found that the nine assassins all were possessed by unfulfilled delusions and were acting out their frustration onto the most tempting of targets, the President of the United States. Weidman would describe the characters as "stalkers with a grievance."

Other historical figures were also written into the show, including presidents Ford and Garfield, Garfield's secretary of state James Blaine, and anarchist Emma Goldman, who would become a major character in *Ragtime* (1998). Dark humor abounds in *Assassins*, but it's left to the audience to decide who is the looniest one in the pack, be it the dyspeptic Byck, dressed as Santa Claus as he rants to conductor Leonard Bernstein through a handheld tape recorder, or the nutty-as-a-fruitcake Moore, rummaging through her handbag searching for her pistol while noshing on Kentucky Fried Chicken. The result is that the audience doesn't know whether to laugh or be horrified by the scenes, which was precisely Sondheim's intent.

In the final and most disturbing sequence, Booth and the other assassins persuade a suicidal, T-shirted Oswald to shoot down JFK. We root against him going through with it but know down deep that history requires that he succeed. When Oswald fires the fatal rifle shot, we are ashamed of our subliminal desire for Oswald to fulfill his historic destiny.

Critics praised *Assassins* as wickedly funny, "an anti-musical about anti-heroes," as Frank Rich of the *New York Times* wrote. Of the nine assassins, only Guiteau had a personal grievance against the president. The others viewed American presidents as symbols, or in Booth's case, a means to gain recognition. "Squeeze your little finger," he oozes to a hesitant Czolgosz, "and change the world." In *Assassins*, Sondheim identified with the characters' cynical, self-centered world by destroying musical theater conventions. *Assassins* has no chronological time frame and no love story; its cast is filled with demented antagonists. Who were audiences supposed to identify with?

The premiere of *Assassins* had the unfortunate timing to coincide with the beginning of the Iraq War in the Persian Gulf. Producer André Bishop recalled President George H. W. Bush riding in a motorcade along West Forty-Second Street on his way to the United Nations and passing by the Playwrights Horizons Theatre, with its posters promoting *Assassins*, a sight that many thought was in bad taste.

The original run of *Assassins* survived for only seventy-three performances. A revival, staged thirteen years later at Studio 54, fared slightly better, but still only lasted for less than three months. Since then,

Assassins has become admired as one of Sondheim's most daring and brilliant musicals, but its appeal depends wholly on timing, and in the gun-conscious world of the twenty-first century, it has become hard for any theatergoer to find humor or amusement in a show about disturbed individuals who, somehow, were able to get their hands on firearms and act on their misguided impulses.

SCORE

Stephen Sondheim's brilliant score drew upon a variety of American musical styles, each of the show's songs suited to the specific era in which each assassin lived. The show's introduction begins with a melodic distortion of "Hail to the Chief," turning it into a carnival-type waltz as the shooting gallery's proprietor (William Parry) cheerily invites the audience to "come in and shoot a president." He then introduces each assassin, justifying their respective actions by singing, "Everybody's Got the Right to Be Happy."

"The Ballad of Booth," sung by Patrick Cassidy as the Balladeer, accompanied by a jaunty banjo, was written in a form that folk song scholar George Malcolm Laws called a native American ballad, one in which the singer relates the story of a criminal's life, deed, and death, ending with a moral and a warning not to follow his example. The Balladeer sings another song in this style, "The Ballad of Guiteau," defined as a badman ballad, structured as a first-person confessional and culminating with a jaunty cakewalk as Charles Guiteau mounts the scaffold for his hanging.

"How I Saved Roosevelt" incorporates a perverted version of John Philip Sousa's "El Capitan" march as a framework, in which a bitter Giuseppe Zangara complains (in broken English) about his persistent stomachaches, blaming the powerful and rich for his ailment. The song ends with his electrocution.

"Gun Song" is reminiscent of "A Little Priest" from *Sweeney Todd*, a sprightly waltz in which Czolgosz, Guiteau, Sara Jane Moore, and Booth croon in barbershop harmony about changing the world. In "Unworthy of Your Love," John Hinckley sings the ballad, which was written in the style of 1980s singer-songwriters.

By taking traditional American song styles and twisting them to fit his characters, Sondheim created a musical counterpoint to the show's nefarious antiheroes and their rationales, forcing the audience to think not only about the motivations of the notorious criminals who changed history by "moving a little finger" but also about the increasingly relevant topic of how Americans view gun rights. In the years since its debut, *Assassins* has only gotten more relevant with time, a true mirror in which Sondheim forced us to look at ourselves, albeit through cracked glass.

SELECTED BIBLIOGRAPHY

Barrett, Mary Ellin. *Irving Berlin: A Daughter's Memoir*. New York: Simon & Schuster, 1994.

Bergreen, Laurence. *As Thousands Cheer: The Life of Irving Berlin*. New York: Viking Penguin, 1990.

Bordman, Gerald. *American Musical Theatre: A Chronicle*. Expanded ed. New York: Oxford University Press, 1986.

Brooks, Tim. *Lost Sounds: Blacks and the Birth of the Recording Industry (1890–1919)*. Urbana: University of Illinois Press, 2004.

Collins, Homer, with John L. Lehrberger. *The Life and Death of Floyd Collins*. Dayton: Cave Books, 2001.

Cusic, Don. *Dang Him!* (Roger Miller biography). Nashville: Brackish Publishing, 2012.

Escott, Colin, with Martin Hawkins. *Good Rockin' Tonight: Sun Records and the Birth of Rock 'N' Roll*. London: St. Martin's Griffin, 1992.

Ewen, David. *Richard Rodgers*. New York: Henry Holt and Company, 1957.

Green, Stanley, revised by Cary Ginell. *Broadway Musicals: Show by Show*. 9th ed. Guilford, CT: Applause, 2019.

Hischak, Thomas S. *The American Musical Theatre Song Encyclopedia*. Westport, CT: Greenwood Press, 1995.

———. *Stage It with Music (An Encyclopedic Guide to the American Musical Theatre)*. Westport, CT: Greenwood Press, 1993.

Horowitz, Mark Eden. *Sondheim On Music*. Lanham, MD: Scarecrow Press, 2003.

Jones, John Bush. *Our Musicals, Ourselves (A Social History of the American Musical Theatre)*. Lebanon: Brandeis University Press, 2003.

Kislan, Richard. *Hoofing on Broadway (A History of Show Dancing)*. New York: Prentice Hall, 1987.

Kissel, Howard. *David Merrick: The Abominable Showman*. New York: Applause, 1993.

Lees, Gene. *Inventing Champagne: The Worlds of Lerner and Loewe*. New York: St. Martin's, 1990.

Mandelbaum, Ken. *Not Since Carrie: 40 Years of Broadway Musical Flops*. New York: St. Martin's, 1991.

Merman, Ethel. *Don't Call Me Madam*. London: W. H. Allen, 1955.

Mordden, Ethan. *Rodgers & Hammerstein*. New York: Harry N. Abrams, Inc., 1992.

Riggs, Lynn. *Green Grow the Lilacs* (play). Norwalk: Heritage Press, 1991.

Rodgers, Richard. *Musical Stages*. Rev. ed. Cambridge: Da Capo Press, 2002.

Secrest, Meryle. *Stephen Sondheim: A Life*. New York: Alfred A. Knopf, 1998.

Silber, Irwin (ed.). *Songs America Voted By*. Harrisburg: Stackpole Books, 1971.

Sobel, Bernard. *A Pictorial History of Vaudeville*. New York: Citadel Press, 1961.

Sondheim, Stephen. *Finishing the Hat*. New York: Alfred A. Knopf, 2010.

Suskin, Steven. *Show Tunes*. 4th ed. New York: Oxford University Press, 2010.

Taylor, Theodore. *Jule: The Story of Composer Jule Styne*. New York: Random House, 1979.

Teichmann, Howard. *George S. Kaufman: An Intimate Portrait*. New York: Atheneum, 1972.

Willson, Meredith. *But He Doesn't Know the Territory*. New York: G. Putnam's Sons, 1959.

INDEX

Hamilton, Alexander, 21–27
Hamilton, Eliza Schuyler, 21, 25, 26
The Hamilton Mixtape, 23–24
Hammerstein, Oscar, II, 12, 13, 65, 145
  Annie Get Your Gun, 72, 73, 75;
  Oklahoma!, 56, 115–22, 192;
  Show Boat, 77, 80–81, 82–85;
  South Pacific, 14, 66, 189–94
Hanley, Ellen, 135, 137
Harbach, Otto, 12, 81
Harburg, E. Y. (Yip)
  Bloomer Girl, 45–51;
  Finian's Rainbow, 203–7
Harnick, Sheldon, 135, 139
Harrary, Nettie, 183
Harriman, Averill, 220
Harris, Phil, 127
Harris, Sam, 173
Harrison, Dorothy, 183, 186
Hart, Lorenz, 7, 9, 11–14, 120
Hart, Moss, 65
Hatch, James V., 227–28
Hauptman, William, 37, 39–40, 42
Hauptmann, Anna, 163, 166
Hauptmann, Bruno Richard, 163, 166, 167
Hawkins, Martin, 212
Hayes, Billie, 220
Hayes, Lucy, 94, 99
Hayes, Rutherford B., 94–95, 99
Hearst, Patricia, 246
Hearst, William Randolph, 88

Heart Mountain Relocation Center, 197
Hemings, Sally, 93, 94
Henry, Joshua, 159, 162
Herman, Jerry, 15, 19
Herold, David, 244
Herzig, S. M. (Sig), 45, 46, 205
Hickok, John, 129
Hickok, "Wild Bill," 69
Hicks, Rodney, 159
Higgins, Ed ("Racetrack"), 88, 89
Hiller, Jeff, 29
Hinckley, John, 243, 247, 249
hip-hop music, 23–24, 25, 26, 27, 127
hippie movement, 237–42
History Theatre, 167, 168
Hitler, Adolf, 173, 174, 187
Hodges, Eddie, 123
Holbrook, Hal, 59
Holland, W. S., 210
Hollis, Tommy, 107
Holm, Celeste:
  in *Bloomer Girl*, 45, *47*, 48, 50, 51;
  in *Oklahoma!*, 115, *117*
Holmes, Michael Thomas, 163
Hooray for What!, 46
Hoover, Herbert, 170, 171, 174, 180
Hoover, J. Edgar, 186–87
Hopkins, James Nathan, 199
Hoty, Dee, 177, 179
Houdetot, Sophie d', 17

Houdini, Harry, 107, 109, 111, 112
Hovick, June (June Havoc), 72, 142, 144
Hovick, Rose, 141–42, 143, 144
Howard, Joseph E., 77
Howard, Ken, 1, *2*, 93, *95*, 97
Howe, William, 9–10
Howes, Sally Ann, 229
How to Succeed in Business Without Really Trying, 40, 229
Huey, Richard, 45, 49, 50
Huffman, Cady, 177, 179, 180
"Human Be-In," 237–38, 239, 240, 242
Hume, Nancy, 101
Hutton, Betty, 74

I Can Get It for You Wholesale, 137, 187
immigration at turn of twentieth century, 107–13
Imperial Theatre, 61, 69, 141, 169, 173
Innvar, Christopher, 153, 157
International Ladies Garment Workers Union (ILGWU), 184
In the Heights, 22, 23, 24, 196
Irene, 102

Jackson, Andrew, 29–35, 101, 243
Jackson, Christopher, 21, 23
Jackson, Clarence Bernard, 227–28

Jackson, Rachel Donelson Robards, 29, 30–31, 32
Jacoby, Mark, 107
Jaffee, Lynne, 183
James, Lilith and Dan, 45, 46
Japanese-American incarceration, 195–98
Jefferson, Martha, 1, 4
Jefferson, Thomas:
 in *1600 Pennsylvania Avenue,* 93–94, 97;
 in *1776,* 1, 4, 5, 7, 97;
 in *Ben Franklin in Paris,* 15;
 in *Hamilton,* 21, 23, 24, 26
Jenkins, Andrew, 155–56
Jenkins, Capathia, 57
Jenkins, Daniel H., 37, 42
Jenkins, Gordon, 67
Johnson, Andrew, 93, 94, 244
Johnson, Bob, 210, 211
Jones, David C., 194
Jones, Kendrick, 159
Joplin, Scott, 112, 125, 162
Jordan, Jeremy, 87, 90
Judd, George, 175

Kaliban, Bob, 19
Kalstedt, Harry, 147
Kander, John, 112
 Chicago, 147, 150, 151, 152;
 The Scottsboro Boys, 159, 160, 161, 162
Kapp, Richard, 101, 104, 105, 106
Karnilova, Maria, 141